REVISE AQA AS/A LEVEL
Business

REVISION
GUIDE AND WORKBOOK

650 7 day

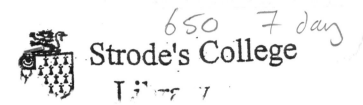
Strode's College
Li... y

Series Consultant: Harry Smith

Author: Andrew Redfern

For the full range of Pearson revision titles across KS2, KS3, GCSE, AS/A Level and BTEC visit:
www.pearsonschools.co.uk/revise

Published by Pearson Education Limited, 80 Strand, London, WC2R 0RL.

www.pearsonschoolsandfecolleges.co.uk

Text and illustrations © Pearson Education Limited 2016
Produced, typeset and illustrations by Cambridge Publishing Management Ltd
Cover illustration by Miriam Sturdee

The right of Andrew Redfern to be identified as author of this work has been asserted by him in accordance with the Copyright, Designs and Patents Act 1988.

First published 2016

19 18 17 16

10 9 8 7 6 5 4 3 2 1

British Library Cataloguing in Publication Data
A catalogue record for this book is available from the British Library

ISBN 9781292111131

 **Pearson**

We are grateful to the following for permission to reproduce copyright material:

Figures
Figure 3.2 from How to Choose a Leadership Pattern, *Harvard Business Review* (Robert Tannenbaum and Warren H. Schmidt, 1973), https://hbr.org/1973/05/how-to-choose-a-leadership-pattern, Reprinted by permission of Harvard Business Review. Exhibit from 'How to Choose a Leadership Pattern' by Robert Tannenbaum and Warren H. Schmidt, 1973. Copyright ©1973 by Harvard Business Publishing; all rights reserved.; Figure 3.2 adapted from *Making Strategy: The Journey of Strategic Management – 978-0-7619-5224-4*, Sage Publications (Eden, C. and Ackermann, F 1998) pp.121–5, pp.344–6, Reproduced by permission of SAGE Publications, London, Los Angeles, New Delhi and Singapore, from Eden, C. and Ackermann, F, Making Strategy: The Journey of Strategic Management, © SAGE Publications, 1998. www.sagepub.co.uk; Figure 3.3 from Bank of England Inflation Report February 2013, *Chart 3 CPI inflation projection based on market interest rate expectations and £375 billion asset purchases. ISSN 1353-6737*, 7 (2013), http://www.bankofengland.co.uk/publications/Documents/inflationreport/2013/ir13feb.pdf; Figure 3.3 adapted from http://www.bcglondon.com/, Adapted from The BCG Portfolio Matrix from the Product Portfolio Matrix,©1970,The Boston Consulting Group (BCG); Figure 3.6 from http://thehrpractice.in/prerana/v4i3/v4i3.html; Figure 3.7.6 adapted from *Business Horizons: The pyramid of corporate social responsibility: Toward the moral management of organizational stakeholders*, Vol, 34, Elsevier B.V. (Archie B. Carroll 1991); Figure 3.8.1 adapted from http://www.ansoffmatrix.com/, reprinted with kind permission of The Ansoff Family Trust; Figure 3.8.2 adapted from Competitive Strategy: Techniques for Analyzing Industries and Competitors., *New York: Free Press* (Porter, Michael E. 1998), Porter, Michael E. Competitive Strategy: Techniques for Analyzing Industries and Competitors. New York: Free Press, 1998; Figure 3.9.1 from *Harvard Business Review: "Evolution and Revolution as Organizations Grow"* Harvard Business School Publishing Corporation (Larry E. Greiner), Reprinted by permission of Harvard Business Review. Exhibit from 'Evolution and Revolution as Organizations Grow' by Larry E. Greiner, May–June 1998. Copyright ©1998 by Harvard Business Publishing; all rights reserved.; Figure 3.9.3 adapted from *Managing Across Borders: The Transnational Solution*, 2.ed, Harvard Business School Press (Christopher. A, Bartlett and Sumantra. Ghoshal 1998), Reprinted by permission of Harvard Business Review Press, exhibit from 'Managing Across Borders: The Transnational Solution' by Christopher. A, Bartlett and Sumantra. Ghoshal. Boston, MA, 1998, 2nd ed. Copyright ©1998 by the Harvard Business Publishing Corporation; all rights reserved.; Figure 3.10.2 from *"Cultures and Organizations, Software of the Mind"*, Third Revised Edition, McGrawHill (Geert Hofstede, Gert Jan Hofstede, Michael Minkov 2010), ©Geert Hofstede B.V. quoted with permission; Figure 3.10.3 from http://www.revisionguru.co.uk/business/critical.htm, Steve Margetts – Revision Guru; Figure 3.10.4 from http://kfknowledgebank.kaplan.co.uk/, from the ACCA P3 Study Text is reproduced by kind permission of Kaplan Financial

Tables
Table 3.3 after http://www.officialcharts.com/, OfficialCharts.com / © Official Charts Company 2015

Text
Quote 3.1 from https://www.oxfamamerica.org, © 2016 Oxfam America Inc. All rights reserved.; Extract 3.1 adapted from Standard Chartered profits to fall for second year in a row, *The Telegraph* 26/06/2014 (James Titcomb), Telegraph Media Group Ltd 2014; General Displayed Text 3.4 adapted from https://www.breitling.com/en/, © BREITLING SA; Case Study 3.7a from Facebook Messenger in transport move with Uber ride ordering deal, *FT.com*, 16/12/2015 (Leslie Hook and Hannah Kuchler), © The Financial Times Limited. All Rights Reserved; Case Study 3.7c from Top 10 Advanced Car Technologies by 2020, *Forbes.com*, 19/01/2015 (Karl Brauer), From Forbes.com, 30/06/2016 © 2015 Forbes.; Case Study 3.7d from UK interest rate rise unlikely until May 2016, CEBR forecasts, *The Guardian.com*, 28/09/2015 (Nick Fletcher)

Photo
The publisher would like to thank the following for their kind permission to reproduce their photographs:

(Key: b-bottom; c-centre; l-left; r-right; t-top)

123RF.com: Olga Serdyuk 52 (a); **Alamy Images:** beata cosgrove 146, Greg Balfour Evans 124, James Hoathly 120, Powered by Light / Alan Spencer 110; **Courtesy of Dyson:** 149; **Courtesy of Toyota (GB) Ltd:** 126; **Fotolia.com:** Altin Osmanaj 75, Arndale 29, chajamp 52 (b), DutchScenery 45, Jacob Lund 108, Jacques PALUT 79, Khvost 80, Kzenon 146r, mastock 158, Michael Schütze 102, Monkey Business Images 109, Nomad_Soul 38c, Sergio Martínez 1, UBER IMAGES 95l, vallefrias 12, Voyagerix 38tl, WavebreakMediaMicro 38tr, yauhenka 80b; **Getty Images:** Britt Erlanson 95r; **Procter & Gamble Professional:** a customer support and advice service for professional customers and products 46; **Shutterstock.com:** Carole Castilli 111, Dmitry Kalinovsky 52 (c), Filipe Frazao 40, Nella 119, nito 10, Vasin Lee 37; **Skullcandy Inc:** 41; **Twitter, Inc:** 7; **2016 Uber Technologies Inc.:** 140; **Courtesy of Boots UK:** 32

All other images © Pearson Education

Contents

Why businesses exist

Businesses are diverse, ranging from the simple to the vastly complex, and are involved in all aspects of life. However, the purpose of all businesses is the same – to meet the needs of people. The incentive to meet these needs may vary from one business to another depending on the industry, sector or the motives of the owners. However, all businesses meet these needs through a transformation process that creates a product (goods or a service).

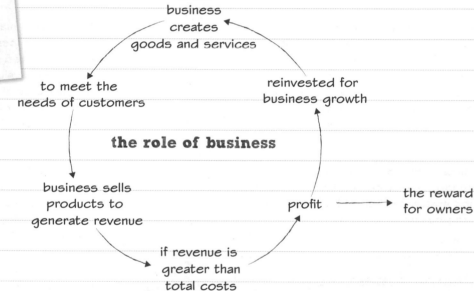

The more value a business can add to its products the more competitive it is. Added value can be achieved through branding, quality, convenience and service.

labour (people)
capital (finance)
land (natural resources and materials)
→ inputs →
transformational process (adds value)
→ outputs →
goods and services

This diagram shows you how businesses add value, meet people's needs and reward their owners.

the role of business

business creates goods and services
→ to meet the needs of customers
→ business sells products to generate revenue
→ if revenue is greater than total costs
→ profit → the reward for owners
→ reinvested for business growth

Why businesses exist

Businesses are important because they:
- create wealth
- create jobs
- develop new products to benefit society
- support other businesses in the country, such as by purchasing materials
- provide a source of tax revenue for the government.

Real world McDonald's

McDonald's adds value to its products through its strong global brand. For example, when customers see the golden arches (the big M) which make up the McDonald's logo, they know exactly what to expect from a McDonald's restaurant wherever they go. Value is also added through the convenience and speed of service.

Now try this

1 What are three different examples of a good and three different examples of a service?
2 Why does the government encourage new business start-ups?
3 What are two ways that a car manufacturer might add value?

Missions and objectives

Although there are slight differences between missions, aims and objectives, they all set out to do the same thing – act as targets and give the business direction. Running a successful business can be very difficult. The owners and employees often have to make decisions in response to external pressures and unforeseen factors. The aims and objectives of a business give clarity to the decision-making process.

Mission statement

A mission statement sets out a business's overall purpose to direct and stimulate the entire organisation.

A mission statement will focus on:

- the organisation's values
- non-financial goals
- the benefits of the business to the community or stakeholder
- how consumers are to be satisfied.

 **Real world** **Oxfam**

Oxfam, the globally renowned aid charity, has the following mission statement:

'To create lasting solutions to poverty, hunger, and social injustice.'

Employees – the mission statement acts as a set of guiding principles for employees. It brings employees together with a shared purpose and communicates the values that underpin the business. A mission statement can have a significant influence on corporate culture – 'the way we do things around here'.

Investors – many shareholders will want assurances that their money is being invested in an ethical business with strong values. A mission will also communicate the ambition of the business to potential stakeholders and its desire to grow.

Mission statement

Owners/directors – directors need to see the bigger picture and think strategically. The mission statement helps the directors form and align the business strategy.

Customers – many organisations use their mission statement as a promise to their customers. It lays down what they can expect from the goods and services they consume.

The objectives hierarchy

The objectives hierarchy shows the relationship between the aims, mission and objectives throughout a business.

aims

mission statement

corporate objectives

functional objectives
finance   marketing   operations   people

The relationship between missions and objectives

The objectives of a business will flow from the mission and aims. Whereas a mission outlines the vision of the business in broad terms, the objectives will be SMART (see page 3). Whereas a mission statement will be communicated to all stakeholders, some objectives may only be shared with managers and employees.

Now try this

1 What is the purpose of a mission statement?
2 What is the difference between business aims and business objectives?

Common business objectives

Objectives are medium- to long-term plans established to coordinate the business and act as targets. Corporate objectives are those set by the owners or directors of the business. These will then influence the functional objectives set at departmental level.

Businesses set objectives to:

- provide quantifiable steps to achieve aims
- clarify direction of the business
- measure success against targets
- provide targets to motivate and reward employees
- influence potential lenders/investors.

SMART

The appropriateness of an objective can be analysed using SMART. All objectives should be:

- Specific
- Measurable
- Agreed
- Realistic
- Time-related

Financial and non-financial objectives

It could be argued that achieving most of these objectives will impact the bottom line and overall aim of most businesses – profit.

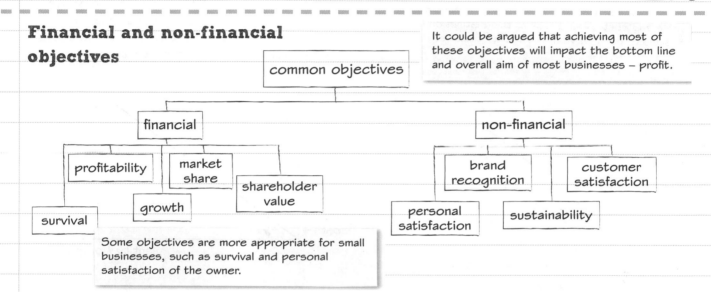

Some objectives are more appropriate for small businesses, such as survival and personal satisfaction of the owner.

Factors which influence business objectives

- **Size** – objectives may change as a business grows and becomes more successful. Most businesses when starting up will aim to survive.
- **Sector** – unlike most private sector businesses, public sector organisations are driven by meeting customer needs, not profit.
- **Market** – some markets are more competitive than others and this will determine objectives, such as targeting market share.
- **Ownership** – a Plc must satisfy shareholders, therefore will set objectives around shareholder value.
- **Owner** – the owner may simply run the business for love of the job.
- **Consumer satisfaction** – how to achieve this.

📝 Exam focus — Business objectives

Aims and objectives are very important when you are evaluating as part of an answer. Always try to identify the objectives of the business in the case study.

Evaluation is about picking out the key issues facing a business. Therefore, if you can argue that a certain course of action will support a business in achieving its objectives then you have a strong point of evaluation.

Now try this

1 Why should objectives be SMART?

2 Are some objectives more important than others?

The importance of profit

Profit is one of the main incentives of running a business. The wealth created through profit allows the owners of a business to reinvest the money into new projects and stimulate economic activity. Profit is also important because it secures the long-term success of a business. Profits can be reinvested to help the business grow and keep up with the demands of the ever-changing business environment. Profit is what is left after all costs have been deducted from revenue.

Revenue

Revenue is the value of sales made during a trading period. It also includes products sold on credit as well as those sold for cash.

A business can increase revenue by increasing the price of its products and by stimulating more demand.

> Make sure you are clear about the difference between price and cost. Always look at this distinction from the business's point of view, not the customer's.

Costs

Variable costs are those that change directly with the level of output or sales, such as the materials used to make a product.

Fixed costs are those that do not change with the level of output or sales, such as rent.

Calculating fixed and variable costs can help when making decisions about profit margins, average costs and pricing decisions. A business can improve profit by reducing either of these costs whilst maintaining value in their products.

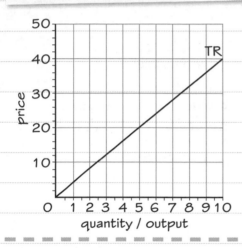

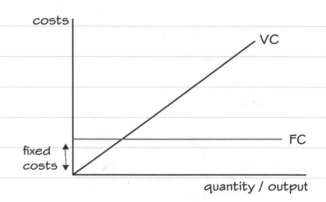

Maths skills: Calculating profit

Revenue is the value of sales made during a trading period. It also includes products sold on credit as well as those sold for cash.

A business can increase revenue by increasing the price of their products and by stimulating more demand.

price	total variable costs
×	+
quantity sold	total fixed costs
=	=

total revenue − total costs = profit

Revenue vs profit

Revenue is an important measure of success for most businesses. Achieving high revenue demonstrates that the business has been able to produce a product that is desirable at the right price for consumers. However, the real test is if the business has been able to turn revenue into profit. As the saying goes, 'revenue is vanity, profit is sanity'.

Exam focus: Profit margin

When **analysing** sales revenue of a business it is also important to consider the **profit margin**. It is difficult to analyse the success of a business without being able to compare revenue and profit.

Now try this

1 How is profit calculated?
2 What is the difference between variable and fixed costs?
3 How might a business increase its revenue?

Exam skills

These pages will give you practical advice, tips and examples on how to approach the different types of questions you will come across in your exams.

Worked example

1 Which one of the following is a reason for having a mission statement?

A To communicate the values of the business   ●

B To communicate the financial performance of the business   ○

C To communicate the product range of the business   ○

D To communicate the strategy of a business   ○

(1 mark)

> When answering multiple choice questions always give an answer even if you're not sure – you may still gain a mark.

2 Which of the following is not a variable cost for a business?

A Wages   ○

B Insurance   ●

C Packaging   ○

D Raw materials   ○

(1 mark)

> Variable costs change with the level of output. So your task is to identify which one of these does not.

3 A business sells 120 units in its first week of trading. The business sells each unit for £15. The variable cost to produce each unit is estimated at £8. The business also acquires fixed costs of £800 per month.

Calculate the profit for one week.

(5 marks)

120 units × £15 each = £1800 revenue

£8 × 120 units = £960 total variable costs

£800 ÷ 4 weeks in a month = £200 fixed costs per week

£1800 − (960 + 200) = £640 profit

> **Maths skills** **Question type: calculation**
> - Write down any formulae.
> - Select the figures you require.
> - Show currency, units and decimals as appropriate.
> - Check your answer – does it make sense? Is it logical?

4 Explain one reason why a new business start-up that sells rare vintage clothing might decide not to set an objective concerned with profitability.

(4 marks)

A new start-up might choose not to set an objective based around profitability because it may initially be concerned with generating enough cash flow to keep the business growing. Therefore the business may initially set an objective to attract X number of customers per week. This is especially important if the clothing is rare as the potential number of customers may be small.

> This question only requires the candidate to explain one reason, but it is important to develop the point and make linked strands of development using appropriate connectives. 'Therefore...' 'As a result...'

Size and form of business

Businesses come in all forms and sizes. The nature and size of each business will determine the most appropriate form of ownership. There are benefits and drawbacks to each type of business and issues that all businesses have to face as they make the transition between different forms of ownership.

Private sector vs public sector

Private businesses are:
- owned by shareholders and private individuals
- most businesses in the UK
- driven by profit motive (most)
- determined by market forces.

Some industries and businesses feature aspects of both the private and public sector, such as the NHS.

Public businesses:
- are owned and funded by national or local government
- account for approximately 19% of UK employment
- are driven by public interest
- are made up of public corporations, public services and municipal services.

100% private	50/50	
		100% public

← **privatisation**
selling of public owned industries to raise capital and improve efficiency

Business forms

The diagram below outlines how a business may change its form as it grows.

Sole traders
- easy to start up – no registration
- requires wide range of skills and flexibility
- own boss but long hours
- keep all profits
- unlimited liability.

sole traders
owned by individuals
self-employed

Private limited company
- must go through process of incorporation
- limited liability
- customers may trust a limited company more than sole trader
- wider access to capital – easier to borrow money as a limited company.

private limited company
owned by shareholders
separate legal entity

Public limited company
- can raise capital through selling shares to the public
- size measured by market capitalisation
- ability to take over other businesses
- can lose control of the business
- pressure to pay dividends to its shareholders.

public limited company
large publicly owned companies

size – as businesses grow they gain more access to capital

Non-profit organisations
A business may also be set up as a charity – a not-for-profit business. A charity may be exempt from tax on most forms of income. Alternatively, a business may take the form of a mutual. A mutual can take any legal form, but it is distinguished by the fact that it is run for the benefit of its members (employees, customers or community).

Incorporation

Incorporation involves the registry of a business with Companies House and includes documents such as a Memorandum of Association and Articles of Association.

Limited liability

Where the liability of the owners is detached from the company. Shareholders can lose their investment in the event of financial difficulties, but their personal belongings are safe, unlike with unlimited liability where there is no distinction in law between the individual and the business.

Now try this

1 What are the benefits of running as a sole trader?

2 Why is limited liability important?

3 Why would a business want to change from a private limited company to a public limited company?

Ownership: aims and objectives

The aims and objectives of a business will be influenced by the type of ownership, its size and the external environment in which it operates.

Aims and objectives of different organisations

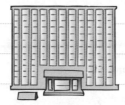

public limited company
large publicly owned companies

- Public limited company (plc) – a public limited company has external shareholders due to stock market floatation. As a result, the aims and objectives of the business are likely to relate to increasing shareholder value. Private limited companies and sole traders do not have this pressure to satisfy external shareholders. As a Plc is more likely to operate in international markets, its objectives may also refer to how it intends to operate in these markets.

- Private limited company (Ltd) – many businesses can be formed as a private limited company. Although the limited status does not necessarily influence aims and objectives, the business may have ambitions to become a Plc. Objectives are also likely to involve growth and expansion.

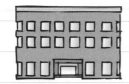

private limited company
owned by shareholders
separate legal entity

sole traders
owned by individuals
self-employed

- Sole trader – sole traders are typically small businesses and owned by one person. If the business is newly formed the objectives are likely to focus on survival, establishing a loyal customer base or building reputation. Objectives may only extend to providing the owner with a comfortable income.

- Charity – a charity is a not-for-profit organisation so obviously its aims and objectives will not focus on the incentive of profit. A charity may set a unique way to measure its success, such as the number of donors, the number of people it has supported or the awareness of the cause it promotes.

charity

Twitter

In 2013 Twitter floated itself on the New York Stock Exchange. The initial public offering was valued at $14.2 bn and the share price for its first day of trading settled at around $44 per share.

Exam focus **Case study and ownership**

In any case study consider the type of ownership of the business in question. Even if the objectives of the business are not explicit in the case study, these can be inferred by the type and nature of the business. For example, a business that has been open for a year may expect returning customers and start to make a profit.

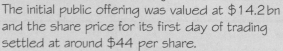

Now try this

1 Why is survival an appropriate objective for a sole trader?
2 Why might the objectives of a private limited company shift as it becomes a public limited company?

Had a look ☐ Nearly there ☐ Nailed it! ☐

The role of shareholders

A shareholder is an individual or an institution that owns a percentage of a company. Shareholders invest in companies to make a profit (return) on their investment. Shareholders can influence the decision making in companies and often have a vote in key company policy.

Shareholders and their percentage stake

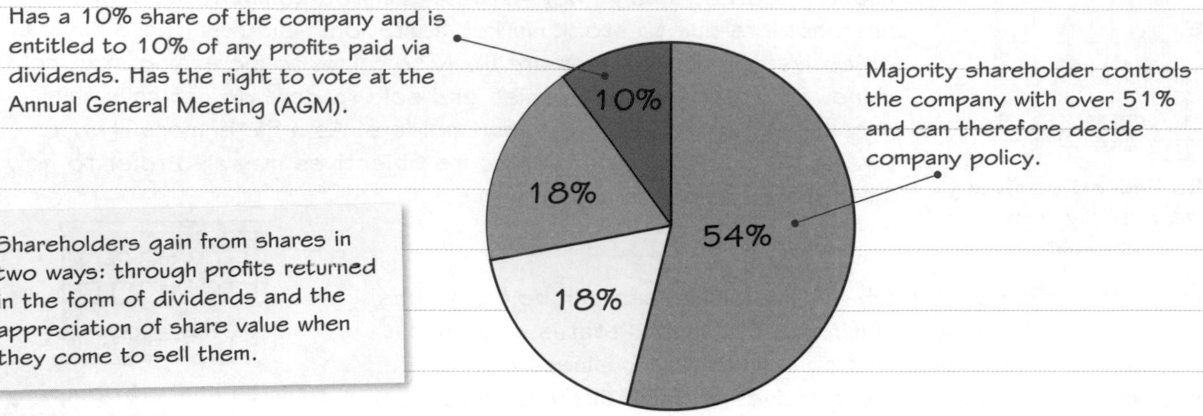

Has a 10% share of the company and is entitled to 10% of any profits paid via dividends. Has the right to vote at the Annual General Meeting (AGM).
10%
18%
18%
54%
Majority shareholder controls the company with over 51% and can therefore decide company policy.

Shareholders gain from shares in two ways: through profits returned in the form of dividends and the appreciation of share value when they come to sell them.

Share price changes

Share prices are affected by the company's performance and the business environment in which it trades. A company's share price could fall even if it is performing well if there are fears for its future.

Example of factors that may affect share price

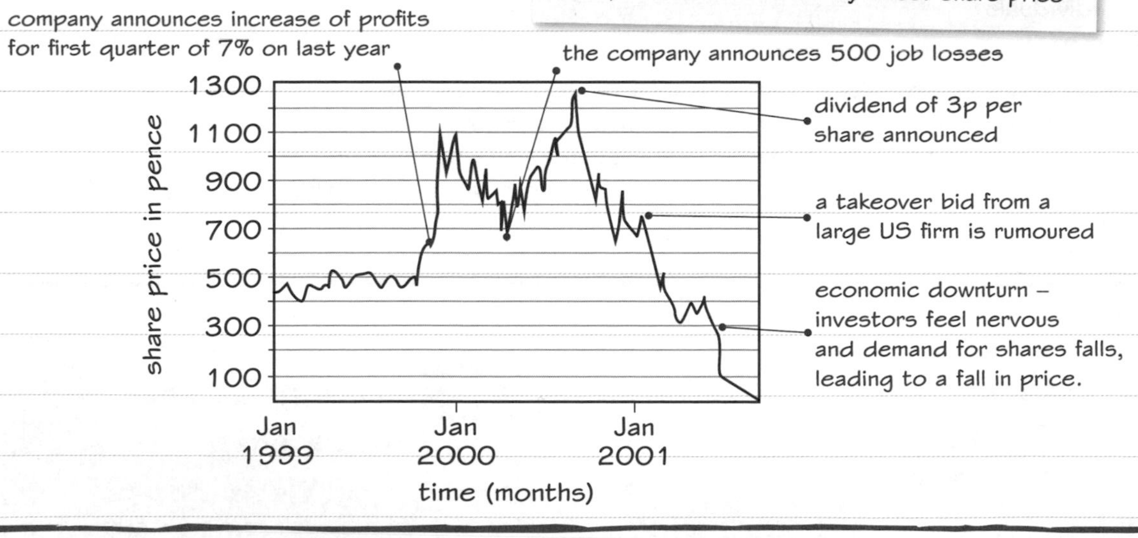

company announces increase of profits for first quarter of 7% on last year
the company announces 500 job losses
dividend of 3p per share announced
a takeover bid from a large US firm is rumoured
economic downturn – investors feel nervous and demand for shares falls, leading to a fall in price.
share price in pence
1300
1100
900
700
500
300
100
Jan 1999
Jan 2000
Jan 2001
time (months)

When share prices rise

- Managers may receive a bonus.
- The company finds it easier to raise capital.
- Consumers with shares feel more confident to spend.
- The business may receive positive publicity.

When share prices fall

- The company may become vulnerable to a takeover.
- Price fall gives an indication of poor performance.
- The company finds it harder to raise capital.
- Consumers with shares feel less confident to spend.

Now try this

1 Why are shareholders important to a company?
2 Give three reasons that the share price of a company might change.
3 Why is share price important for a company?

Exam skills

Have a look at the examples of exam-style questions below. Each question refers to the issues facing different forms of business ownership. Note how context is still important for these types of questions.

Worked example

Which one of the following is a benefit of limited liability?

A The owner keeps all of the profits   ⬭

B The owner's personal belongings are safe   ⬤

C The business can sell shares to the public   ⬭

D The business is easy to set up   ⬭

(1 mark)

Options A and C are both good distractors. It is possible for the owner of a limited company to keep all of the profits if they are the sole shareholder. A public limited company can also sell shares to the general public. However, these are not the benefit of limited liability. B is the only correct answer.

Question type: explain

When answering on an 'Explain' question you should:

👍 identify the reason/purpose benefit, and so on

👍 say why – state the cause

👍 show an understanding of the relevant issues

👍 apply your answer to the question context

👍 develop your explanation with cause and/or consequence.

Worked example

Explain one reason why the decision of a company to recall faulty products could lead to a fall in their share price.   **(4 marks)**
Recalling faulty products could lead to a fall in a company's share price because the market will anticipate a fall in profits. If a company has to recall faulty products it will have to refund customers and this is likely to impact their profits and reputation. As a result there will be less demand for their shares and share prices will fall.

The candidate has shown an understanding of factors that may reduce the share price of a company. They have also applied the context by explaining how a product recall would lead to the anticipated fall in profits and impact the company's reputation.

Worked example

Explain one way that a photographer with little experience of running a business might benefit from setting up as a sole trader.   **(5 marks)**
A photographer might benefit from setting up their business as a sole trader because the process is relatively straightforward and the photographer could start trading immediately. A sole trader does not need to be registered with Companies House which saves time and money. As a result the photographer can start trading and see if there is sufficient demand for his/her photographs without committing too much capital to starting the business.

The candidate has started by clearly identifying the benefit – easy to set up. They have then gone on to say why it is easy to start as a sole trader (no need to register with Companies House) and have then applied their answer to the context of the photographer.

An easy way to apply your answer to the context on a short answer question is to refer to the product of the business. In this case 'photographs'.

9

The external environment 1

All businesses operate within an external environment. Unlike the internal functions, a business cannot control these external forces but instead must adapt and respond to these pressures. If a business responds quickly to a change in the external environment, it can gain advantages over its competitors.

External forces

competition

market conditions

economic factors such as consumer incomes, interest rate changes

The business

demographic factors such as birth rates, migration, consumer tastes

environmental issues such as consumer preference for fair trade products and green business practices

market conditions such as consumer incomes, competition, growth in demand

Market conditions and competition

There are a range of factors that might determine how attractive or changeable a market is. These factors may determine how responsive and flexible a business needs to be in order to succeed within its market. Some of these factors include:

- the growth rate of the market
- the typical profit margin that businesses can generate
- the number and size of competitors in the market
- the pace of innovation and new product development
- the bargaining power of suppliers and customers
- the level of differentiation between competitors
- the seasonality of the product
- the volatility of costs incurred by businesses, such as commodity prices.

 Real world **Mobile phone industry**

The pace of technology and new product development is a key market factor in the mobile phone industry. Most smartphone manufacturers launch a new product every 6–8 months. Furthermore, sales growth for smartphones in Western Europe and the USA is declining, whilst Africa and Asia Pacific offer considerable growth opportunities for manufacturers and network providers.

 See page 133 for more on Porter's Five Forces.

Exam focus **Case studies and market factors**

Whenever you are reading a case study, try to pick up on the key issues within the business. However, it is just as important to understand the market factors that may influence the business in question. You should always try to think about the market issues listed on the left. Even if these are not explicitly referred to in the case study, you can always infer the market factors by considering the industry, type of business and nature of the product. Another way to remember this is by using MOPSS as an acronym for the factors you might consider when analysing a market – market, organisation, product, stage and state.

Now try this

1 What factors might determine the bargaining power of a customer?

2 What might be the impact on a business operating in a market with a large number of competitors?

3 Give examples of three products that have seasonal demand.

The external environment 2

Economic factors

A key economic factor is the income of consumers. Incomes are determined by the gross domestic product (GDP). GDP is a measure of the output of an economy in terms of the goods and services it produces over a year.

High GDP will increase the incomes of consumers leading to increased spending on a range of goods and services.

Remember that consumer spending on luxuries will respond differently to that on necessities to a change in incomes. Consumers may purchase more luxury items as their incomes rise, but there may be little change in demand for necessities as incomes fall.

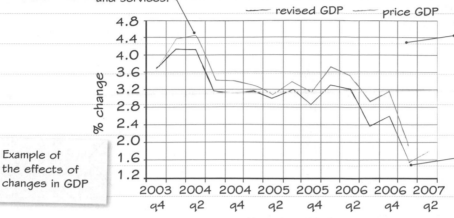

— revised GDP   — price GDP

Example of the effects of changes in GDP

Low GDP may result in unemployment and falling incomes. Spending will fall for certain goods and services.

Interest rates

An interest rate is the cost of borrowing money or the reward for saving.

Interest rates are closely linked to the level of inflation and the exchange rate.

High interest rates

- cost of existing loans may increase
- consumers may have less disposable income (consequence of increased mortgage payments)
- demand for products bought on credit may fall
- consumers more likely to save their money

3.5%

2.0%

1.0%

Low interest rates

- cost of existing loans may fall
- demand for products bought on credit may rise e.g. luxury goods
- consumers more likely to spend
- disposable income rises
- savers lose out on earnings from investments

Demographic factors

Demography is the study of the human population. There are a number of key demographic issues affecting the UK. These are:

- the UK population is growing, leading to an increase in demand for most goods and services.
- migration to the UK from Eastern European countries is growing, fuelling growth in the labour market.
- the UK population is getting older, changing the demand for different products and services.

Stakeholder groups

Remember that the population forms two key stakeholder groups.

Changes in the population will impact the size of a potential market and their wants and needs.

Changes in the population will impact the size of the labour market and the skills of those workers.

Now try this

1 How might consumers react to an increase in interest rates?

2 Identify three consequences of an increase in average incomes.

3 What are the benefits of a growing population?

The external environment 3

Environmental factors

Government tries to ensure businesses pay for the total cost of production including the external costs, such as pollution, which ultimately has to be paid for by society. There are benefits and drawbacks for a business of being environmentally friendly.

for   against

avoid negative publicity from the media

opportunity for differentiation

avoids fines or penalties imported through environmental legislation

opportunity for government incentives such as tax relief

creates a sustainable business

environmental business practices

increased cost of raw materials

increased cost of waste disposal

lower profit margin on fair trade goods

The benefits and drawbacks of environmentally friendly business practices.

UK environmental legislation includes:

- the Environmental Protection Act, 1990
- the Environment Act, 1995
- the Climate Change Act, 2008.

 Real world **Fairtrade**

Global retail sales of Fairtrade products such as coffee, sugar and bananas increased by 15% in 2014. The UK is currently the world's largest market for Fairtrade produce.

 Exam focus **Environmentally friendly businesses**

In the past, environmentally friendly businesses have gained an advantage over others that are less 'green'. However, as consumer attitudes change, they expect businesses to be environmentally friendly as standard. Therefore, it becomes less of a competitive advantage and more of a prerequisite to be able to operate successfully in a competitive market. This is a good point of balance to consider whenever discussing environmentally friendly business practices.

Now try this

1 What is Fairtrade produce?

2 Why does the government impose environmental legislation?

3 Identify three external environmental factors that might have an impact on a business.

Exam skills

The following exam-style questions with exemplar answers cover the topic **The external environment**.

Worked example

1 Which of the following refers to a demographic factor that may influence business activity?

Demographics is the study of the human population.

A Trends increasing for consumers who want ethical products ○

B The population of the UK getting older ●

C Gross domestic product increasing by 1.2% in the last 3 months ○

D Interest rates falling by 0.5% ○

(1 mark)

2 Explain one market factor that might affect an independent restaurant that has recently opened on a busy high street in a wealthy suburb of a large city. **(4 marks)**

There are three pieces of context that the student should take from this question. 1. independent restaurant, 2. recently opened and 3. wealthy suburb.

One market factor that may affect this business is the extent to which other local restaurants are differentiated from this one. As the restaurant has set up in a busy suburb it is likely that there will be lots of competition. For customers to be drawn away from other more established restaurants the new restaurant must offer something different. For example, as it is a wealthy area it is likely that competitors will be up-market restaurants. The new restaurant could differentiate itself by selling unique dishes or having a specific theme, such as a seafood restaurant if there are no other seafood restaurants in the area.

This answer identifies a relevant market factor 'differentiation' and applies the explanation to the context given. The student has made good use of an example.

3 Analyse how a small business that sells building materials for landscape gardening might be affected by the economic trends in Table 1. **(9 marks)**

Two different economic variables are included in this question. Is there any relationship between the two?

Table 1

	Qtr 1	Qtr 2	Qtr 3	Qtr 4
GDP % change	0.2	0.2	0.5	0.4
Interest rate	2.0	1.5	1.5	1.0

The economic forecast suggests that the rate of growth in the economy is likely to increase at a steady rate. This growth is likely to boost demand in the economy as people spend more money. It is also likely that unemployment will be falling. For this reason people may choose to spend more money on home improvements such as their garden. As a result, small gardening businesses are likely to see a rise in sales revenue. However, this may depend on the time of year as gardening is seasonal.

Interest rates are also falling and this could encourage people to borrow more money and spend instead of saving. Many people may choose to borrow money to landscape their garden and this is another factor that could lead to increased demand for the small supplier of building materials.

Question type: analyse

When answering an 'analyse' question you should:

- 👍 demonstrate a good understanding of the concept/s in the question
- 👍 use appropriate key terms
- 👍 apply your answer effectively to the question's context
- 👍 identify and analyse at least one issue
- 👍 develop your analysis with cause and/or consequence.

Exam-style practice 1

Have a go at the questions below that apply the concepts covered in Unit 3.1. They are examples of question types that you will find on both sections of Paper 1. There are answers on pages 195 and 196.

1 Which one of the following is not a benefit that a business can bring to society?

   A Enhance the country's reputation ☐

   B Create employment opportunities ☐

   C Improve equality in a country ☐

   D Create wealth for individuals ☐

   (1 mark)

> Remember to eliminate one answer at a time.

2 What is meant by the term 'real income'?

   A Incomes adjusted with inflation ☐

   B The measure of a country's total output ☐

   C The amount people take home after tax ☐

   D The level of income required to achieve basic necessities ☐

   (1 mark)

> Start by narrowing this answer down to two options. What might 'real income' take into consideration?

3 A business spent:

* £10 000 on raw materials
* £30 000 on fixed costs
* £7500 on other variable costs

The business now buys its raw materials 10% more cheaply from a new supplier.

What effect will this have on its profit level?

The profit level will:

A increase by £2500 ☐

B fall by £2500 ☐

C increase from £2500 to £3500 ☐

D increase by 10% ☐

   (1 mark)

> Always write out the formula to help ensure you reach the right answer. The alternative options are always possible answers if you calculate the numbers incorrectly, for example get something the wrong way round.

4 Based on the data shown in Table 1, calculate the fixed costs for the business. Show your workings. **(4 marks)**

> What number do you need to find the fixed costs for this business?

Table 1

Selling price	**£8.50**
Total revenue	£25 500
Total contribution	£17 700
Total costs	£21 000

Exam-style practice 2

5 Explain one way that an electrician, registering their business as a private limited company, might benefit when operating in a competitive local market. **(5 marks)**

Only one benefit needs explaining. Remember to apply the context. Your answer might take into account 'electrician' or 'competitive local market'.

6 Explain how a fall in GDP might affect a national delivery company. **(4 marks)**

A good way to start an 'explain' question is to clearly define the concept being addressed in the question, for example, GDP.

Standard Chartered

Standard Chartered has warned investors that it will experience a second-successive fall in annual profits after an unexpectedly poor performance from its trading division. The bank reported a 44% drop in half-year profits. The UK-listed bank halved its dividend payout plans and is considering the possibility of raising more capital from investors.

Tougher economic conditions in emerging markets and a wave of new regulation have created difficulties for Standard Chartered, which rode out the financial crisis far better than most banks.

Read the context before answering the question.

7 To what extent is the payment of dividends important for the long-term success of a public limited company?
(16 marks)

Remember to show balance in your answer by discussing factors other than dividend payments or a limiting factor. You might use examples from the context to make your point.

Question type: to what extent

When answering a 'To what extent' question you should:

👍 demonstrate a good understanding of the concept/s in the question

👍 use appropriate key terms

👍 apply your answer effectively to the question's context

👍 analyse reasons for and against

👍 develop your analysis with cause and/or consequence

👍 bring a comparative issue of factor into your answer

👍 evaluate the extent to which you agree with the statement and justify your answer.

This style of essay is likely to appear on Section D of the A level Paper 1 so only answer this question if you are revising for your A level exam. It requires the same skills as all the other essay questions but is not directly linked to a specific case study context.

8 A large supermarket chain operating in a competitive market is considering a review of its environmental policies around its food produce and packaging. The economy in which the supermarket operates is also facing recession. To what extent are environmentally friendly business practices a key to the success of such a business?
(25 marks)

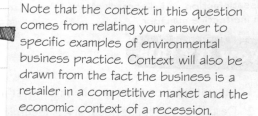

Note that the context in this question comes from relating your answer to specific examples of environmental business practice. Context will also be drawn from the fact the business is a retailer in a competitive market and the economic context of a recession.

Management and leadership 1

This unit looks at the importance of managers and leaders in running a successful business. In this unit you will revise several theoretical models for analysing management and leadership and the benefits and drawbacks of each model.

The role of managers

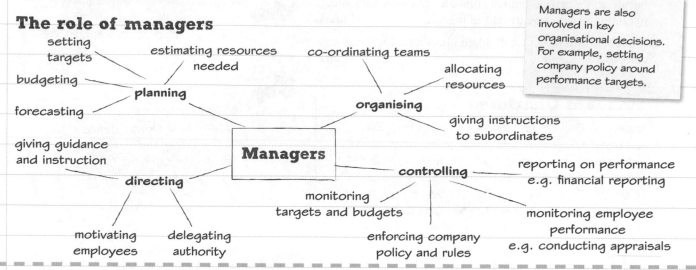

planning
- setting targets
- estimating resources needed
- budgeting
- forecasting

organising
- co-ordinating teams
- allocating resources
- giving instructions to subordinates

Managers

directing
- giving guidance and instruction
- motivating employees
- delegating authority

controlling
- monitoring targets and budgets
- enforcing company policy and rules
- reporting on performance e.g. financial reporting
- monitoring employee performance e.g. conducting appraisals

> Managers are also involved in key organisational decisions. For example, setting company policy around performance targets.

Trait theory

The belief that leaders and managers hold certain traits that distinguish them from other people. There is disagreement about the exact traits that constitute a successful leader. One argument against this theory is that successful leaders have been found to possess very different traits from one another.

Behavioural theory

The behavioural theory of leadership suggests that there is an appropriate style of management or leadership determined by the context, situation and nature of the task. There are a number of theories that explore behavioural management and consider different styles based on a number of different factors. For example, task vs relationship styles (the Blake and Mouton Grid) or the extent to which a manager tells employees or listens to their opinions (the Tannenbaum–Schmidt Continuum).

The Blake and Moulton grid

This grid identifies a number of approaches to leadership based on the extent to which a manager is focused on their concern for production and their concern for people.

> Neither aspect is focused on entirely. Manager might care, but does not get the balance right. Hence neither the task nor employees' well-being are completely satisfied.

> A relaxed working environment. Manager is concerned with relationships and motivation of employees. Task may not get done.

> Overall the Blake and Mouton Grid can be used to help managers reflect on their own practice and identify strategies to improve their management/leadership skills.

> Perhaps focused on self and not leading the organisation. Dissatisfaction and disorganisation. An ineffective manager.

	low concern for production	high
high concern for people	country club	team leader
	middle of the road	
low	impoverished	produce or perish

> High focus on both. In theory this should be highly successful as the employees' needs should be aligned to those of the organisation. Employees feel involved and have a stake in the success of the business.

> Authoritarian. Driven by targets and getting the task done. Cares little for well-being or feelings of employees.

1 In your opinion what are the three most important roles of a manager?
2 Describe two management styles identified on the Blake and Mouton Grid.

Management and leadership 2

The Tannenbaum–Schmidt Continuum

This shows where a manager's approach lies on a continuum, ranging from the manager imposing strict authority at one extreme, through to employees having full freedom to act as they choose at the other extreme.

Continuum can be used to make choices about which approach to adopt, but no advice is given on how the approach should be chosen based on the circumstances.

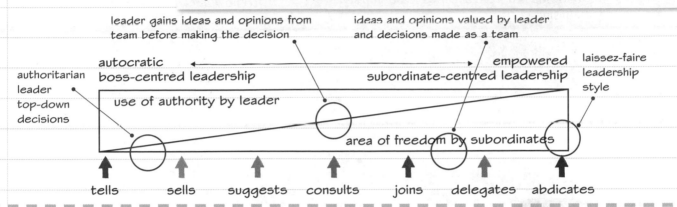

leader gains ideas and opinions from team before making the decision

ideas and opinions valued by leader and decisions made as a team

autocratic → boss-centred leadership

empowered

laissez-faire leadership style

subordinate-centred leadership

authoritarian leader top-down decisions

use of authority by leader

area of freedom by subordinates

tells   sells   suggests   consults   joins   delegates   abdicates

Advantages and disadvantages of different leadership styles

Leadership style	Advantages	Disadvantages
Autocratic (authoritarian)	• focused on getting the task done • high levels of control suitable for unskilled workforce • speeds up decision-making process – important in times of crisis • suitable for implementing a clear vision held by the leader	• can lead to low levels of motivation if employees don't feel respected or valued • no opportunity for employees to be involved in decision making • no opportunity to collect ideas and opinions of the workforce that might be valuable • employees might not feel as though they have a stake in the business
Democratic	• develops a team spirit – more opportunity for employees to 'buy in' to the task if they feel they have had a say • allows a manager to collect ideas and opinions from the whole workforce	• decision making can take a long time when done by committee • employees may not see the 'bigger picture' and vote for decisions that benefit them
Laissez-faire	• allows employees autonomy to make their own decisions, often leading to higher levels of creativity and motivation amongst workers	• lack of control over the workforce – deadlines and targets might be missed • tasks may not be coordinated very well

Leadership theories

In an exam you could be asked questions directly linked to one of the leadership theories. These might be questions such as 'To what extent is the Blake and Mouton Grid a useful tool in helping X improve her leadership skills?' For this reason it is important to understand the uses of these theories, but also their limitations.

Choosing a management/leadership style

There are a number of factors to take into account when trying to identify the best approach to management/ leadership.
These are: labour force, nature of task, timescale, personality and tradition.

Now try this

1 What is a laissez-faire leader?

2 What factors might determine the type of leadership style suitable for a situation?

17

Exam skills

The questions below apply the concepts of management and leadership. For these questions refer to the Print Eastwood case study on page 28.

Worked example

Which of the following is not a recognised leadership style associated with business?

A Autocratic ⬭

B Democratic ⬭

C Theocratic ⬤

D Laissez-faire ⬭

(1 mark)

> Three of these terms relate to how a manager will deal with their subordinates.

Worked example

With reference to the Blake and Mouton Grid. Explain the management style adopted by Dave Nutton. **(5 marks)**

Dave's leadership style is 'produce or perish' meaning he is more concerned about the task than he is about people. Dave Nutton shows little evidence of being people orientated as he insists on making the final decisions about artwork himself. Dave does seem to be task driven as he has acted quickly to ensure he can make the most of the opportunity of the imminent closure of a competitor.

> In this answer it is important to show an understanding of this leadership theory. It is not enough just to describe Dave Nutton's leadership style based on the information in the case study.

> The candidate makes a statement identifying the leadership style of Dave Nutton. The candidate has used evidence from the case study and clearly understands the Blake and Mouton Grid.

Worked example

Analyse how important it is for Dave Nutton to delegate responsibility to his workforce. **(9 marks)**

Delegation is passing on authority to a subordinate to make their own decisions on a specific task or project. Delegating tasks will allow Dave to concentrate on other managerial roles such as the planning of Print Eastwood's expansion. As Dave hopes to expand his business it is likely that he will be involved in organising and planning new projects and this is likely to increase his workload. Dave must be able to delegate more responsibility to his workforce in order to keep them motivated and ensure he is not overworked.

> The key term in this question is delegate. It is a useful approach to start your answer by defining the key concept addressed in the question.

> This is a good start to the answer. The candidate has explained the benefit of delegation and has applied this to the context of the question by referring to the fact that the business is growing. The candidate could now go on to mention how delegation would help Dave to empower his workforce. The candidate could potentially refer to the Tannenbaum–Schmidt Continuum too.

Management decision making 1

Decision making is a key role of management. Business decisions will be made on both quantitative and qualitative information and use both scientific techniques (data, logic, rationale) and the intuition of the manager (experience and hunches). Ultimately, business decisions are based on a wide number of factors and you need to understand the usefulness and value of these techniques.

The decision-making process

A range of techniques might be used to evaluate the success of a decision or project. For example, financial ratios or the Triple Bottom Line.

In Unit 3.1.1 we looked at businesses setting objectives.

In order to make the most appropriate decision factors such as risk, reward and uncertainty will be taken into account.

set objectives

review

gathering information

In Unit 3.2.1 we revised how leaders manage others to implement business decisions.

implementation

choosing the course of action

The process is key if decisions are to be made scientifically. However, managers are just as likely to use their own experience and intuition. A decision might be strategic or tactical.

Key decision-making factors

Risk the chance of an occurring misfortune or loss. Risk is calculated by multiplying the extent of the impact by the probability of its occurrence. In business risk generally refers to financial loss.

Reward – generally translates into greater revenue and profit. Sometimes a risk might be worth taking if the reward is substantial. For example, the first to enter a new market or secure a patent on a new product.

Uncertainty – very little is certain in business. Managers have to question the reliability of the information (scientific or hunches) that a decision is based upon.

Opportunity cost – the next best opportunity forfeited and all things remaining equal (ceteris paribus). Managers must always make decisions to gain the best returns from the resources they have available.

Data vs intuition

Decisions based on **data** such as financial forecasts or using business tools such as break-even analysis or investment appraisal.

Decisions based on **experience** and 'gut feeling' without having supporting data.

The extent to which decisions are made at a point along this continuum depends on a number of factors.

scientific decision making (data)

intuition or 'hunch'

👍 Data can help reduce the risk in decision making and help identify the likely outcome. Data can help compare alternative options.

👎 Sometimes data can be hard to collect or very expensive to collect, especially for small businesses. Sometimes data is not available, out of date or unreliable.

👍 Intuition might come from the experience of the manager and this is useful when making qualitative decisions, such as the character of a new employee or the potential success of a new marketing campaign or brand name.

👎 Without evidence in the form of data decisions based on intuition can be high risk.

Now try this

1 What is risk?

2 How can a business reduce uncertainty?

3 When might a decision based on intuition be better than using data?

Management decision making 2

Decision trees

This is a model that represents the likely outcomes for a business of a number of courses of action showing the financial consequences of each.

Benefits

👍 clarifies possible courses of action

👍 adds financial data to decisions

👍 makes managers account for risk.

Drawbacks

👎 probabilities are often estimated

👎 does not consider qualitative information

👎 does not take into account dynamic nature of business.

Influences on decision making

There are other factors that may play a part in shaping management decisions. These include:

- the objectives and mission of the business
- ethics – using a 'moral compass' to guide decisions
- the level of risk involved – some managers and businesses are more risk adverse than others
- the external environment including competition – most decision-making models do not take into account these factors that are constantly changing
- resource constraints – a business can only make decisions if they have the resources available (labour, capital, knowledge) and this is where opportunity cost comes in.

Decision tree example

This example shows a business with two investment decisions (or do nothing). The expected value (EV) is the highest on the marketing campaign and therefore the option the business should take.

The **expected value** is the weighted average of the outcomes taking into account their probability.

Subtract the initial cost to work out the **net gain**.

EV £20m

marketing campaign

£4m

A

high revenue
0.3
£20m

low revenue
0.7
£3m

calculating the marketing campaign's net gain = (0.3 × 20) + (0.7 × 3) = 8.1m − £4m = £4.1m

do nothing

// through the options not chosen

decision node

staff training
£1m

B

EV £3.5m

high impact
0.5
£5m

low impact
0.5
£2m

Staff training has two outcomes. The financial benefit is shown at the end of the arrows.

possible outcome node

The possibility goes below the line. The probability of all outcomes, no matter how many, should always add up to 1.

This example shows a business with two investment decisions (or do nothing). The expected value is the highest on the marketing campaign and therefore the option the business should take.

Now try this

1 How might a manager use a decision tree?

2 What is the expected value in a decision tree?

Management decision making 3

Constructing a decision tree

The five stages below will help you to construct a complete decision tree, which can then be used to make investment decisions.

1 Add information to the decision tree:
  • decisions
  • costs
  • outcomes
  • financial benefits
  • probability.

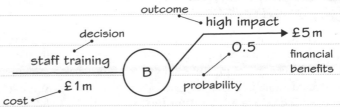

2 Multiply each financial benefit by its probability for each outcome and add them together to get the **expected value**.

> e.g. staff training = (0.5 × 5m) + (0.5 × 2m)
> EV = £.3.5m

3 If there is an initial cost (£1m to train staff), subtract this to get the **net gains** of the decision.

4 Repeat this process for each decision.

5 Cross through the options not taken.

Now try this

1 What are the limitations of decision trees?

2 What other decision-making tools might a manager use alongside a decision tree?

3 Using the guide above and the blank decision tree diagram below, come up with your own set of business decisions with probable outcomes. When you have created a scenario that fits the decision tree, work through the five stages to complete the decision tree.

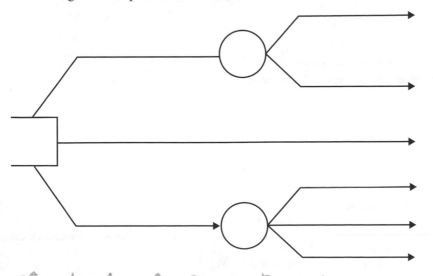

Exam skills

The questions below apply the concepts of management decision making. For these questions refer to the Print Eastwood case study on page 28.

Worked example

Apart from the option of purchasing a new 'direct to garment' printer, Print Eastwood also has the option of spending £50 000 on a regional advertising campaign. Referring to the figure below, calculate the expected value and the net gain of the advertising campaign. Using these calculations advise Print Eastwood which of the two options it should choose. Show your workings. **(6 marks)**

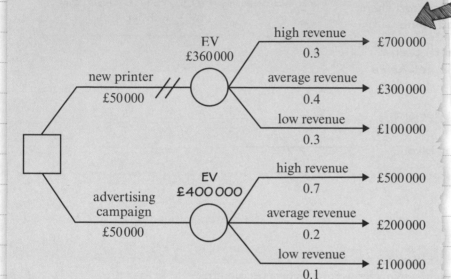

> Expected value of new printer calculated by:
> (0.3 × 700) + (0.4 × 300) + (0.3 × 100)
> = 210 + 120 + 30
> = £360 000

(0.7 × 500) + (0.2 × 200) + (0.1 × 100)
= 350 + 40 + 10
= £400 000 expected value
− £50 000 = £350 000 net gain

Print Eastwood should opt for the advertising campaign because it has a higher expected value and net gain than buying the new printer.

> The candidate has clearly shown their workings in stages and has made sure they have answered the question by stating which of the two investments Print Eastwood should opt for. The candidate has also labelled the diagram correctly and crossed through the less profitable option with //.

Worked example

Explain one disadvantage of Dave basing his business decisions on intuition. **(4 marks)**

One disadvantage of Dave basing his decisions on intuition is that he has no evidence in order to calculate the likely risk and probability of success (which he would have if he completed a decision tree). If he has no evidence on which to base his decision to buy a new printer for £50 000 then he may struggle to convince a lender to loan the money to purchase the printer.

> The candidate has identified a disadvantage of basing management decisions on intuition. They have then gone on to apply this to the context of Print Eastwood.

The importance of stakeholders 1

Stakeholders are groups or individuals who have an interest in a business. It is important for all businesses to manage the needs of their stakeholders if they are to be successful. Stakeholders can have a considerable impact on the actions and fortunes of a business, but not all stakeholders have the same needs and wants. Therefore, the key is being able to manage these often-conflicting interests.

Stakeholders in a business

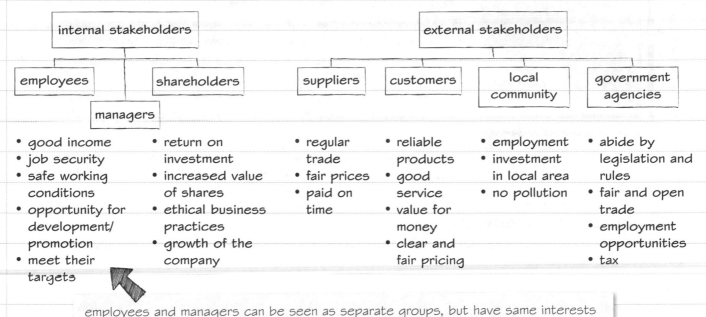

internal stakeholders

- employees
- shareholders
- managers

external stakeholders

- suppliers
- customers
- local community
- government agencies

employees / shareholders / managers
- good income
- job security
- safe working conditions
- opportunity for development/ promotion
- meet their targets

- return on investment
- increased value of shares
- ethical business practices
- growth of the company

suppliers
- regular trade
- fair prices
- paid on time

customers
- reliable products
- good service
- value for money
- clear and fair pricing

local community
- employment
- investment in local area
- no pollution

government agencies
- abide by legislation and rules
- fair and open trade
- employment opportunities
- tax

employees and managers can be seen as separate groups, but have same interests

Shareholder vs stakeholder concept

The concept of managing stakeholder expectations is closely linked to that of social responsibility. Meeting the needs of stakeholders, especially the external stakeholders, encourages ethical practices by reducing the negative impact of a business's decisions on a third party. Meeting stakeholders' needs can be expensive and time-consuming. Indeed, it can often compromise profitability in the short term. For example, investing in employee medical cover may benefit the business in the long run, but will increase short-term costs. The major conflict that many large businesses face is focusing on the needs of shareholders or the wider stakeholder groups.

Overlapping and conflicting interests

Sometimes stakeholder interests are aligned, but often satisfying one set of needs can lead to conflict elsewhere. In any situation you should try to consider where conflicts might exist and what the business could do to resolve these conflicts. Look at the diagram and think how a business opening a new high tech factory could have an impact on the stakeholders shown.

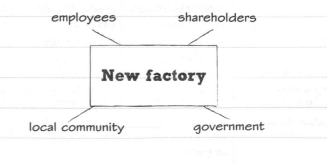

employees　　　shareholders

New factory

local community　　　government

Now try this

1 State three stakeholder groups.
2 Outline the interests of the local community.
3 What is the most important stakeholder group in a business?

The importance of stakeholders 2

Stakeholder mapping

A stakeholder map is a tool to assess the interest and power of stakeholders in order to make decisions about how to manage them.

A – High power but low interest. May be key shareholders who are only interested in return on investment. Satisfy needs but try to increase their interest and involvement in the business.

B – May be key customers who account for a significant percentage of sales. Keep them happy, consult and involve them in key decisions.

C – Minimal effort – make sure information is available to this group through newsletter or website.

D – Perhaps local residents who are concerned with the business actions. Communicate key decisions only. Possibly consult on low-impact decisions.

> Stakeholder maps, like a market map, are useful decision-making tools to generate discussion and give structure to decision making. However, they do not provide businesses with clear solutions on how to manage stakeholders.

Stakeholder engagement

The likelihood of stakeholder conflict can be reduced through effective communication and in some circumstances consultation. The extent can be determined through stakeholder mapping.

high power /
high interest

low power /
low interest

partnership	participation	consultation	'push' communication	'pull' communication
• decisions taken jointly • implement actions together • shared responsibility	• extensive two-way communication • given responsibility for certain decisions	• collect views / opinions • share ideas as proposals	• inform • one-way communications • emails, newsletters, mailshots	• information available for stakeholders if they choose to access e.g. website

Influences on stakeholder relationships

internal factors			external factors		
management and leadership	**objectives**	**size / ownership**	**market conditions**	**stakeholder power**	**government policy**
Differing leadership styles will determine how managers view employees. For example the Blake and Mouton Grid explored in 3.2.1.	Profit objectives will be more aligned to shareholder interests. Growth objectives may be more aligned with employees' interests.	A sole trader will not have the pressures of meeting shareholder expectations and may not have as big an impact on the local community.	Demand and the competitiveness of a market will change the priorities of a business.	Majority shareholders and key customers will be given greater focus than a stakeholder with limited power to influence the business.	A business will have to meet its legal requirements, no matter how this impacts its stakeholders. For example new employment legislation.

Now try this

1 What might determine the interests of a stakeholder group?

2 What might determine the influence/power of a stakeholder group?

Exam skills

Read the Print Eastwood case study on page 28 and have a go at the following questions that cover the concepts explored across Unit 3.2.

Worked example

1 Explain **one reason** why Dave Nutton should consider the interests of his employees when making decisions about the future of Print Eastwood.   **(4 marks)**

Question only requires one reason to be explained.

Dave should consider the interests of his employees because they have considerable power in the organisation. This is because they are a skilled workforce and he relies on them for designing and printing. As it is a small workforce he cannot afford to lose any employees, considering that he wants the business to expand. The employees may also be glad of the opportunity to develop their roles within the business and the chance of promotion.

The answer refers to the power of the stakeholder group and explains why employees should be considered to have high power within Dave's business.

2 Analyse the **reasons why** Dave Nutton should carry out stakeholder mapping.   **(9 marks)**

This question requires the candidate to explore at least one benefit of stakeholder mapping and apply it to Print Eastwood.

A stakeholder map is a business tool that helps managers to identify and categorise stakeholders in order to make decisions on how to engage them. If Dave carried out stakeholder mapping he would be able to identify the stakeholders who have the most influence on his business. By doing this he would then be able to put in place measures to ensure he is able to meet the needs of these stakeholders and therefore secure the long-term success of his business. For example, Dave may find out that his suppliers of garments are a major stakeholder. He could then try to put in place a long-term supply agreement with the supplier to secure the best prices and build a strong relationship...

At the end of the answer the candidate uses an example. The example applies the concept of stakeholder mapping to Print Eastwood. This is an effective way to add context to your answer. In this instance, the candidate has only analysed one reason, but could go on to explain a second. However, this may not be necessary if the reason given is well-developed, is applied to the context and shows understanding of cause and consequence.

3 The recent announcement of the potential closure of one of Print Eastwood's major competitors has created a number of new opportunities for the company to expand. To what extent are market conditions important to how Dave Nutton manages his stakeholder relations?   **(16 marks)**

Ideally this answer should consider other factors that are more/just as important as market conditions. For example, the student could discuss the trends and tastes of customers. This will provide balance to the answer.

...Another factor that is important to how Dave manages his stakeholders is size and ownership of his business. Dave is the sole owner of the business – he has no other shareholders to worry about satisfying. However, as the business grows he may decide to take on other investors and this might change his priorities.

This would be a good second paragraph to the answer. The candidate has brought in a second factor – the ownership of the company – to give the answer balance. The evaluation could then justify which of the two factors is the most important.

Exam-style practice 1

The questions below apply the concepts of managing stakeholders. For these questions refer to the Print Eastwood case study on page 28. There are answers on page 196.

1 Which of the following is not a scientific decision-making technique used by business?

A Decision tree ◯

B Ratio analysis ◯

C Manager's experience ◯

D Investment appraisal ◯

(1 mark)

 Which of these options does not involve a business model, statistics, probability or financial information?

2 Which of the following best describes the term opportunity cost?

A The next best alternative forgone ◯

B The benefit of choosing an option ◯

C The benefits of not choosing an option ◯

D The disadvantage of the alternative forgone ◯

(1 mark)

Read the options carefully. Each answer is very similar and it is easy to select the wrong option if you do not read the question carefully.

3 Dave Nutton is considering two new investment projects for Print Eastwood:

• increasing advertising of current products

• launching a new product range

Using Figure 1, calculate the expected values of both options and identify which option Dave should choose.

(6 marks)

Think about the suitability of different leadership styles to different contexts. Then consider what the demands might be on Dave's business as it expands.

Figure 1 Decision tree for Print Eastwood

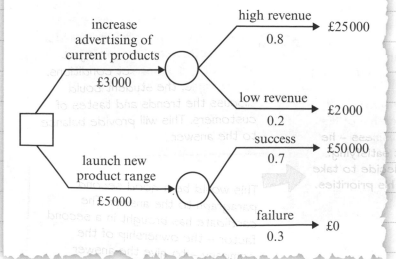

Exam-style practice 2

4 Explain one reason why Dave Nutton might need to change his leadership style as Print Eastwood expands. **(5 marks)**

First start by thinking about what leadership style characterises Dave Nutton. What are the requirements of a leader as a business expands?

5 Analyse the **level of risk** involved in Dave Nutton's decision to invest in a new garment printing machine. **(9 marks)**

6 Figure 2 represents a stakeholder map carried out by Dave Nutton. Using the diagram analyse the reasons why Dave should work closely with his suppliers. **(9 marks)**

Risk will concern the likelihood of the purchase of the printing machine failing and the impact of this happening. Start by demonstrating your understanding of risk and then consider the context of Print Eastwood.

Figure 2 Stakeholder map for Print Eastwood

influence / power of stakeholders ↑		
meet the needs • local community	key player • employees
least important	• suppliers show consideration

interest of stakeholders →

First, show your understanding of stakeholder mapping and consider where Dave Nutton has placed suppliers on his diagram. You might also consider the interest of suppliers in your answer.

7 To what extent is the local community important to the long-term success of Print Eastwood? **(16 marks)**

This style of question will appear on both AS and A level exam papers. On A level papers this style of question could be worth 20–24 marks.

Evaluate the importance of the local community considering how closely Print Eastwood has worked with its community in the past. It is also important to compare the importance of the local community to other stakeholders before you evaluate your answer. Your evaluation might identify what you believe to be the most important issue, given the Print Eastwood context.

Case study

Print Eastwood

PRINT EASTWOOD

Dave Nutton has run his small garment printing business based in Eastwood, Nottinghamshire for 8 years. Since opening his business in 2007, Dave has seen his company grow to the point where he employs three full-time employees and two part-time. Dave has a background in graphic design. His business is able to compete with other printing firms through the inexpensive design service they offer to other businesses, clubs, societies and private events such as bachelor parties.

Over the years Print Eastwood has developed a number of ties with the local community. Dave has secured contracts to print garments for the local schools and worked closely with the local council to print garments for the annual Eastwood Fair. Print Eastwood also sponsors the local football team and uses a local supplier for their garments such as t-shirts and hoodies.

Print Eastwood has developed logos and designs for many of their customers and although Dave employs two in-house designers, he still insists on having a hand in all new artwork and makes sure he sees every design before it is approved for print.

Rumour has it that a major competitor, with a 20% market share, is in financial difficulty and expects to stop trading by 2016. Dave sees this as an opportunity to expand his company's services nationwide. Dave has never really conducted research into the national printing market, but has based most of his decisions on intuition. Dave also knows that for his company to expand he needs to look elsewhere for a larger supplier and invest up to £50 000 in a new direct to garment printer.

Within the week Dave has decided to go ahead with the expansion plans without consulting his employees. He knows time is of the essence and he wants to start a regional advertising campaign to raise awareness. With the expansion it is likely that the company will require an additional three to four full-time employees and he knows his two part-time staff cannot increase the number of hours they currently work. It was also likely that he will have to take his attention away from Eastwood if his printing company is going to capitalise on the gap created by the imminent closure of his competitor.

Marketing objectives

Marketing is the function within a business concerned with communicating with customers. Marketing is a two-way process whereby the business learns about its customers in order to provide goods and services that meet their needs. It is then concerned with ensuring customers are aware, understand and desire the product. The role of marketing overlaps with that of other business functions.

The importance of marketing

The process of marketing allows a business to:

- 👍 understand the market it is operating in
- 👍 understand what customers want
- 👍 understand the relative strengths and weaknesses in comparison to competitors
- 👍 build a strong brand
- 👍 build relationships with customers
- 👍 understand the nature of pricing for its products.

The market

A market is where buyers meet sellers. A market exists wherever there are potential customers who want to buy a product, and where there is a business able to produce and sell that product. All markets have unique characteristics, can grow or shrink and can be distinguished on a local, regional, national or global scale; for example, the UK housing market or the global market for oil.

The UK domestic tourism market was worth £23 billion in 2014.

Marketing objectives

Marketing departments typically set objectives around growth, brand image, share and brand loyalty.

Market and sales growth – measured in volume (units) or value (pounds). Marketing can increase the awareness, desire and ability of customers to buy the product – leads to increased revenue.

Brand image – building brand characteristics. If a business develops a good reputation (for example, high quality) it can attract and reassure customers and allow them to charge a premium price.

Objectives

Market share – the amount a business sells as a percentage of the whole market. Increasing market share gives a business more influence and power in the market and means it has increased its number of customers.

Brand loyalty – businesses need regular custom in order to succeed. Brand loyalty involves building a relationship with customers in order to encourage repeat purchasing.

Internal and external influences on marketing objectives and decisions

All business functions are interlinked and influence each other. For example marketing will negotiate its advertising budget with finance and work closely with operations to develop a product that meets customer needs.

Now try this

1 Why is marketing important to a business?

2 Identify three marketing objectives.

3 How is marketing closely linked to other functions of a business?

Market research

Marketing research is the first stage of the marketing process and involves gathering and analysing qualitative and quantitative market data. Market research is the key indicator of customer needs, which drives decision making across all business functions, not just marketing.

The market research process

define problem / question → develop market research plan → collect data → analyse data → interpret and report findings

Questions market research will attempt to answer:

- Who are our potential customers?
- What do our customers want?
- How big is the market – is it growing?
- Who are our competitors?
- What are customers willing to pay?
- Is there a gap/opportunity in the market?

Primary market research

This is research collected first hand:

👍 specific to the needs of the business

👍 more up to date and reliable

👍 gives more opportunity for two-way communication and follow up questions

👍 often better if you want to collect qualitative data

👍 **sampling** provides an insight into the market, but saves money as the whole population is not needed; a sample must be representative, unbiased and large enough to represent the whole market

👎 can be more time-consuming and therefore more costly

👎 difficult to conduct a large sample size

Examples include questionnaires, consumer panels, interviews, focus groups and customer observations.

Secondary market research

This is research that already exists, conducted by another organisation:

👍 easily accessible and a good starting point

👍 fast and less time-consuming

👍 often better if you want to collect quantitative data

👎 some data can be free but detailed reports can be expensive to purchase

👎 not always up to date or specifically tailored to the business's needs

Examples include market research reports, competitors, websites, government statistics and newspaper articles.

Market mapping

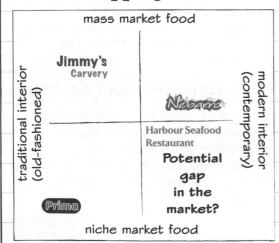

Market mapping is a technique used to understand how products/businesses are viewed relative to competitors based on two relevant characteristics. Market mapping:

- helps businesses decide whether to set up in a market – is there a 'gap'/opportunity?
- a useful process for comparing similarities and differences between businesses – market positioning
- helps a business gain a better understanding of its competition
- useful as a market research tool to gain an understanding of customer perceptions.

A limitation might be that it only considers two main variables – markets and customer perceptions are often very complex.

Now try this

1 Why is market research important for a business?

2 What is the best form of market research for a new business start-up?

3 How could a large supermarket chain use market mapping?

Interpreting marketing data

Correlation

Correlation helps businesses understand the relationship between two factors. If a business can understand the key factors determining demand for its products, then it can manipulate them to achieve greater sales.

a strong correlation does not necessarily mean that one variable leads to another

correlation is given as a value between −1 and +1

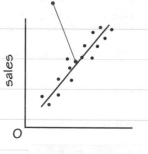

customer satisfaction + 0.9 strong positive correlation

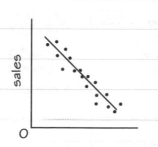

price − 0.8 strong negative correlation

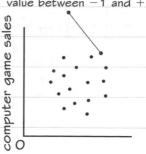

GCSE performance of school 0 no correlation

Sampling

Sampling involves selecting a representative group of people from the target population.

👍 It is quicker and easier than trying to collect research from everyone – this is often impossible!

👍 The bigger the sample size, the more representative it will be.

total target population

sample size 15%

Confidence levels and intervals

The sample size and the method of conducting the research will determine its accuracy and reliability.

Anything less than the whole population cannot be 100% accurate.

Confidence level – an indication of how accurate the research findings are, for example 80% = 80% confidence that the results are accurate.

Confidence interval – the possible range of outcomes for a given confidence. As the interval narrows the confidence level will fall.

Extrapolation

Extrapolation means predicting future trends, for example sales trends based on past results. Extrapolation is reliable when conditions remain the same. The further into the future we extrapolate, the less confidence we have in the certainty of the prediction.

80% confidence level rate of inflation will be 2% in 2016

98% confidence interval rate of inflation will be −0.5 and +4 in 2016

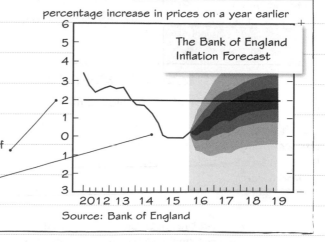

percentage increase in prices on a year earlier

The Bank of England Inflation Forecast

Source: Bank of England

Now try this

1 What does a correlation of 0.7 suggest?

2 What factors might determine the success of sampling in market research?

3 What is a confidence level?

Price and income elasticity

Price elasticity of demand (PED) and income elasticity of demand

Price elasticity is the effect of a change in price on the quantity demanded.
Income elasticity is the effect of a change in consumer income on the quantity demanded.

	Price / income elastic	Price / income inelastic
Price increase	Leads to a bigger percentage decrease in demand. Revenues fall.	Leads to a smaller percentage decrease in demand. Revenues rise.
Price decrease	Leads to a bigger percentage increase in demand. Revenues rise.	Leads to a smaller percentage increase in demand. Revenues fall.

PED scale

⟵　3　　　1　　　0　⟶

elastic　　　　　inelastic

Factors influencing elasticity

- number of substitutes/competitors
- relative effort/costs of switching to another product
- extent to which the product is considered a necessity
- perceived value of the brand.

> Ignore the negative when calculating PED. Just focus on the decimal number. An inelastic PED means price has little impact on demand – not that demand will not change at all.

Key calculations

Market size
Expressed in terms of units sold or value (£)

Market share
$$\frac{\text{total company sales}}{\text{total market sales}} \times 100$$

Market and sales growth
$$\frac{\text{increase in market size/sales (the difference)}}{\text{original size/sales}} \times 100$$

The uses of market research

product development

cash flow forecasting

workforce forecast

Uses

budgeting

production forecast

developing marketing activities – such as promotional campaigns

sales forecasting

Technology and market research

Technology can make the collection of market research data much faster and more specific to individual customers. This data can also be processed more effectively so that trends, patterns and correlations can be uncovered and used to help make marketing decisions. For example, store and loyalty cards are an extremely effective way for businesses to collect data on their customers.

Now try this

1 What does a PED of 0.2 mean?
2 What is the difference between market size and market share?
3 How can technology aid market research?

Exam skills

The following questions relate to the case study Round Round Records on page 45.

Worked example

What is meant by market share? **(2 marks)**

Market share is the percentage of total market sales occupied by a business. For example, a restaurant may serve 300 customers per week representing 10% of the local market.

This type of question requires a concise definition. This can be supported by an example.

Worked example

Using the data from Figure 2 calculate the growth in sales of vinyl records between 2013 and 2014. **(4 marks)**

$$\frac{\text{Increase in market size}}{\text{Original size}} \times 100$$

1288 − 780 = 508 (increase)

$$\frac{508}{1288} \times 100$$

= 65%

Always write down the formula and show your workings on a calculation question.

Note how the candidate has substituted the relevant numbers from the table into the formula at the second stage.

Worked example

Assess the importance of Round Round Records using market mapping to analyse the local record market.
(16 marks)

...Overall, market mapping is a useful tool to help understand the perception customers have of a business and help a business position itself within a market. However, as Round Round Records sells records that are a standard product it might be difficult to identify suitable variables to base the market map on. Nor are there a number of competitors locally for them to be compared against.

Ideally the answer here should consider the limitations of market mapping as well as the benefits for Round Round Records.

This would be the conclusion to this question. The candidate has started by summarising both sides of the argument. The candidate could have also gone on to suggest other tools or market research techniques that might be as/more useful than market mapping. This would have been a recommendation and a good feature to include in your evaluations.

Segmentation, targeting and positioning

Segmentation, positioning and targeting (STP) is the process a business will use to ensure it is able to succeed in a market without necessarily competing directly with other companies. Market segmentation also allows a business to specialise in order to better meet the needs of customers.

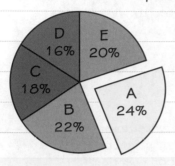

The process of dividing customers within a market into distinguishable groups based on their characteristics and needs to allow positioning of the business and customer targeting to take place.

The value of market segmentation

Market segmentation allows a business to:

- differentiate itself from its competitors
- develop and build its brand
- identify and satisfy the needs of a specific group of customers
- reach its customers with relevant marketing activities such as advertising
- focus the business activities
- build loyalty towards its brand and products.

Methods of segmentation

Businesses may use a variety of factors by which to segment a market. The most common factors are shown below.

geographic – based on where people live

behavioural – considering factors such as when people buy, why people buy, loyalty towards a brand

Methods of segmentation

demographic – based on characteristics such as age, gender, occupation

income – how much people earn

Positioning

Businesses might use a market map to help them position their business within the market. Positioning involves a business considering the combination of benefits and price relative to competitors.

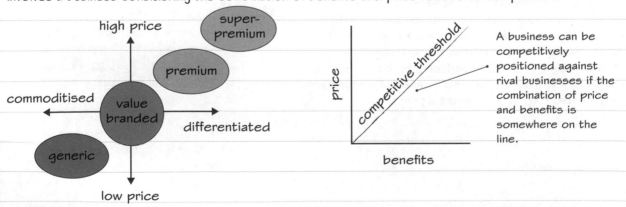

A business can be competitively positioned against rival businesses if the combination of price and benefits is somewhere on the line.

Now try this

1 State three ways that a business could segment the market.
2 How can a business ensure it is positioned effectively in the market?
3 What are the benefits of market segmentation?

Mass and niche markets

Where businesses tend to focus on a specific segment of the market with particular needs this is known as niche marketing. A business targeting a mass market will produce a generic product that meets the needs of most people. This will determine how a business markets its products and positions itself in the market.

The scale of segmentation in a market

- targeting a large population of the market with a generic product
- requires production on a large scale and investment in capacity
- potential for high sales revenue
- may compete with many other businesses in the market
- promotion will involve mass market techniques such as TV and newspapers
- business will have to be competitive on price in order to succeed

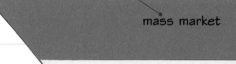

mass market

market segment

niche market

individual

- targeting a small population of the market with a specialised product
- production on a small scale (possibly bespoke)
- low volumes but high profit margins
- few competitors but limited number of potential customers
- promotion through specialist mediums
- direct marketing
- business will have to compete on quality and customisation in order to succeed

In some industries technology has allowed businesses to profile individuals and customise their products so that they can target customers as individuals, such as online bespoke greeting cards.

The STP process: a summary

Identify target market based on business strengths, potential for sales, profitability of segment and presence of competition.

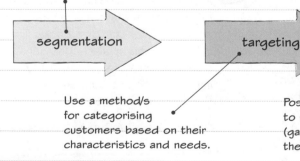

segmentation → targeting → positioning

Use a method/s for categorising customers based on their characteristics and needs.

Position business relative to competitors in order to meet customer needs currently not satisfied (gap in the market) or alongside a business where they can do it better.

1 What is 'targeting'?
2 What is a niche market?

Exam skills

The following questions explore the topics covered in Unit 3.3.3 and relate to the case study Round Round Records on page 45.

Worked example

1 Explain how **Round Round Records** could use market segmentation.   **(4 marks)**

Round Round Records might use age as a basis for segmenting their market. They could then identify their target market based on this classification. By doing this they could then develop a strategy to meet the needs of their customers. For example, Round Round Records could stock records of artists and genres that are popular with that age range. This would therefore help them build good relationships with their customers and encourage repeat sales.

It may be fairly easy to explain how a business might use market segmentation, but the answer has to be in the context of Round Round Records.

This answer is clearly in context as it specifically refers to the product Round Round Records sells — records!

2 Assess two factors that Rick White might consider when positioning Round Round Records.   **(8 marks)**

...Rick may also position his business based on price. Price is an important factor for all businesses when positioning themselves in the market. If Rick decides on a high price then he must be able to justify this by ensuring his business provides sufficient benefits to the customer, for example excellent customer service. Rick might choose to do this if he believed a rival business had set a relatively low price point for their records. This might mean that customers who are willing to pay a higher price for a better service would be attracted to Round Round Records instead of Rick's rivals.

This is the second paragraph of the student's answer. In the first paragraph they might have discussed how the type of music might be used to position his business against the competition. For example, Round Round Records might specialise in rock music.

The final paragraph would need to explain how important these factors are and identify which of the two is the most relevant for Round Round Records.

3 Although the UK market for vinyl records is growing, Rick still considers his business to operate in a niche market

Assess the importance of Round Round Records being a 'niche marketer' for the success of the business.   **(10 marks)**

A niche market is a small segment of the market where customers have specialist needs. By operating in a niche market Round Round Records is able to avoid high levels of competition from other businesses that sell music, for example HMV and Amazon. As Round Round Records is a small business it is unable to compete on price with other larger companies, but it may be able to provide a specialist service for the small number of customers. This may allow it to charge a higher price and maintain a loyal customer base because it is able to understand its customers better than a large business. However, as Round Round Records has a smaller number of potential customers, every sale is extremely important and it will have to rely on repeat purchasing for long-term success.

A student might approach this answer by discussing the benefits of operating in a niche market, but also consider the drawbacks. The candidate might also consider other factors that are similarly important to the success of Round Round Records.

This is a good opening paragraph. The student starts by defining what a niche market is. They have also identified a limitation of working in a niche market at the end of the paragraph. The student could now go on to discuss a second reason why working in a niche market is beneficial for Round Round Records.

Using the marketing mix

The Marketing Mix, also known as the '7 Ps', is a collection of factors that a business must consider when marketing its products in order to meet the needs of its customers. In order to be successful these seven factors must complement each other if the marketing mix is going to be successful. Through the 7Ps a business will be able to achieve its marketing objectives.

The marketing mix

product – everything that the customer buys – brand, features and benefits of a good or service

price – set to match the expectations of customers and the features of the product

promotion – communicating the product offer, creating an awareness and desire to buy

The 7 Ps

place – using the right channels to get the product to the customer

people – adding to the product by using the right people in the transaction

process – making the transaction convenient, efficient and effective for the customer

physical environment – matching the physical environment in which the transaction takes place to the product and brand

 Real world **Breitling**

Breitling is a premium watch maker that specialises in making watches for professionals, in particular the aviation industry. Breitling also has a number of partnerships, including with Bentley, a premium UK car manufacturer. Breitling makes several watches in the 'Breitling for Bentley' range. Breitling also has a number of its own boutiques in major cities across the UK.

The Marketing Mix for a consumer product, such as an Breitling watch, will be very different from an industrial product such as a CCTV system sold to a local council. For example, the CCTV seller may use sales agents instead of a retail outlet.

 Real world **Synectics**

Synectics sells surveillance solutions to large organisations and local government. Its sales team are experts in their field and are able to build unique security solutions for their clients. Synectics provides long-term solutions and maintenance contracts for its products and sells through international trade fairs and word of mouth. Its prices have to be very competitive and it often has to bid for contracts.

People are sometimes more important in relation to selling industrial products because relationships have to be built up over a long period of time, whereas, with a consumer product it is sometimes bought on impulse. Therefore, the use of colour, emotion and branding can be more important.

Now try this

1 What are the 7Ps?

2 What is the difference between a consumer product and an industrial product?

3 Why is it important for the elements of the marketing mix to complement each other?

Product

Customers go through a different process when buying different types of products. Therefore, different products require different forms of marketing.

Types of consumer products

Convenience items	Shopping goods	Speciality products
 • bought on impulse • not brand loyal • consumers are sensitive to price changes • products must be widely available	• consumers will 'shop around' • consumers take their time and will compare product features • brand and price become more important in the purchasing decision • consumers are susceptible to promotion techniques	• there are high levels of engagement • consumers take a long time to process information and make a decision • people involved in the transaction are very important • physical environment is very important • consumers are willing to travel far

> When analysing a business it is important to consider the type of product and the elements of the marketing mix that are the most important.

The whole product

When analysing the product it helps to consider the 'whole product'. The three levels are:

- the core benefits – this is what the product actually does and how well it does it. How well does the product do its function?

- the actual product – this includes all of the product features. The details and benefits that add value. This might include features to improve quality, convenience, efficiency, style and reliability.

- the augmented product – this includes everything the business builds around the product. Service, advice, after-sales care and features to build loyalty and a long-term relationship with the brand.

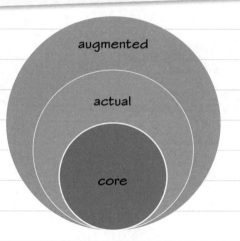

Influences on and value of new product development

When developing products, a business must consider the 'whole product' along with the three factors shown in the diagram opposite. All products must have a balance of design, function and cost. Influencing any one of these features can have a detrimental impact on the other two. For example, improving the design could reduce the functionality of the product, or improving the functionality could increase costs.

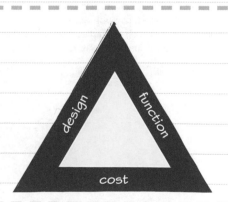

Now try this

1 Why is 'function' an important factor to consider when developing a product?

2 What are the key characteristics of a 'speciality good'?

Product portfolio analysis

Product portfolio analysis (PPA) can be used to analyse and track the development of multiple products over time taking into account a number of factors such as growth, sales and market conditions.

The product life-cycle

Price may be low to initial sales. Heavy promotion to create awareness. Low number of product variations launched.

Price may increase with popularity. New varieties and distribution methods introduced. Business must keep up with demand growth.

The market is 'full' – all potential customers have the product and there are other better / cheaper alternatives. Price may be cut to maintain competitiveness.

Consider cutting price to maintain demand, promotion slows as customers are aware of product, introduction of new customers slows down – focus instead on retention and repeat purchase.

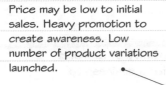

Further price cuts to maintain demand. Variety of products streamlined to the most popular. Business may consider discontinuing product if replacement can be introduced. An **extension strategy** may be used to re-launch the product to boost new growth. For example, slight modifications may be made to the design and packaging of a product to make it appear new or 'fresh'.

Life-cycle curve

Not all products have the same life-cycle curve. Fad products may grow and decline very quickly whereas some products will maintain maturity for a long time.

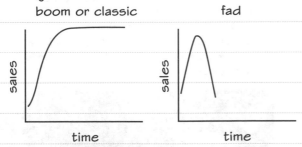

boom or classic   fad

The value of PPA

👍 Useful analysis tool for a business with a wide product range.

👍 Useful for making decisions about where funds should be allocated.

👍 Can be used to predict future sales and therefore plan production/distribution.

👎 Products and markets are complicated and do not necessarily follow a pattern.

👎 Does not provide clear solutions for a business.

👎 As with all models, PPA simplifies what can be a complex issue.

The Boston Matrix

Possibly a leading brand in the market. Distribution must be effective to ensure product availability.

Fast growing market but not yet an established product. Normally requires heavy investment to develop and ensure success. Usually lots of competition from rival brands.

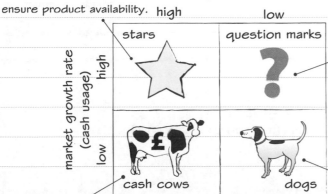

relative market share (cash generation)

Invest to revitalise or discontinue the product.

Successful products in mature markets. Cash cows generate high revenue for a business that can be invested in other areas. Relatively little promotion is required.

Source: Adapted from The BCG Portfolio Matrix from the Product Portfolio Matrix, ©1970, The Boston Consulting Group

Price

Price is a key factor in any product decision. Price will not only determine the demand for a product, it will also determine the contribution of a product and the overall profit margin for the business.

What influences price

costs – what profit margin is the business hoping to achieve?

other elements of the marketing mix – the 7Ps must complement one another

the price elasticity of demand – the potential for a business to change the price

Influences on price

branding – the perceptions customers have of the brand and how much value they place on it

competition – the level of competition and the price set by the market

product life-cycle – the stage of the life-cycle the product is in

Price is very subjective. A price of £10 for a product might be appropriate one day and disastrous the next.

Pricing strategies

expensive – high price

Dynamic pricing – applied to products where price can fluctuate with the level of demand, such as hotel rooms.

Price skimming – used to capitalise on 'first movers' (those people willing to pay a premium to be the first to own a product). The initial price is high so the profit in the market can be 'skimmed'. Suitable for established brands where anticipation for a new product is high. Particularly effective in technology markets.

Penetration pricing – applied to a new product attempting to enter the market. Initial price is low in order to penetrate the market by undercutting competitors. Over time price may increase as demand grows and reputation/popularity builds.

Queuing to purchase at the launch of a branded product.

cheap – low price

Now try this

1 Why is the profit margin an important factor to consider when setting a price?
2 In what circumstance might a business decide to set a premium (high) price for a product?
3 What is penetration pricing?
4 Why is price subjective?

Promotion

Promotion is the key method a business will use to communicate with its customers and potential customers. Successful promotion will create awareness, understanding, and a desire for the product.

What influences promotion

The target audience – choosing the right method and channel to reach the right people. For example, placing an advert in a magazine for a product that matches the demographic of the readership, such as an advert for a new face cream in a fashion magazine aimed at older women.

Competition – a business may use similar channels to its competitors in order to challenge their message or use strategies that allow it to stand out and be unique.

Promotion budget – the promotion budget will determine which methods are available and the geographical reach of the campaign.

Influences on promotion

Technology – can help a business narrow down its promotion so that it only reaches the right people. Subscription services also allow a business to target customers with personal messages and relevant information.

The message – a public apology might be posted on a company's website, but a sneak peek at a new product line might be shared via Twitter. Sponsoring a sporting event might encourage an association with healthy living.

The appropriateness of advertising

Factors such as focus and reach are important when choosing the right medium for advertising.

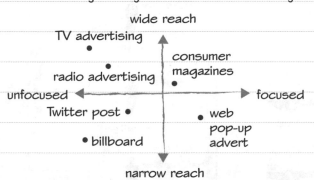

wide reach

TV advertising

consumer magazines

radio advertising

unfocused ←——————→ focused

Twitter post

web pop-up advert

billboard

narrow reach

Promotion methods

- Advertising – above-the-line (mass media) and below-the-line (small and focused promotion) techniques.
- Direct marketing – direct communication with the customer, often personal.
- Sales promotions – special offers to encourage sales.
- Sponsorship – paid association with a business or product.
- Social media – promotion through networks such as Facebook and Twitter.
- Public relations – media attention generated through a third party, such as a review from a blogger.

The importance of branding

adds value to the product

brands can be traded

allows a premium price to be charged

Strong brands — builds trust

helps a business to position itself in the market relative to other competitors

makes a product recognisable

product might become the natural choice for the novice customer

Skull Candy Headphones

1 What is the purpose of promotion?
2 Identify three promotion methods.
3 What promotional methods might be suitable for targeting children aged 5–8?

Distribution (place)

Distribution refers to how the product gets to the customer. Many products use multi-channel methods to reach the customer. The key is to make distribution easy and convenient for the customer in order to maximise sales.

What influences distribution

Scope / scale – a product sold internationally may require distribution through an extensive network of wholesalers, agents and distribution companies. By contrast a local business may simply require one retail outlet.

Nature of the product – some products are not suitable for certain channels. For example, it can be difficult and costly to ship plants, flowers and other delicate objects.

Influences on distribution

Control over promotion and pricing – a business may opt to use its own website or retail chain if controlling these factors is important.

Expectations of customers – will customers expect to access the product via multi-channels or will one suffice?

Channels of distribution

The factors above will determine the mix of channels used to get the product from the business to the customer. Many modern products use multiple channels, such as direct, click and collect and in-store purchasing.

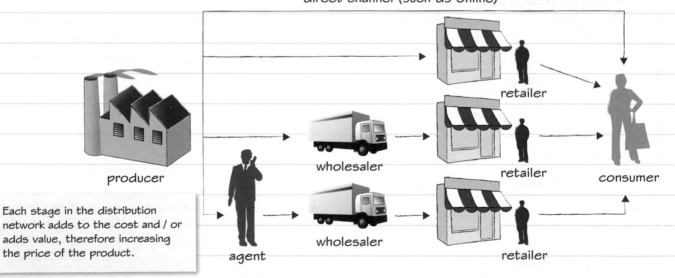

direct channel (such as online)

producer

agent

wholesaler

wholesaler

retailer

retailer

retailer

consumer

Each stage in the distribution network adds to the cost and / or adds value, therefore increasing the price of the product.

Digital marketing and e-commerce

allows small businesses to target a global market

allows businesses to gather customer information easily

opportunities for personalisation and involving customers in the design of products

The value of digital marketing and e-commerce

builds relationships through a more personal service by tracking buying habits

targeting specific segments is much easier – even on an individual basis

---

Now try this

1 What is the role of a retailer in the distribution process?

2 What is the role of a wholesaler in the distribution process?

3 Why might a business opt to sell through a direct channel such as their own website?

Exam skills

These exam-style questions explore the topics covered in Unit 3.3.4 and relate to the case Study Round Round Records on page 45.

Worked example

What is meant by the term 'distribution channel'?
(2 marks)

A distribution channel is the means by which a business will distribute its product to its customers. A distribution channel should be appropriate for the type of product and needs of the customer.

This definition could be supported with an appropriate example such as, wholesaler, retailer or e-commerce.

Worked example

Explain why Round Round Records might use a price skimming strategy for newly launched records.   **(5 marks)**

Price skimming is where a high price is initially set for a new product. When a new album is launched, perhaps by a popular artist, there will be high demand for it. As a result, Round Round Records could capitalise on the high demand by setting the price high to maximise the contribution made by the early sales of the album. Over time Round Round Records may reduce the price after the initial launch so that the price is in-line with similar albums. This may help maintain demand and steady sales revenue.

The answer starts by explaining what price skimming is. This is always a good approach and demonstrates that you understand the concepts in the question.

Worked example

Analyse the possible benefits to Round Round Records of using the product life-cycle to make marketing decisions.
(9 marks)

Round Round Records could use the product life-cycle to make decisions on how it should promote and price its products. For example, Round Round Records will sell a wide variety of records from a range of artists. It could use the product life-cycle to analyse its product sales and identify which records have reached maturity and might be entering decline. Round Round Records could then use special promotions to boost sales such as 'bargain basket' in order to clear its stock. This would help it ensure it is not stocking a high volume of records that are not popular. This would help it maximise sales.

An effective approach to this question might be to identify two possible benefits and then explain each in the context of Round Round Records.

This is a good first paragraph. The second paragraph could then go on to explain another benefit of using the product life-cycle, for example analysing sales figures and determining when an extension strategy might be appropriate.

Exam-style practice

Have a go at the questions below that apply the concepts covered in Unit 3.3. For these questions refer to the Round Round Records case study on page 45. There are answers on pages 196–197.

1 Which of the following is not an objective of the marketing function?

A increase market share ⬭

B increase productivity ⬭

C increase sales value ⬭

D increase brand awareness ⬭

(1 mark)

> Draw up your own list of marketing objectives before answering this question.

2 Which of the following best describes the term 'correlation'?

A forecasting a trend into the future ⬭

B the position of one brand in relation to another ⬭

C the relationship between two market factors ⬭

D the level of income required to achieve break-even ⬭

(1 mark)

> All of these responses are linked to market research data.

3 Rick White has set a five-year growth target for Round Round Records to gain 3% share of the UK vinyl record market by 2020.

Using Figure 1 in the case study, calculate the number of vinyl records Round Round Records would have sold if it had achieved 3% market share in 2014. **(4 marks)**

> Start by writing down the formula for calculating market share and then substitute the relevant information from Figure 1.

4 Analyse the benefits of Rick White using market segmentation. **(9 marks)**

> Consider what market segmentation will help Rick understand his customers and make marketing decisions.

5 Do you think that Round Round Records should distribute its products solely through e-commerce? Justify your answer. **(16 marks)**

> Your answer should consider the relative merits of selling through e-commerce and the limitations of not using other techniques, such as retail.

6 'People' is one of the 7Ps from the Marketing Mix.

To what extent is 'People' important to successful marketing of Round Round Records? **(16 marks)**

> Think about the nature of the business and the product Round Round Record sells. It might be a good idea to compare the value of another 'P' against 'People'.

7 Rick White believes that he will be able to charge a premium price for his rarer vinyl records. To what extent is price the most important factor in ensuring Round Round Records is able to maximise profits? **(20 marks)**

> This question does not simply require you to discuss the importance of price in terms of Round Round Records. Your answer must specifically relate to maximising profit. Is there anything that is more or just as important as price?

Case study

Round Round Records

Rick White had a passion for music and since being a teenager had played in bands. Rick had always collected vinyl records which he bought from around the world. In 2014 Rick decided to set up his own record store, Round Round Records, specialising in vintage records and music memorabilia. Originally Rick decided to set his business up as a sole trader and invested £20 000 from the short-lived success of the band to rent premises and purchase stock. Before opening his store, Rick carried out some secondary market research into the UK music industry.

Figure 1: UK music industry data 2015

Key facts

- Music streaming – The rate of music streaming doubled in 2014, with 14.8 billion tracks streamed digitally.

- CD sales – The ongoing shift to digital from CD slowed in 2014, which may suggest LP or CD collecting is more resilient than expected.

- In 2015 the UK's first vinyl chart was launched following the growth of vinyl album and single sales.

- Vinyl record sales reached a 20 year high in 2015.

Figure 2: Vinyl record sales figures 2010–2014

Year	2010	2011	2012	2013	2014
Sales (000s)	234	337	388	780	1 288
% share of UK Albums Market	0.2%	0.3%	0.4%	0.8%	1.5%

Source: Official Charts Company 2015

Although the UK music market continues to grow, a significant proportion of album sales are now bought digitally or steamed via music download sites. The vinyl market is certainly having a comeback with sales tripling over the past 3 years. However, it is still a niche market and accounts for a small segment of the overall market.

The store Rick rented was on the old high street in Derby, which suited the retro nature of his business. Rick anticipated his main customer to be men aged 35 plus, but found that the average age of his customers was early twenties, both men and women, and typically university students. Rick believed that customers visited the stores as much for the shopping experience and the opportunity to meet other enthusiasts, as to buy the records.

Rick knew that he would have to have an online presence if his business was going to succeed and set up a website with an online blog, stock inventory and e-commerce facility. Within weeks Rick found that his website was receiving a lot of hits, especially his vinyl record blog. By the end of 2015 his website accounted for 60% of all sales.

With the changing trend in the market, Rick found that he was able to charge a premium price for his rare vinyl albums that many of his collectors wanted. The most expensive was a rare Led Zeppelin album that sold for £1 000.

Operational objectives

Operations is the function of a business that is concerned with providing customers with a product that they want in a timely, effective, efficient and profitable way. Operations is about the actual production of the good or service sold by a business.

The importance of operations

Effectively managing operations allows a business to:

- 👍 control costs of production
- 👍 add value to its products
- 👍 guarantee the right level of service
- 👍 guarantee the right level of quality
- 👍 adapt to the needs of customers
- 👍 provide itself with 'green' credentials
- 👍 meet the demand for its products and services.

Operations and added value

Operations management is the key factor in the transformational process by which a business creates its products and services. Therefore, operations is the key to adding value to what a business does.

Adding handles to a heavy box of washing powder may add value to a product by making it easier to carry.

Setting objectives

Operations departments typically set objectives around the issues shown in the diagram below.

Costs – the operations department must be able to control the costs of production in order to maximise profit margins.

Environmental objectives – the production process can cause many negative externalities, such as pollution. Businesses will set targets on a number of environmental factors such as recycling and waste disposal.

Quality – the operations department is responsible for setting quality standards and ensuring these specifications are met, ensuring the product or service is fit for purpose.

Operational objectives

Speed of response and flexibility – opportunities and sales can be lost if a business cannot meet order volumes in a specific time frame. Operations is also responsible for ensuring the product is suitably flexible to meet the needs of different customers.

Dependability – businesses cannot afford to let their customers down. Those that do tend to lose loyalty and repeat purchases. Dependability can be the key factor by which a customer chooses its supplier, especially in industrial markets.

The 4Vs of operations

Just like the 4Ps of the marketing mix, the 4Vs of operations can be used to analyse key issues in the operational decisions of any business.

volume	variability
variety	visibility

Internal and external influences on operational objectives

- Legal / political factors – such as health and safety legislation and industry regulation.
- Economic factors – operations must be able to adapt to changing levels of demand in the market.
- Employee skills – these may determine objectives, such as the level of quality.
- Nature of the product – minimising cost may be very important for a product sold for £1.99.
- Social factors – such as consumers continue to expect more personalisation of the products they buy.
- Technological factors – technology drives all operational decisions, in particular new product development and processes of manufacture and distribution.

Now try this

1 How can operations give a business a competitive advantage?

2 Identify three factors that operational objectives might be set around.

3 How are operational decisions linked to the other functions of a business?

Analysing operational performance

The following formulae can be used to analyse operational performance in a business. They cover issues such as productivity and efficiency. You need to be able to calculate this data and interpret what it tells you about the performance of a business.

Labour productivity

This measures the output per employee and is a measure of how productive the workforce is. Productivity is a measure of output in relation to the input – in this case, the workers.

It is calculated using:

Labour productivity =
$$\frac{\text{output per time period}}{\text{number of employees}}$$

For example:

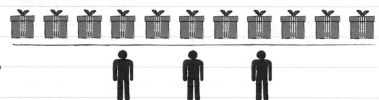

= 3.7 🎁 per employee

Unit costs

The unit cost is sometimes referred to as the average cost because it takes into account the total costs of a business (fixed + variable) and divides this by the level of output.

It is calculated using:

Unit costs =
$$\frac{\text{total costs of production}}{\text{number of units of output produced}}$$

For example:

= £X per 🎁

Capacity utilisation

The capacity of production is the maximum amount a business can produce over a period of time given the resources it has available. Capacity utilisation measures existing output as a percentage of the maximum possible output.

It is calculated using:

Capacity utilisation =
$$\frac{\text{actual output in a given time period}}{\text{maximum possible output in a given time period}} \times 100$$

× 100

= 42% of maximum capacity

Now try this

1 What is meant by productivity?

2 What is the difference between labour productivity and unit costs

3 How is capacity utilisation measured?

Uses of operational data

Labour productivity data

use data to set targets and motivate the workforce

use as a tool for performance-related pay

use to identify training needs of the workforce

Ways to increase efficiency and labour productivity

use as a tool to identify employees for praise and reward

use to test different production techniques, such as teamworking or cell production

use to measure the efficiency of the workforce

Unit cost data

use to set prices based on profit margin target

use as a target to drive operational decisions such as how, where and what to produce

use to make decisions about which products to produce

Using unit cost data

use alongside variable costs to analyse distribution of overheads

use to make decisions about scale of production – what level of output will achieve sufficiently low costs

Using capacity utilisation data

Capacity utilisation data can be used in a number of ways including:

👍 setting targets for output

👍 identifying when a business should increase capacity (growth)

👍 identifying when a business should decrease capacity (retrenchment)

👍 identifying the maximum level of output before production becomes ineffective (diseconomies start to occur).

Capacity utilisation data becomes most effective when used alongside the other measures of performance, such as labour productivity and unit costs.

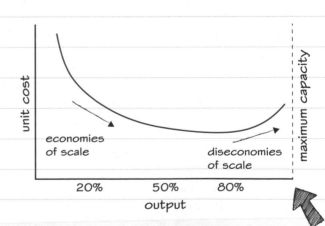

As capacity utilisation increases unit costs will fall as the business experiences economies of scale. Unit costs may rise as a business approaches maximum capacity due to stress, mistakes and diseconomies.

Now try this

1 How could labour productivity data be used to manage the workforce?

2 Why might a business want to operate at high capacity utilisation?

3 What is the difference between variable costs and unit costs?

Exam skills

These exam-style questions use knowledge and skills you have already revised. They relate to the Tasty Tapas case study on page 60.

Worked example

1 Calculate capacity utilisation for the Cleethorpes branch on Friday 12 June. **(3 marks)**

$$\frac{\text{Current capacity}}{\text{maximum capacity}} = 100$$

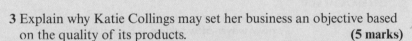

$$\frac{40}{65} \times 100 = 61.5\% \text{ capacity utilisation}$$

> Always start your answer to a calculation question by writing down the formula.

2 Explain one way that Tasty Tapas could improve labour productivity in its restaurants. **(4 marks)**

Labour productivity is the output per employee per hour that they work. Improving labour productivity lowers the costs per unit and means that more customers will be served. The best way for Tasty Tapas to do this would be to ensure all of their staff have sufficient training to use the IT system which has recently been having 'teething problems'. If employees are better trained to use the system it will not take them as long to process customer orders and will allow them to turn over a greater number of tables each hour.

> Where possible try to define any key terms at the start of your answer. This will ensure you secure the marks for knowledge. In this case the student opens by defining what labour productivity is.

3 Explain why Katie Collings may set her business an objective based on the quality of its products. **(5 marks)**

Quality is how well a product or service achieves its purpose. Quality is also very subjective and can mean different things to different people. Many customers have been complaining about poor service and wait times in the restaurant. Quality could refer to the overall experience of the customer and therefore a quality focused target might help improve overall service. Quality could also refer to the standard of the food and if quality is of a premium Katie will be able to charge a premium price and customers may also be willing to wait longer for their food.

> See how the student has taken the concept of quality and applied it to the nature of the business and some of the issues that the business is facing – poor/slow service in its restaurants.

4 Analyse the reasons why it is important for Tasty Tapas to be able to adjust the capacity of its restaurants. **(9 marks)**

Capacity refers to the maximum number of tables each restaurant can serve each night. One reason why adjusting capacity is important is so that each restaurant can maximise its capacity utilisation. For example, during busy periods it is important for each restaurant to be able to increase the number of tables and waiters so that they do not need to turn away bookings. This will increase capacity and allow them to generate more revenue.

On the other hand, Tasty Tapas may also need to reduce its capacity when demand is low...

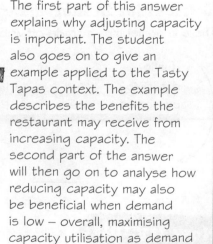

> The first part of this answer explains why adjusting capacity is important. The student also goes on to give an example applied to the Tasty Tapas context. The example describes the benefits the restaurant may receive from increasing capacity. The second part of the answer will then go on to analyse how reducing capacity may also be beneficial when demand is low – overall, maximising capacity utilisation as demand changes so that there are no underutilised/idle resources.

Increasing efficiency and productivity

Improving efficiency means getting more output from a given level of input. Another way to consider efficiency is using the minimum level of resources to achieve the desired product at the right quality. As efficiency is directly linked to unit cost it is a key route to maximising profits.

Productivity and efficiency are directly connected. Greater productivity means the workforce is more efficient and efficiency across the business allows more resources to be devoted to production.

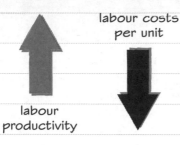

labour costs per unit

labour productivity

The benefits of improved efficiency

- 👍 labour productivity increased
- 👍 unit costs fall
- 👍 resources such as labour, expertise and time can be reallocated
- 👍 profit margins increase
- 👍 improved flexibility across the business
- 👍 opportunity to explore new ventures – such as a new product lines
- 👍 ability to charge lower prices and therefore improve competitiveness

Increasing efficiency and productivity

introduce new reward systems – in order to create an incentive to work harder (incentives linked to output)

new ways of working – design the job of the workforce to be more effective

Ways to increase efficiency and labour productivity

better management – improve supervision, direction and leadership of the workforce

training – invest in training to improve workers' skills and motivation

new technology – speed up processes and reduce human error

Difficulties in increasing efficiency and labour productivity

There is sometimes a trade-off when increasing labour productivity.

quality
creativity
customer service

labour productivity

Increasing the output of a worker may increase productivity and unit costs in the short term. But high levels of output can cause stress and burnout. It is also true that a focus on output can compromise quality, customer service and creativity. Costly mistakes and faults are also more likely to occur leading to product returns and complaints.

Now try this

1 Why is efficiency important?

2 Identify three ways a business could increase labour productivity.

3 What are the potential drawbacks of increasing labour productivity?

Lean production

Lean production involves practices that reduce waste in the operational process. The main forms of lean production are focused on reducing defects, time wasted and inventory levels.

Waste

In business, waste can be considered anything that does not add value to the product. There are seven types of waste a business can reduce:

1 motion – unnecessary movement of people

2 transport – unnecessary movement of the product or materials

3 inventory – too much stock

4 defects – faulty products

5 waiting – for processes to finish before others can begin

6 extra processing – adding features that do not add value

7 overproduction – producing products that cannot be sold easily.

Ways of reducing waste

👍 designing the work areas within a business so that employees are close together and in close proximity to the resources they require

👍 designing production facilities to minimise movement

👍 using effective stock control systems

👍 adopting quality assurance techniques to minimise defaults

👍 designing products and services to meet the exact needs of customers

👍 using a range of forecasting techniques to predict demand and match production accordingly.

Lean production method 1: just-in-time

Supply of products and raw materials triggered by demand from customers

supply of materials and services → demand for products and services

Stock levels kept to a minimum and resources and capital are freed up. Relies on effective communication and systems for order processing and delivery.

Lean production method 2: Kaizen

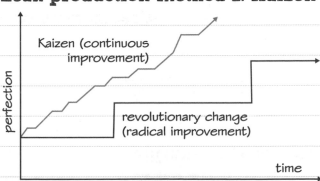

Kaizen (continuous improvement)

perfection

revolutionary change (radical improvement)

time

This is a Japanese concept of continuous improvement, for example by making marginal improvements in efficiency.

Lean production method 3: lean organisations

Only use processes that add value and are effective. Remove anything that is not necessary. For example, the following aspects of an organisation could be re-designed.

   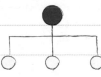

meetings   processes   organisational structure

The difficulties of adopting lean production

• If there are disruptions in production, business may be vulnerable if there is no inventory.

• It creates over-reliance on suppliers to deliver on time.

• There is the danger of stripping away processes and features that employees and customers value.

• It puts pressure on workforce to 'self-check' and monitor their own work – does the workforce have the skills?

• Kaizen can bring about change that may be resisted by the workforce.

Now try this

1 What does a business need in order for JIT to be successful?

2 Identify three barriers to effective lean production.

Capacity and technology efficiency

As we have seen, low capacity utilisation is inefficient and can increase unit costs. Similarly, reaching maximum capacity can also cause problems. A business can use a range of techniques to control its capacity in the short term.

Increase capacity

- sub-contract out production to another business
- offer overtime pay to the workforce
- employ workers on temporary contracts.

Decrease capacity (or utilise idle resources)

- rationalisation (redundancies or sale of assets)
- sub-contract in work from another business.

Choosing the optimal mix of resources

A business's production process can either be labour intensive or capital intensive. The balance of the two might depend on the nature of the product and the target market.

capital intensive: mass production, standardisation, efficient production ⟷ labour intensive: highly specialist, personal, service industry, high level of skill required

Capital intensive: high level of capital investment (such as use of machinery)

Labour intensive: high level of human input in the production process

Real world examples

Robots in the production process speed up production and reduce human error.

Communication systems such as group messaging apps and mobile phones allow workers to communicate individually and as a group more effectively.

Online ordering systems link in with stock management systems to improve efficiency in logistics. These processes also allow for greater customisation for the customer.

Now try this

1 Why would a business want to decrease its capacity?

2 What is the difference between labour intensive and capital intensive?

3 How can technology improve efficiency?

Exam skills

These exam-style questions use knowledge and skills you have already revised. They relate to the Tasty Tapas case study on page 60.

Worked example

1 What is meant by the term 'lean production'?
(2 marks)

Lean production involves reducing the inputs into a business.

The definition given by the candidate is partially correct and is therefore an imperfect definition. There are often two points that a student can give for a definition. Lean production might involve reducing the inputs into a business but the student has made no reference to the fact that lean production is about efficiency. A better definition would be, 'Lean production involves reducing waste in a business in order to improve efficiency.'

2 Explain one way that Tasty Tapas could improve labour productivity in its restaurants. (4 marks)

By installing new ovens Tasty Tapas will be able to increase its capacity by cooking more food at once and offering a wider range of dishes. This will increase its capacity and allow it to serve more customers each day. This is likely to improve revenue and profit. The new ovens are also more efficient because they use less energy than the old ovens. This will reduce the restaurant's utility bills, which will also help maximise profits.

Think about what this question requires the candidate to do. Although the question is referring to ovens, the student must consider this from a business perspective. What business factors might be influenced by installing new ovens?

3 Despite some of the teething problems with the new integrated IT system, Katie has decided to persist and ensure all employees have comprehensive training in using the hand-held devices.

To what extent is technology such as the touch screen device ordering system key to achieving operational efficiency? (20 marks)

As you can see, the student has linked new ovens to capacity and efficiency. Two key operational issues.

... Overall, technology is very important in a restaurant business because the key to an effective restaurant is being able to provide a fast and efficient service. Technology such as the touch screen devices can do this by streamlining communication and speeding up the process. However, many other factors are important in maintaining operational efficiency, such as the stock management system. If the right stock is not delivered to the restaurant the touch screen ordering devices will have little impact on improving service.

Ultimately, the extent to which these devices improve operational efficiency depends on whether Katie's employees make use of the system as it will fail in the long term if staff keep resorting back to the paper based system. For IT to be a success Katie must make sure that all staff are trained sufficiently and any problems with the system are resolved very soon.

You will find a 20 mark question at the end of your Unit 2 exam paper. The difference between the 16 mark question and the 20 mark question is the extent to which you have to provide a justified and balanced evaluation and go on to provide recommendations for the organisation. On A level papers this style of question could be worth 20–24 marks.

This is an example of an evaluation for this answer. The candidate will have analysed both sides of the question before writing this.

As you can see, the student's evaluation is clearly justified and shows an awareness of other important factors. At the end of the answer the student has made a recommendation relevant to the context of Tasty Tapas. This is appropriate for a 20 mark question.

Improving quality

Quality is the extent to which a product or operation meets its customers' requirements. This means that it is 'fit for purpose'. Achieving the desired quality has a number of benefits for a business, but quality is a subjective concept. What one customer considers high quality, another may consider low quality.

The importance of quality

Quality is the key to achieving customer needs. A high quality product is one that meets customer expectations. A pizza for £2 can have a higher quality than a more expensive pizza priced at £15 if it is more 'fit for purpose' (i.e. it is tasty with good quality ingredients).

Products must have high quality to be able to compete at the right price point. Some businesses will differentiate themselves on having a premium quality. For example, Steveston Pizza Company in Vancouver Canada sells a pizza for $850 featuring ingredients such as smoked salmon, caviar and other exotic seafood.

Achieving quality improvement

have a clear understanding of customer needs

train employees in quality procedures

achieve a quality award / mark (recognition from external organisation)

Methods of achieving quality

invest in technology

involve all employees in managing quality

work with high quality suppliers

adopt processes that assure quality

Achieving high levels of quality can improve customer satisfaction, help the business differentiate its product from competitors and above all, add value to the product allowing a premium price to be charged.

Quality control and quality assurance

Below are two perspectives on implementing quality management systems.

Ⓠ = focus on quality

start — end   start — end

- quality control is about the **product**
- quality is checked at the end of the production process
- focus on identifying faults
- quality control is a specific role – maybe one person

- quality assurance is about the **process**
- all employees are involved in quality assurance
- quality is considered at every step of the production process
- focus on continual improvement of quality

Difficulties in improving quality

Quality can be difficult to improve because:

- customers' perception of quality is constantly changing
- a successful business could let quality slip if there is no incentive to outperform rival businesses.
- improving quality can add more work so might be naturally opposed by the workforce
- measuring quality can be difficult and expensive.

Consequences of poor quality

Poor quality can cause a number of problems for a business:

- If products need recalling this can be extremely expensive.
- Poor quality can damage brand reputation.
- There may be legal costs if customers sue the company.
- Correcting poor quality can be very expensive.

Now try this

1 Why is quality important?

2 How can a business improve quality?

3 Why can improving quality be difficult for a business?

Exam skills

These exam-style questions use the knowledge and skills you have revised in Unit 3.4.4. Question 3 directly relates to the Tasty Tapas case study on page 60.

Worked example

1 A business employs a quality manager to verify the quality of production and identify product faults. This quality measure is most associated with which of the following quality management principles?

   A Quality inspection ⬭

   B Quality assurance ⬭

   C Quality control ⬤

   D Quality guarantee ⬭

                      (1 mark)

> The correct answer is C. Only B and C are actually quality management principles. Quality control is closely associated with inspecting the product at the end of the process to identify faults.

2 Analyse one way that a small contract cleaning business could implement quality assurance.

                      (5 marks)

Quality assurance is about achieving high standards of quality through focusing on each stage of the production process. A small contract cleaning business could do this by using the highest quality supplies of cleaning chemicals and involving its employees in evaluating how effective these supplies are. This will allow the business to get feedback on the most effective chemicals to inform future decisions about which supplies to purchase. This will then improve the standard of cleaning from its employees and improve customer satisfaction.

> This is a good answer because the student has started by demonstrating knowledge of quality assurance. They have also clearly analysed one way that a business could implement quality assurance and they have applied it to the context of a small contract cleaning business.

3 Evaluate how Katie Collings could improve the customer reviews of Tasty Tapas. **(16 marks)**

> An evaluation question requires you to make a judgement from the available evidence.

Katie Collings could reduce the number of negative reviews at her restaurant by adopting quality assurance. Quality assurance would ensure that every step of the production process is of the highest quality. For example, this would help ensure the ingredients are of the highest quality right through to the service given by her waiters. As each restaurant is operating at near full capacity it will allow her to analyse whether the high level of capacity utilisation is affecting the quality of service. It might also allow her to focus on how effectively the touch screen ordering system is working. One limitation on this system is that she might not have the time or money to train employees properly in how to monitor quality in their particular area.

> There are a number of ways that a student could answer this question and a number of functional issues they could consider. This is an example of how you might start your answer. The student has begun by discussing how quality assurance could help reduce the number of negative reviews at Tasty Tapas.
>
> The second paragraph could go on to explain how introducing a system of employee rewards could also help Tasty Tapas reduce the number of negative reviews.

Inventory and supply chains 1

Inventory refers to the supplies and stock held by a business. Coordinating inventory and managing the supply chain effectively can influence the competitiveness of a business.

Factors to consider when managing inventory and the supply chain

 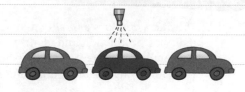

Some industries rely on speed. For example, parcel delivery companies. Even where speed is not as important as other factors, like quality, it can still mean the difference between a customer choosing one business over another.

Meeting a deadline is very important for some industries. For example, the travel industry. All businesses can claim to meet a deadline, but reputation precedes a business when it comes to dependability. Some businesses may provide 'money back' guarantees if a deadline is not met.

Flexibility is about customisation. The greater level of customisation a business offers, the better it is able to meet customer needs. However, often greater customisation increases unit costs. For example, all Dell computers are manufactured to their customers' inventory specifications. This is known as mass customisation.

Managing inventory

meeting demand – holding stock allows a business to meet demand

costly – holding stock ties up cash which could be used in other investments (opportunity cost)

Issues in managing inventory

risk – some inventory poses a greater risk than others. Inventory can be perishable (food), easily damaged in storage (glassware) or become outdated quickly (fashion and technology)

Inventory includes raw materials, work in progress and finished goods.

Choosing the right supplier

A business will consider the following factors when choosing a supplier:

- 👍 the cost and quality of materials
- 👍 dependability
- 👍 ethical practices
- 👍 availability of trade credit
- 👍 level of service
- 👍 flexibility
- 👍 speed.

📝 Exam focus   Nature of the product

Whenever analysing inventory issues in an exam, always consider the nature of the product and how this might affect the need for inventory. It is also worth considering how important the supply chain is in terms of competitiveness. Can the business gain a competitive advantage through speed, dependability or flexibility? If so, how might the supply chain and inventory support this?

Now try this

1 How can inventory management give a business a competitive advantage?

2 Why might holding large quantities of inventory be a risk?

3 What might determine the level of customisation a business offers its customers?

Inventory and supply chains 2

Inventory control charts

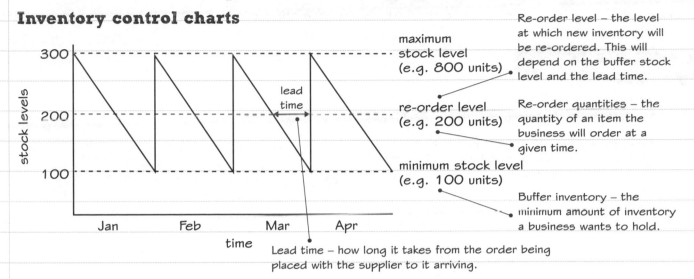

Re-order level – the level at which new inventory will be re-ordered. This will depend on the buffer stock level and the lead time.

maximum stock level (e.g. 800 units)

re-order level (e.g. 200 units)

Re-order quantities – the quantity of an item the business will order at a given time.

minimum stock level (e.g. 100 units)

Buffer inventory – the minimum amount of inventory a business wants to hold.

Lead time – how long it takes from the order being placed with the supplier to it arriving.

Managing inventory

A business must consider the following issues when using inventory control charts:

👎 unexpected changes in demand

👎 long lead times which make inventory planning more difficult

👎 suppliers who fail to deliver

👎 choosing the right buffer stock level can affect efficiency and cash flow

👍 human or computer error when re-ordering stock.

When choosing a supplier a business might consider: the price, the flexibility in terms of size and customisation, the discounts offered on scale and potential for trade credit.

Managing the supply chain

The supply chain refers to the network of providers involved in the process of getting the product to the customer. This may involve a wide number of people and organisations.

Effective management of the supply chain may involve:

* supplier strategy – such as long-term vs short-term agreements

* agreeing contracts with suppliers – service level agreement or a code of conduct

* deciding on what aspects of the process the business will do itself and which it will outsource

* vertical integration – will the business take control of the supply chain for itself?

Supply and demand

Employ a flexible workforce (part-time employment and temporary contracts).

Produce to order – only producing a product when an order comes in.

Managing supply to meet demand

Outsource production to other businesses when demand is high. Outsourcing can help a firm subcontract a specialist task, such as payroll, and help manage capacity utilisation.

Queuing systems – automated queueing can help manage supply during high demand periods.

Now try this

1 Identify three pieces of information shown on an inventory control chart.

2 How can a business increase flexibility when managing inventory?

3 What is the supply chain?

Exam skills

These exam-style questions relate to the Tasty Tapas case study on page 60.

Worked example

1 Explain one factor Tasty Tapas might consider when managing its inventory. **(5 marks)**

Tasty Tapas might consider the speed at which it is able to convert its inventory into a finished meal ready for serving. Tasty Tapas is operating at high capacity utilisation and this has led to poor reviews for its slow service. By focusing on processes to increase the turnaround of an order it will be able to avoid poor reviews. As a result, this will also allow Tasty Tapas to increase its capacity and turnover more tables each day with the possibility of increasing revenue.

> The student has chosen a relevant factor in 'speed' because this directly links to one of the issues identified in the case study. The student goes on to explain why speed is important and gives at least one consequence of serving meals faster.

2 Below is an inventory control chart for a Tasty Tapas restaurant. Using the chart identify the following pieces of information.

(a) the maximum inventory level

500 units

(b) the re-order quantity

400 units

(c) the buffer inventory level

100 units

(d) the lead time on an order **(4 marks)**

2 weeks

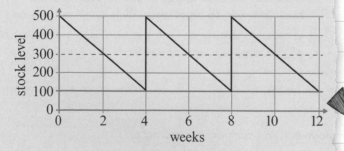

3 Analyse the importance to Tasty Tapas of having a flexible workforce. **(9 marks)**

A flexible workforce might involve employing workers on a part-time basis or employing workers on temporary contracts. A flexible workforce is very important for a restaurant because demand fluctuates greatly at weekends. By using part-time workers Tasty Tapas will be able to ensure they have enough staff at busy periods, but reduce their labour costs when the restaurants are less busy...

> This question involves interpreting information on an inventory control chart. (a) is a relatively straightforward question and most students would guess this even if they were not sure what it meant. Some students might think the answer to (b) is 300 units. This is the re-order level and not the re-order quantity that can be interpreted by how much the chart increases by when the inventory is delivered. (d) – the lead time is the difference from the point at which inventory is ordered (shown as 300 units on the chart) to the point when it arrives. Each time inventory is ordered it takes two weeks to arrive according to the chart.

> This is a relatively good start to the answer. The student has shown understanding of what could increase flexibility. However, the student has not yet explained why it is really important for Tasty Tapas. There are a number of relevant issues that the student should go on to explore. These include efficiency and profitability. The student should also analyse the benefits of flexibility for a business like Tasty Tapas.

Exam-style practice

Have a go at the questions below that apply to the concepts covered in Unit 3.4. There are answers on pages 197–198.

1 Which of the following is correct for calculating capacity utilisation in a business?

> How is capacity utilisation expressed? As a ratio or as a percentage?

A $\dfrac{\text{total output}}{\text{number of employees}}$ ◯

B $\dfrac{\text{actual output in a given time period}}{\text{maximum possible output in a given time period}} \times 100$ ◯

C $\dfrac{\text{total costs}}{\text{total output}}$ ◯

D $\dfrac{\text{revenue}}{\text{total labour costs}} \times 100$ ◯

(1 mark)

> Start by writing down the formula for calculating unit costs and then substitute the relevant information from the table.

2 The table below represents information taken from the Cleethorpes restaurant for one week of trading in June.

Direct costs	£12 000
Running costs	£7000
Overheads	£5750
Average customers served per week	1300

Calculate the unit costs for one week of trading at the Cleethorpes restaurant. **(3 marks)**

> Use the information from the case study to link the benefits of new ovens to the impact it could have on the output of the workforce. Maybe start by explaining what labour productivity means.

3 Explain how introducing new ovens into the kitchens of each restaurant could improve labour productivity at Tasty Tapas. **(4 marks)**

> If you can use calculations from the case study this will show good application to the context.

4 Explain one way that Tasty Tapas might benefit from operating at high capacity utilisation. **(5 marks)**

> This is a very open question. Read the case study and choose an aspect of operations management that you can link to the Tasty Tapas context.

5 Analyse how operations management could help Tasty Tapas achieve a competitive advantage. **(9 marks)**

6 Do you think that outsourcing some of the basic food preparation will 'ease pressure on the kitchens'? Justify your answer. **(16 marks)**

> Remember to consider this question from both perspectives. What could be the drawbacks of outsourcing? Remember to ensure your answer is rooted in relevant operational concepts.

7 To what extent is working with a good supplier key to effectively managing the operational side of a business like Tasty Tapas? **(20 marks)**

> Remember that 'to what extent' questions require you to consider other issues in your answer. It might also be worth explaining what a 'good supplier' means.

Case study

Tasty Tapas (TT) operates a small chain of tapas restaurants serving 'an authentic variety of Spanish food and drink'. The chain is owned by Katie Collings who set up the first restaurant in 2007. In every TT venue the aim is to deliver a traditional Spanish-style customer experience, ranging from the food and drink on the menu to the classic iron railings and hand-painted tiles inside every restaurant, as well as each member of staff speaking Spanish as their first or second language. The chain currently consists of four restaurants situated in seaside towns on the east coast of the UK.

One initiative Katie recently introduced is a sophisticated and integrated IT system. Every manager and waiter uses a small touch screen device to place orders. Each of these is wirelessly connected to the restaurant's intranet and can be used to record data. This allows staff to manage customer bookings, take food and drinks orders and to issue or redeem special offer vouchers. There have been some 'teething problems' with the technology, occasionally leading to some staff having to revert to using the old-fashioned paperbased systems.

All four restaurants are successful, and are fully booked on most nights of the week. In particular, customers at the Cleethorpes restaurant have to book several weeks in advance to reserve a table at the weekend. During the weekend the manager of the Cleethorpes restaurant believes the restaurant can serve a maximum of 65 tables in an evening shift.

The table below shows the number of tables the Cleethorpes restaurant served during the weekends of June 2015.

Date	Fri 5/6	Sat 6/6	Fri 12/6	Sat 13/6	Fri 19/6	Sat 20/6	Fri 26/6	Sat 27/6
Tables served (evening)	52	62	40	62	64	68	63	71

Recently Katie has been concerned with some of the reviews her restaurants have received on a well-known review website. Several people have given TT poor reviews, stating that service was poor and complaining about long wait times for their meal. One customer wrote, '*I almost felt like marching into the kitchen to cook the food myself*'.

To maintain this success and grow the business, Katie has decided to install new ovens in each of the kitchens. These new ovens will increase the number of dishes that can be cooked at one time and lower energy costs by 20%. To ease pressure on the kitchens Katie is also considering outsourcing some of the basic food preparation tasks, such as chopping vegetables and preparing sauces, to a contractor who will deliver the ingredients each morning.

Setting financial objectives 1

Financial objectives are often the most important objectives in a business. This is because without sufficient financial security the business will cease to trade. Financial objectives, such as profit maximisation, are also the incentive for which many businesses are run.

Why set financial objectives?

Poor financial management is a key reason why a business might fail.

The level of long-term debt in a business increases risk. A business may set objectives to reduce the proportion of long-term funding that is debt.

Financial measures such as profitability and shareholder value are two of the key reasons why people invest in businesses.

Importance of financial objectives

Financial objectives are easier to manage than other functional objectives, often with a numerical element and timescale.

Financial measures determine the success of all other functional areas such as marketing, operations and human resources.

Cash vs profit

Profit is measured over a given period of time. Cash flow considers the timing of payments and receipts.

There is a difference between cash balance and profit:

cash balance = cash inflows − cash outflows

profit = revenues earned − expenses incurred

A business can be very profitable but still run out of cash!

The profit hierarchy

revenue

direct costs such as materials are taken away from revenue

gross profit

indirect costs such as salaries and overheads are taken away from profit

operation profit

other incomes such as interest are taken into account and taxation to be applied to the business profit also referred to as **net profit**

profit of the year

Revenue, costs and profit

Costs – lowering costs may be important where a business is trying to improve efficiency. Cost is also an important factor in a recession or where a business competes on price.

Revenue – this is earnings generated by a business from its trading activity.
Setting revenue objectives helps drive a business's ambition to grow. Increased revenue indicates the popularity of a particular product. Also suitable where profit is less important, for example a charity.

Revenue, costs and profit objectives

Profit – profit objectives are clear to understand and one of the key performance indicators of a business. Profits are often shared with all stakeholders and as such are the indicator that most businesses will be judged against. Even though the business may be performing well, shareholders and the public may judge a business as underperforming if profits have fallen.

Now try this

1 What is operating profit?

2 Why might cash flow be more important than profit?

3 Why might a business set itself a financial objective to reduce costs by 10%?

Setting financial objectives 2

Cash flow objectives

A business will fail if it is unable to meet its financial obligations and pay bills. For this reason, some businesses will set specific objectives to help manage cash flow. Businesses with long cash cycles will find it more challenging to manage cash flow. Specific cash flow objectives might include:

👍 maintaining a specific level of cash reserves

👍 extending payment periods to suppliers

👍 shortening payment periods from customers.

Investment and return objectives

A business may set a target for capital investment over the year. This will support a strategy of growth. Similarly, a business may set an objective to reduce capital over the year in order to reduce debt.

Investment objectives may also refer to the returns received on the investment. This may be calculated as the operating profit as a percentage of the investment.

$$\text{Return on investment} = \frac{\text{operating profit}}{\text{capital invested}} \times 100$$

Capital structure objectives

Capital structure is the balance between capital from borrowing (loan capital) and the capital from selling shares (share capital) in the company. Some businesses will want to balance these two sources.

* low gearing
* danger of losing control of the business
* high dividend payments to shareholders

* high gearing
* may be at risk of increasing interest payments
* difficult to find further lending

Exam focus: Financial performance measures

When analysing financial objectives it is important to take as many factors into account as possible, such as profitability, growth, cash flow and return on investment. Even if profits have fallen, the business might still be making progress if its liquidity has improved and sales have risen. Financial performance is always relative and certain measures, such as capital investment in new machinery, may not come into fruition for a number of years. Always look for the reasons behind the figures – they only tell part of the story.

Internal and external influences

Corporate objectives – all functional objectives will flow from these.

Technological – new technology may determine how a business invests. It may also create opportunities to cut costs and increase revenues.

Economic environment – a business may set lower profit objectives if indicators suggest the market is shrinking.

Financial objectives

Nature of the product – a product with a short life-cycle may dictate that sales revenue is an important financial objective to set.

Other functions – if the business sets operational objectives to improve efficiency, financial objectives around reducing costs may be appropriate.

The competitive environment – businesses will naturally set objectives that will allow them to compete. For example, aggressive investment targets.

Now try this

1 What is meant by low gearing?

2 What is the calculation for return on investment?

3 Why is the economic environment an important factor when a business comes to set financial objectives?

Exam skills

These exam-style questions use knowledge and skills you have already explored in Unit 3.5.1. The questions refer to the three case study extracts on pages 79–80.

Worked example

The following question refers to Extract B.

Jaume has set himself the objective of achieving a cumulative three-year profit of £22 000 after the bank loan has been repaid.

Based on the total capital that Jaume put in to starting his business, calculate the return on investment over the 3 year period.

(3 marks)

> Often in calculation questions, new pieces of information will be given to you that you then have to combine with information given in the case study.

$$ROI = \frac{profit}{capital\ invested} \times 100$$

$$£22\,000 \times 100 = \frac{2\,200\,000}{£12\,000} = 183.3\%$$

$$\frac{2\,200\,000}{£12\,000} = 183.3\%$$

Worked example

The following two questions refer to Extract A.

1 Explain why Harmeet might set an objective to build a good cash reserve in her business.

(4 marks)

> The student has considered that Harmeet is opening a new business. They have used this context and linked it to the problems small businesses face when trying to manage cash.

Harmeet has opened a new business and many small businesses will fail because they are unable to manage their cash flow. It is likely that it will take time for Harmeet to build a loyal customer base and create awareness of her business. In this time she will still have to pay overheads and other business costs. If she is able to maintain a healthy balance in her bank account her business will be able to meet any unexpected costs as the business grows.

2 Analyse how Harmeet's financial objectives might change as her business grows.

(9 marks)

> This is a good start to the answer. The student has identified a relevant financial objective and applied it to Harmeet's cake making business. The student has also used other relevant concepts within their answer, such as 'economies of scale'. You should always try to make links between different functions and business concepts.

As her business grows, Harmeet might decide to set herself capital investment targets as the business becomes established. For example, Harmeet might decide that she wants to set an objective to invest £5000 in new cake making facilities that will increase her output. This might be a suitable financial objective because growth could help her achieve economies of scale and this will help improve the profitability of the business...

Budgets

A budget is a financial plan for the future. An effective budget should drive many of the decisions taken across the functional areas of a business. For example, the number of products to make, how to promote the product and the number of workers to employ. Budgets can also be used to motivate the workforce when used in target setting.

Types of budgets

Setting budgets helps a business achieve its financial and wider objectives. A business looking to grow will increase its revenue budgets. This in turn will inform the expenditure budgets which will then determine the business's budgeted profits.

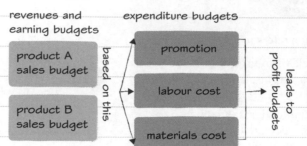

A business may set separate revenue budgets for different products or areas of earning, for example online sales and in store sales.

The budgeting process

analyse the market such as trends and average prices

↓

set financial objectives

↓

set revenue budgets

↓

forecast expenditure such as labour costs

↓

set expenditure budgets

↓

set profit budgets

↓

review and monitor budgets – adjusting as appropriate

Managers will rely heavily on market research, past sales trends and internal forecasts, such as quotes from suppliers, when setting budgets.

The problems with budgets

- A budget is only as accurate as the data on which it is based.
- Past trends can be a poor indicator of what is likely to happen in the future. Therefore, it can be very difficult to forecast sales.
- New decisions taken by governments and public bodies – such as interest rate changes (interest to be paid on business loans might increase) and employment legislation (leading to more costs for employers).
- Unexpected changes – such as a rise in commodity prices.
- An unrealistic budget loses all value as a motivational tool.

Variance analysis

Variance analysis compares the forecast data to the actual figures. It can be used to analyse the accuracy of the budgeting process and help make decisions about budget adjustments. A favourable variance is one that is better than budgeted and an adverse variance is one that is worse. Here are some key questions when analysing budgets.

Which adverse variances are due to unexpected factors?

Budget	2015 budget	2015 actual	Variance
Staff salaries and training	1.5 m	2 m	0.5 m adverse
Revenue	6 m	7 m	1 m favourable
Maintenance	2.3 m	4 m	1.7 m adverse
Marketing	0.5 m	0.5 m	no variance
Overheads	7 m	6.5 m	0.5 m favourable

How effectively has the business budgeted revenue?

What are the key areas that have led to the budget being inaccurate?

How effectively has the business budgeted expenditure?

Which adverse variances are due to poor forecasting?

Now try this

1 Give two examples of an expenditure budget.

2 What is an adverse variance?

3 Give two reasons why it is difficult to forecast accurate budgets.

Cash flow forecasts

A cash flow forecast will predict the cash inflows (receipts) for a business and the cash outflows (expenditure). A cash flow forecast should then determine the cash funds a business has at any one time. If a business knows what cash funds it needs at any one time, it can take measures to ensure finance is available.

Constructing a cash flow forecast

A cash flow forecast is generally made up of three sections:

Generally a longer list of items than cash in.

Difference between monthly inflows and monthly outflows.

		January	February	March
Cash in	cash sales			
	credit sales			
	total inflow			
Cash out	raw materials			
	salaries			
	other costs			
	total outflows			
Net cash flow	net cash flow			
	opening balance			
	closing balance			

Cash flow forecast is calculated as: (inflows − outflows = net cash flow) + opening balance = closing balance

Net cash flow + opening balance. Closing balance is the available cash a business is forecast to have during that trading period.

Cash carried forward from previous trading period for example February's opening balance will be January's closing balance.

Analysing cash flow forecasts

When analysing cash flow forecasts, managers should consider the following questions:

Are our monthly inflows greater than our monthly outflows?

↓

What are the forecast periods of high expenditure?

↓

Is a positive cash flow sustainable? For example, is it simply due to a large inflow of capital?

↓

Are inflows increasing over time?

↓

Is there a seasonal trend?

↓

Do we have enough cash reserves to cover unexpected costs?

The value of cash flow forecasting

There are a number of reasons a business should construct a cash flow forecast:

- used to support an application for lending (perhaps as part of a business plan)
- supports the budgeting process
- identifies any potential cash flow crisis.

A business must analyse the timings of its payables and receivables in order to manage cash flow effectively.

- **payables** – amount of time (days) taken for the business to pay creditors
- **receivables** – amount of time taken for debtors to pay the business.

Now try this

1 What is an opening balance?

2 Identify three outflows for a business.

3 What might a cash flow forecast be used for?

4 How is a cash flow forecast calculated?

5 What is net cash flow?

Break-even 1

The break-even output is the point at which a business's revenue generated through the sales of its products will cover the total costs. At break-even the business is making neither a profit nor a loss. Break-even analysis can be used to help a business make important decisions about costs, prices and expected profit.

The uses of break-even analysis

👍 Decide whether a business idea is profitable and viable.

👍 Identify the level of output and sales necessary to generate a profit (and therefore the scale of the business).

👍 Assess changes in the level of production.

👍 Assess the effects of costing and pricing decisions.

$$\text{Break-even point} = \frac{\text{contribution per unit}}{\text{fixed costs}}$$

Contribution

Contribution is the difference between the variable costs of one unit and its selling price. Total contribution is total output × contribution per unit.

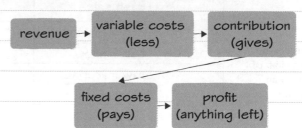

Understanding break-even

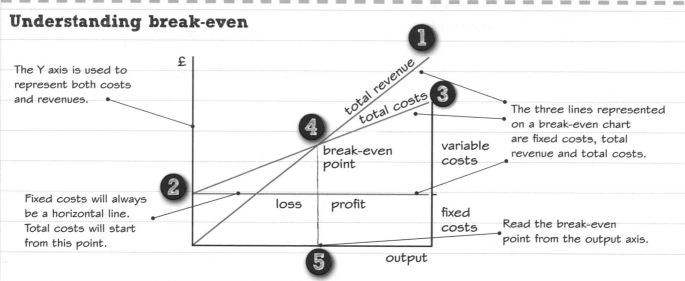

The Y axis is used to represent both costs and revenues.

The three lines represented on a break-even chart are fixed costs, total revenue and total costs.

Fixed costs will always be a horizontal line. Total costs will start from this point.

Read the break-even point from the output axis.

1 Plot total revenue line (price × quantity sold) at each level of output. You only need two points on a graph to draw a line. You know total revenue will start at 0 so you only need to calculate revenue at one other output level to draw your line.

2 Plot fixed costs line. As fixed costs will not change at any level of output, you know this will be a horizontal line.

3 Plot total costs line. Add variable cost at each level of output to the fixed costs. As your total costs line at 0 will start at the same point as fixed costs you only need to calculate one other point to get your line.

4 Where total costs meet total revenue is where break-even is identified. Label this.

5 If the current level of output is below break-even the business will make a loss. If it is above break-even it will generate a profit.

Now try this

1 How is the break-even point calculated?

2 What three pieces of information are included on a break-even chart?

3 Give three reasons why a business might use a break-even analysis.

Break-even 2

Changing variables and break-even analysis

Analysing and manipulating break-even charts can help a business make decisions on whether to accept prices on orders different from those normally charged or the impact on profitability of a change in costs and output levels.

For example:

A Raising the price by £2 will increase revenue at each level of output and lower the break-even point.

B Using a cheaper supplier might lower variable costs by £1. This would move the total costs line down and lower the break-even point.

C An increase in rent of £200 per month would raise the fixed cost line, which in turn would increase total costs. The break-even point would rise.

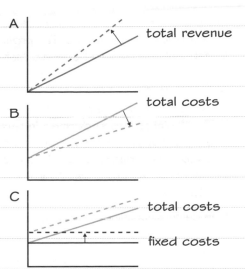

The margin of safety

This is the difference between the break-even point and the current level of output. The size of the margin of safety will determine the risk of the business – the margin of safety should be as high as possible.

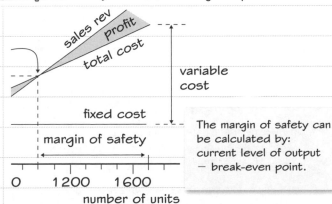

The margin of safety can be calculated by: current level of output – break-even point.

📝 **Exam focus** **Break-even analysis**

When analysing financial information, break-even analysis can be used to evaluate the potential of a business to make a profit based on its output. For example, a business with a high break-even point will have to produce and sell a lot before it starts to make a profit. A small margin of safety could also suggest any negative impact on output or demand could lead to the business making a loss. As you will see below, break-even has its limitations and this should also be taken into consideration when analysing break-even data.

The value of break-even analysis

Benefits

👍 Can be used to analyse the impact of varying customers, prices and costs on a business's profit.

👍 It is simple and easy to use.

👍 The break-even point is a useful guideline to help businesses make decisions.

Limitations

👎 Break-even analysis simplifies what can be a very complex process – most business sell multiple products, which makes break-even more difficult.

👎 Costs are rarely constant – break-even analysis presumes that costs stay the same over various levels of output.

👎 Break-even focuses on output – it presumes that the business will sell all of its output at the same price.

Now try this

1 Identify two ways a business could lower its break-even point.

2 What is the margin of safety?

3 Give two limitations of break-even analysis.

Profitability

Profit is a key measure of business success. However, as a single figure the profit a business makes tells us little about its performance. For profit to be useful we have to compare it to the level of sales and the level of investment required to generate that profit. To do this a manager might use a number of profitability ratios.

Gross profit margin

Gross profit margin is a useful indicator to analyse how a business has performed in terms of its direct trading activity. It helps a business answer the question 'have our products been successful?'. However, gross profit has its limitations as it does not take into account indirect costs.

It is calculated using:

$$\text{Gross profit margin} = \frac{\text{gross profit}}{\text{sales revenue}} \times 100$$

Operating profit margin

Operating profit takes into account the performance of a business more fully, as the calculation takes into account direct and indirect costs. It is a useful tool when used alongside the gross profit margin.

It is calculated using:

$$\text{Operating profit margin} = \frac{\text{operating profit}}{\text{sales revenue}} \times 100$$

Profit for the year margin

This ratio takes into account all revenues and costs incurred by the business. It is a good measure of how effectively the business performed over the financial year. This ratio may be used to identify the potential to pay a dividend to shareholders.

It is calculated using:

$$\text{Profit for the year margin} = \frac{\text{profit for the year}}{\text{sales revenue}} \times 100$$

Exam focus Profitability

When analysing profitability, the best answers will be able to identify exactly where a business is falling short. For example:

- Are direct costs too high (analyse the gross profit margin)?

- Is the business not managing its overheads (compare to the operating profit margin)?

- Has performance been impacted by factors outside the business's trading activity (large income from selling off a large asset)?

Always look for the reasons why a business is profitable or not.

Budgets and cash flow forecasts are important in making business start-up decisions and attracting investment.

Return on investment analysis can be used to compare projects for potential investment.

Profitability ratios can be used to analyse which aspects of a business are being run effectively and where improvements are needed.

Using financial data to make business decisions

Break-even analysis can be used to answer 'what if' scenarios.

Financial information is very important in business decision making because all business decisions must be financially viable. However, managers must also take into account the issues behind the numbers. For example, financial information will not take into account human or ethical factors.

Now try this

1 What is profit for the year?

2 Why are financial ratios important?

3 What is a limitation of financial information when making business decisions?

Exam skills 1

The following exam-style questions use the knowledge and skills you have already revised in Unit 3.5.2. The questions refer to the case study extracts on pages 79–80.

Worked example

The following question refers to Extract A.

1 Complete the cash flow forecast below for Harmeet's Cakes by filling in the cells labelled (a)–(e). **(5 marks)**

Harmeet's Cakes cash flow forecast

	Jan	Feb	Mar	Apr
Income				
Specialist cakes	400	500	900	1200
Parties	500	1600	1900	2200
Total income	**(a) 900**	**2100**	**2800**	**3400**
Expenditure (payments)				
Rent	400	400	400	400
Materials	450	**(c) 600**	800	900
Delivery costs	65	80	120	150
Advertising	200	40	40	40
Total expenditure	**1115**	**1120**	**1360**	**1490**
Net cash flow	**(b) −215**	**980**	**1440**	**1910**
Opening balance	100	−115	**(e) 865**	2305
Closing balance	−115	**(d) 865**	2305	4215

By knowing the calculations necessary to complete a cash flow forecast the student was able to work out the five missing numbers:

(a) the sum of the two inflows in January

(b) — Net cash flow = total income − total expenditure for January

(c) the difference between total expenditure for February and the sum of the other three expenditures in February (400 + 80 + 40)

(d) Net cash flow for February + opening balance for February

(e) the opening balance for March will be the same as the closing balance for February.

2 Label the break-even chart below. **(4 marks)**

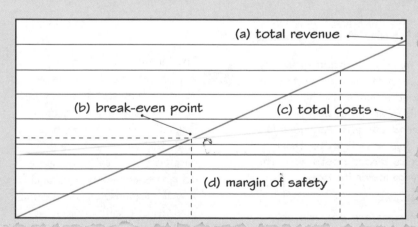

(a) total revenue

(b) break-even point   (c) total costs

(d) margin of safety

Exam skills 2

Worked example

The following question refers to Extract A.

Using the information in Figure 2, calculate the budget variance for Harmeet's Cakes (1–5) for 2016 Quarter 1. For each variance identify whether it is favourable or adverse.   **(5 marks)**

	2016 quarter 1 forecast	2016 quarter 1 actual	Variance
Income budget			
Income from parties	6300	5850	
Income from specialist cakes	2700	2900	**1 200** favourable
Total income	**9000**	**8750**	2 250 adverse
Expenditure budget			
Fixed costs	6000	6500	3 500 adverse
Cost of specialist cakes	1575	1575	
Other variable costs	675	575	**4 100** favourable
Total expenditure	**8250**	**8650**	5 400 adverse

> The key to calculating variance is to first identify the type of budget. In 1 the variance is favourable by 200 because the business exceeded its sales budget for specialist cakes. On the other hand, 3 is adverse because this is an expenditure budget and fixed costs are £300 higher than forecast.

Worked example

The following question refers to Extract C.

Based on the financial information presented in Figure 4, to what extent is Hands on Puzzles Plc a profitable business?   **(16 marks)**

Figure 4 shows that the gross profit margin has been gradually rising over the past 4 years. The gross profit margin compares the profit generated from selling products minus the direct costs compared to sales revenue. This is an indication of how profitable Hands on Puzzles Plc products are. As there is consistent growth in gross profit the business is potentially selling lots of products and managing its direct costs well. This might be due to growth and its ability to lower its cost of sales.

On the other hand, operating profit margins are considerably lower and this suggests that the business has high overhead costs. Furthermore, the operating profit margin has been falling slightly over the past 4 years. With gross profit rising I would expect a similar trend with operating profit. This might suggest that the business has problems managing its indirect costs such as rent, salaries and loan repayments...

> This answer has good application because the student has clearly used and analysed the information in Figure 4. The student has analysed why the business might be profitable based on its gross profit margin, and why it might not, based on its operating profit figures. For each, the student has tried to interpret why. To evaluate the student might go on to explain that the extent to which Hands on Puzzles Plc is profitable might depend on the industry average and other internal factors.

Sources of finance 1

A business may require a range of financing options. These can be internal or external sources and the availability will depend on a number of factors including the type of business.

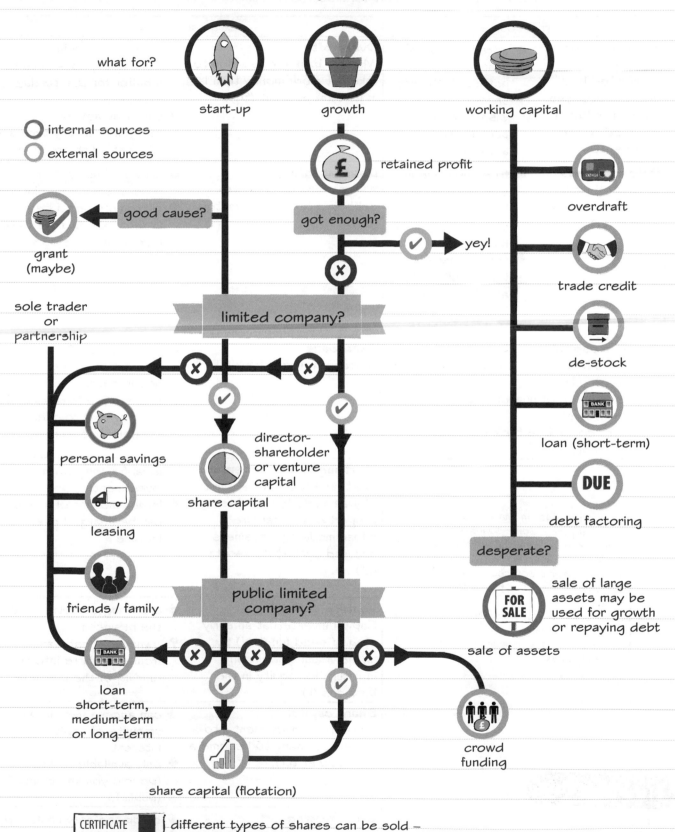

what for?

start-up   growth   working capital

○ internal sources
○ external sources

retained profit

good cause? ←

got enough? ✓ → yey!
✗

grant (maybe)

overdraft

trade credit

sole trader or partnership

limited company?

de-stock

✗ ← ✗
✓   ✓

personal savings

director-shareholder or venture capital

share capital

loan (short-term)

DUE

debt factoring

leasing

desperate?

public limited company?

✗ ✗ ✓ ✗
✓   ✓

friends / family

FOR SALE

sale of large assets may be used for growth or repaying debt

sale of assets

loan short-term, medium-term or long-term

crowd funding

share capital (flotation)

CERTIFICATE different types of shares can be sold –
• ordinary shares
• preference shares
• debentures

Sources of finance 2

Benefits and drawbacks of sources of finance

LT = Long-term source of finance ST = short-term source of finance

Internal sources		External sources	
Retained profit Net profit reinvested back into the business instead of being returned to the owners. (LT)	👍 a free source of finance that does not incur interest 👎 shareholders may wish to receive back in the form of a dividend.	**Overdrafts** Where a bank allows a firm to take out more money than is in its bank account (ST).	👍 flexible way to fund working capital – acts as a buffer for day-to-day expenses 👎 bank may ask for repayment at any time and interest rates are high.
Sale of assets Selling off items of value to free up capital (LT)	👍 frees up value in unwanted assets to be invested in other areas of the business 👎 the business loses the benefit of the asset, such as no longer owning a delivery vehicle.	**Debt factoring** Where a firm sells on its debt to a third party factor (ST).	👍 allows a business to receive cash immediately 👎 customers could be aware if debts are factored and lose faith in the company.
Owner's capital Personal savings used to start or expand a business (LT) • a free source of finance that does not incur interest • owners could lose their personal investment.		**Bank loans** Borrowing from a bank (LT).	👍 can be negotiated to meet business requirements 👎 business has to pay interest and may have to offer collateral to secure it.
		Mortgages and debentures Mortgage is a special type of loan made for purchasing property. A debenture is a loan made to a business secured against its assets (LT).	👍 ideal for long-term investments 👎 large amounts of interest can be charged over its lifetime.
Factors to consider in finance sourcing: • Legal structure – some sources, such as share capital are only available to companies. • Flexibility – some sources are highly adaptable to meet the business's precise needs. • Cost – some sources have very high interest repayments. • Risk – sources that require collateral can be high risk.		**Venture capital** Capital invested at an early stage ('seed funding') by an individual or company in return for equity in the business (LT).	👍 can bring expertise into the business 👎 owner may not want input from elsewhere into the running of the business.
		Share capital An owner's investment into a limited company to become a shareholder (LT).	👍 can access very large amounts of capital and no interest 👎 only available to Ltd (people you know) and Plc (public).
		Crowdfunding Raising monetary contributions from a large number of people, today often performed via crowdfunding websites (LT).	👍 cheap and easy to set up 👎 not suitable for raising large amounts of money.

Now try this

1 Give three short-term sources of finance.
2 Why is retained profit low risk?
3 What types of businesses can raise share capital?

Exam skills 16

The following exam-style questions use the knowledge and skills you have already revised in Unit 3.5.2. The questions refer to the three case studies on pages 79–80.

Worked example

The following question refers to Extract A.

Harmeet has decided that she wants to expand her cake business and has decided to invest £3000 of her personal savings.
Explain the benefits of Harmeet expanding her business using personal finance. **(5 marks)**

The benefits of Harmeet expanding her cake business with personal finance is that this is a low risk method of finance. Although she might stand to lose the £3000 investment, she will not have to pay interest and is not subject to making regular repayments. This means that she will find it easier to manage her cash flow as the business gradually grows.

This is a good answer explaining the benefits of personal finance. However, the student could develop the benefits further and ensure the answer is rooted in the context of Harmeet Cakes. They could do this by linking it to the type of business or giving specific examples pertinent to the case.

Worked example

The following two questions refer to Extract B.

1 Analyse the reasons why Jaume may find it difficult to secure a bank loan. **(9 marks)**

Jaume is setting up a new business therefore he has no track record of success and the bank may find that this is a high risk venture. Furthermore, it is unclear whether Jaume has produced a business plan or financial planning documents and a bank will want to see these in order to be able to assess the level of risk...

It is OK to discuss things not mentioned in the case study. We don't know whether Jaume has produced a business plan, but the student has shown good understanding of the requirements of securing a bank loan.

2 Evaluate alternative sources of finance Jaume could use to finance his leavers hoodie business other than using a bank loan. **(16 marks)**

As Jaume is starting a new creative business he could opt to raise finance through crowdfunding. This would require Jaume submitting a proposal online through a crowdfunding website and hope that his project attracts investors. The benefit is that this is easy to do and he would avoid paying high rates of interest. Nevertheless, Jaume still requires £7000 and it might be difficult to raise this amount through crowdfunding if potential investors don't feel that a hoodie printing business is unique. In order for crowdfunding to work, Jaume would have to submit a very convincing proposal to attract potential investors.

In this answer the student might go on to analyse other reasons why Jaume might find it difficult to secure a bank loan. For example, the fact that the bank might require collateral before it offers lending.

When answering questions on sources of finance, make sure the sources you suggest are appropriate for the situation, context and type of business.

This is a good start to this answer. The student has selected a relevant source of finance for a small business and analysed the issues in relation to Jaume's business. The second paragraph might go on to suggest a second source of finance and then evaluate which of the two is the most appropriate for Jaume.

Improving cash flow

A key decision managers have to make is how they will improve the financial performance of the business. In particular, managers must know how to improve cash flow and profitability.

Improving cash flow

The key to managing cash flow is to speed up the process of cash coming into the business (receivables) and slow down the process of money leaving the business (payables).

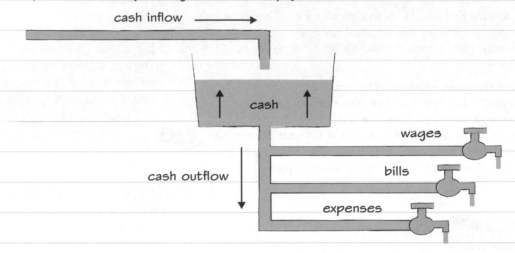

Speed up inflows

👍 Incentivise early repayment – give customers a discount for paying early.

👍 Reduce trade credit given to customers.

👍 Sell off stock at a discounted price to free up cash.

👍 Inject fresh capital into the business.

A business should always plan to keep a minimum cash reserve in its bank account.

Slow down outflows

👍 Delay payments to suppliers.

👍 Increase trade credit agreements with suppliers.

👍 Cut costs – find cheaper alternatives or postpone spending in areas such as training or advertising.

The best way to ensure the business has a positive cash flow is to invest time and effort in researching and planning effective cash flow forecasts.

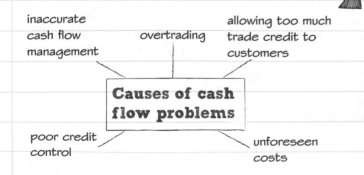

📝 **Exam focus** **Improving cash flow**

There is always a consequence of taking measures to improve cash flow or profitability. For example, lowering costs might adversely affect quality. There is often also a condition. For example, an advertising campaign could boost sales revenue if the right medium and message is used in the campaign. Always think about the **consequences** and the **conditions**.

Now try this

1 Identify two ways a business can increase cash inflows.

2 Identify two ways a business can reduce cash outflows.

3 Identify three reasons why a business may have difficulty managing its cash flow.

Increasing profitability

Profitability can be improved through measures taken by each functional area of the business.

Ways to increase revenue

1 Increase prices.

2 Reduce process (dependent on price elasticity of demand).

3 Create awareness and desire through marketing.

4 Add value to the product – increase benefits and features.

Improving profit

Profit is the difference between total revenue and total costs. Therefore, there are two general ways that a business can improve its profits. Increase revenue or/and decrease costs.

revenue

profit

costs

Why businesses are unprofitable

There are a number of reasons why a business might be unprofitable:

- ✔ no demand for the product
- ✔ selling at the wrong price
- ✔ low contribution per unit
- ✔ poor management of costs
- ✔ expansion of the business – profit retained and not available for return to shareholders.

Ways to reduce costs

1 Reduce production costs.

2 Improve efficiency.

3 Use capacity more fully.

4 Eliminate unprofitable processes – such as unprofitable product lines.

5 Reduce variable costs – negotiate better deals with suppliers.

6 Lower overheads – move to a cheaper location.

The problems with managing finance

- **Impact on stakeholders** – some actions can damage relationships with stakeholders, for example, delayed payment could upset suppliers and higher prices could deter customers.

- **Spend money to make money** – measures to improve profits and cash flow often cost the business, for example an advertising campaign to boost sales or lower prices to incentivise early payment from customers.

- **Short-term solutions** – sometimes efforts may boost profits and improve cash flow in the short term, but hinder long-term success, for example, lowering reinvestment to return profits for shareholders.

Now try this

1 Identify three costs a business could reduce in order to improve profits.

2 Why is price an important factor in a business's profitability?

3 Identify three problems a business might face when trying to improve profits.

Exam skills 1

These exam-style questions use the knowledge and skills you have already revised in Unit 3.5.4. The questions refer to the case studies on pages 79–80.

Worked example

The following question refers to Extract A.

The table below represents Harmeet's cash flow forecast for the first 4 months of trading in 2016. Harmeet is concerned that she may find it difficult to manage her cash flow during the first few months of the year.

Analyse how Harmeet could ensure she has a positive cash flow at the start of the year. **(9 marks)**

Harmeet's Cakes cash flow forecast

	Jan	Feb	Mar	Apr
Income				
Specialist cakes	400	500	900	1200
Parties	500	1600	1900	2200
Total income	**900**	**2100**	**2800**	**3400**
Expenditure (payments)				
Rent	400	400	400	400
Materials	450	600	800	900
Delivery costs	65	80	120	150
Advertising	200	40	40	40
Total expenditure	**1115**	**1120**	**1360**	**1490**
Net cash flow	**−215**	**980**	**1440**	**1910**
Opening bank	**100**	**−115**	**865**	**2305**
Closing bank	**−115**	**865**	**2305**	**4215**

Harmeet could improve her cash flow position at the start of the year by trying to secure better trade credit arrangements with her suppliers. This would then free up funds in January which could be used to pay other bills such as the rent of her premises. Harmeet is currently forecast to pay £450 for materials and if this could be postponed until February or March it could avoid the net cash flow of − £215 she forecasts for January. However, she might only be able to do this if she has a good relationship with her suppliers and as she has not been trading for very long this might be difficult....

The student has clearly applied the financial information from the cash flow table in their answer. The student has suggested one method that Harmeet could use to improve her cash flow position and analysed the consequence. The student could now go on to analyse a second option. For example, does Harmeet need to pay £200 on marketing in January? Or perhaps she could find a way to boost revenue?

Worked example

The following question refers to Extract B.

Using the information in Figure 3, calculate the profit that Jaume is anticipated to make in his first year of trading. **(4 marks)**

Profit = total revenue − total costs
Total revenue = £21.20 × 9000 = £190 800
Total costs = £13 × 9000 = £117 000 + (20 000 + 15 000)
= 152 000
Profit = £190 800 − £152 000 = £38 800

Exam skills 2

Worked example

The following question refers to Extract C.

Using the information in Figure 4 explain the importance of profit to a business like Hands On Puzzles Plc. **(5 marks)**

Hands On Puzzles Plc is a public limited company with external shareholders. It is important for a Plc to satisfy shareholders and provide a return for its investment. If Hands On Puzzles Plc is able to generate a net profit, some of this may be returned to shareholders in the form of a dividend. The achievement of profit is also a sign that the business is healthy. Hands On Puzzles Plc is currently making a profit, but the operating profit has been falling in recent years.

When a question asks you to use certain information, such as a table, extract or figure, always make sure you do!

Worked example

The following question refers to Extract C.

Hands On Puzzles Plc plans to launch a new line of products in the near future. Assess how the company could ensure the new line of products is profitable. **(16 marks)**

A business can improve profitability by maximising sales revenue with a high price and minimising overall business costs. Hands On Puzzles Plc could ensure its new product line is profitable by researching potential suppliers of bamboo and ensuring it receives the lowest possible price. If the variable cost of bamboo is kept low, this will maximise the profit margin (or contribution) of its new product line. The danger of trying to buy raw materials at the lowest price is that this can possibly compromise the quality of its products. Considering that most of its products are shipped to the USA and Western Europe, quality will be very important...

This is a very open question. There are many aspects that the student could consider to answer this question. The trick is to choose those methods that are most relevant to the Hands On Puzzles Plc's context.

A good opening paragraph. The student has answered in context and shown balance in their answer by discussing the benefits and drawbacks of purchasing low cost raw materials.

Exam-style practice

Have a go at the questions below that apply the concepts covered in Unit 3.5 and the finance function of a business. Refer to the three case studies on pages 79–80. There are answers on page 198.

The following two questions refer to Extract A.

1 Harmeet estimated that her average monthly fixed costs for 2016 would be £900. The average price she planned to sell her cakes for was £45 with variable costs per cake being £16.

On average, how many cakes would Harmeet have to sell each month in order to break-even? **(3 marks)**

> Start with formula for break-even and remember to round your answer to the nearest whole unit.

2 Using Figure 1, calculate the percentage growth in forecasted sales of Harmeet's Cakes between Qtr1 and Qtr 4. **(3 marks)**

> Start by working out the actual increase between Qtr 1 and Qtr 4.

The following three questions refer to Extract B.

3 Using the information in Figure 3, construct a break-even chart for Jaume's business. Clearly label your chart including the break-even point and margin of safety. **(6 marks)**

> In this question the axis is drawn for you. Start by drawing on the fixed cost line and then move on to calculate the total revenue line. Try working out the revenue for 1000 hoodies. Once you know this you have your second line. Total revenue will always start at £0 and you only need two points on a graph to draw a line. Remember to label all parts of your graph.

£ (1000s)

units (hoodies)

> You will need graph paper to answer this question. If you need to draw a graph in your exam, the graph paper will be printed on your exam script

4 Explain how Jaume could increase revenue for his business. **(5 marks)**

> This is a very open question. Try to choose a method that you can easily apply to the context of Extract B.

5 Evaluate the value of cash flow forecasting for a business like Jaume's Hoodies. **(16 marks)**

> Consider the nature of Jaume's product and the stage that his business is at.

The following two questions refer to Extract C.

6 To what extent is raising the finance through issuing new shares an effective way for Hands On Puzzles Plc to raise capital for its new line of products? **(16 marks)**

> Have a look at the gearing ratio for Hands On Puzzles Plc.

7 What do you believe would be appropriate financial objectives for Hands On Puzzles Plc in 2017? Justify your answer. **(20 marks)**

> Flick back to Unit 3.5.1. There are a range of financial objectives a business might set. Discuss two areas that you think might be appropriate for Hands On Puzzles Plc considering its current activity and financial position.

Case study 1

Extract A – Harmeet's Cakes

Harmeet was a skilled baker of confectionery goods. For the past 2 years, she had been a part-time confectionery chef in a local cake store. As she felt that she knew the market well, she decided to open her own catering business making one-off specialised cakes for special occasions and baking for parties such as birthdays and weddings. She had built up a loyal customer base and had gained an insight into the types of cakes that worked best for different occasions.

Harmeet knew that her business would have the most demand during the summer when people tended to have weddings and around the Christmas period. However, she also knew that the market was becoming more competitive and that demand would fall sharply if the economy was weak. Harmeet constructed a forecast for demand (see Figure 1).

Figure 1: Forecast demand for Harmeet's cake business

	2016 Quarter 1	2016 Quarter 2	2016 Quarter 3	2016 Quarter 4
Number of parties	45	45	60	75

Figure 2: Harmeet's budget forecast

	2016 Quarter 1	2016 Quarter 2	2016 Quarter 3	2016 Quarter 4
Income budget				
Income from parties	6300	6300	8400	10500
Income from specialist cakes	2700	2700	3600	4500
Total income	9000	9000	12000	15000
Expenditure budget				
Fixed costs	6000	3000	3000	3000
Cost of specialist cakes	1575	1575	2100	2625
Other variable costs	675	675	900	1125
Total expenditure	8250	5250	6000	6750

Case study 2

Extract B – Jaume's Hoodies

Jaume planned to open a business selling hoodies to school leavers. Jaume had noticed that this was a growing market and that most schools in the region purchased hoodies for students leaving in Year 11 and Year 13. Jaume calculated his business start-up costs for the first 3 months of trading to be £12 000. Jaume had managed to invest £5000 of his own savings and considered raising the remaining funds through a bank loan.

Jaume had limited funds available but was able to use his skills in website design to create a website to promote his business and, once the business started trading, to allow online purchasing in the electronic market.

Figure 3: Jaume's financial information

Decision	Options chosen
Selling price	£21.20 per hoodie Expected sales 9 000 units per annum
Variable costs	Purchase high quality hoodies at £13.00 each
Rent premises	£20 000 per annum
Other overheads	£15 000 per annum

Extract C – Hands On Puzzles Plc

Hands On Puzzles Plc is a large manufacturer of wooden puzzles and brain teasers based in China. The company manufactures around 2 million puzzles each year, which it exports all around the world, its main markets being the USA and Western Europe. The company is looking to invest in a new line of traditional wooden toys for children. The line of products will be made from locally supplied bamboo, an ecologically sustainable resource. The company is looking to finance the new product line through the issue of new shares.

Figure 4: Hands On Plc Financial Performance 2013–16

	2013	2014	2015	2016
Gearing	60%	54%	38%	30%
Gross profit margin	42%	45%	39%	53%
Operating profit margin	7%	5%	5%	4%

Human resource objectives

Human resources is the function of a business that is concerned with ensuring that the organisation has a workforce who are able to do their job effectively in order to meet the needs of the business and its customers. Human resources are concerned with anything related to the people within the organisation.

The importance of human resources

Effectively managing human resources allows a business to:

- 👍 control costs of production (through controlling labour costs)
- 👍 add value through expertise and customer service
- 👍 ensure employees are driven and motivated.
- 👍 identify and develop leaders
- 👍 adapt to the internal and external pressures on the business.

Human resource perspectives

There are two competing perspectives on human resources:

- Hard HRM – this refers to managers who see employees as just another resource in the business that needs to be utilised efficiently and effectively
- Soft HRM – this refers to managers who see people as the most valuable asset a business has. Therefore, they need to be nurtured and developed to achieve their potential.

Managers with the latter perspective are more likely to invest in people.

Human resource objectives

- Employee engagement and involvement – ensuring employees feel involved, valued and part of the organisation, and maximising intellectual input and effort from the workforce.
- Alignment of values – ensuring the values of the organisation are embraced by all employees.
- Talent development – ensuring talent in the organisation is developed and promoted.
- Diversity – such as ethnicity, gender, disability, religion or sexuality.
- Number, skills and location of employees – ensuring the business has the right number of employees with the correct skills, in the right places.
- Training – ensuring the workforce has the right training to do their jobs properly considering the changing nature of business.
- Labour productivity – maximising output from its workers.

Influences on human resource objectives

Legal/political factors – for example, health and safety legislation and industry regulation may influence job design.

The product – labour intensive production will often require a highly skilled workforce.

Social factors – employee values must match that of the consumer (ethical consumers).

Attitudes and beliefs of managers – the extent to which the business adopts a 'soft' or a 'hard' approach to HRM.

Technological factors – employees might require training to use new technologies or processes.

Internal and external influences

Competitive environment – a business may need to move fast and offer competitive remuneration packages in order to attract the best employees.

Make-up of the current workforce – an ageing workforce may necessitate the need for training of new employees and dissemination of expert knowledge.

Economic factors – it may be difficult to employ the right people when there is a lack of skills in the labour market.

Now try this

1 What is 'hard HRM'?

2 How can human resources add value to an organisation?

3 Identify three factors that may be considered when a business sets its human resource objectives.

Exam skills

The following exam-style questions use the knowledge and skills you have already revised in Unit 3.6.1 and refer to the Retro Homes case study on page 101.

Worked example

Which one of the following is a reason for having a mission statement?

A The perspective that employees are the most important asset to a business

B The perspective that employees must be motivated in a business

C The perspective that employees are an asset to be utilised efficiently and effectively

D The perspective that employees should receive training

(1 mark)

> Both B and D might seem like logical answers as both would require managers to care about the welfare and development of their employees. However, A is most closely linked to the perspective of soft HRM.

Worked example

Explain why Retro Homes might set itself an objective to develop the skills of its workforce. **(5 marks)**

Retro Homes might set itself a HR objective to develop the skills of its workforce so that it can improve the quality of the products and service it offers customers. If the furniture workers have improved skills, the furniture will be of a higher quality. As people will pay more for better craftsmanship, this will add value to their products and make them more competitive than rival furniture manufacturers. Furthermore, if Retro Homes invests in the workforce this could boost motivation which will directly improve labour productivity if it leads to employees working harder and more effectively with improved skills.

> The student has developed their answer well. There is a logical chain of development which explains the consequences of improving the skills of the workforce. The answer is also in the context of Retro Homes by referring to 'furniture' and 'craftsmanship'.

Worked example

Analyse why Retro Homes might decide to appoint a specialist company to recruit new employees. **(9 marks)**

Retro Homes may decide to appoint a specialist recruitment company as this would remove the burden of recruitment from Paul and Louise. Neither have a background in recruitment and this would allow them to concentrate on running the business instead. The very high rate of labour turnover that Retro Homes has experienced might suggest that it is not employing the right people for the job. Furthermore, a specialist recruitment company would be able to reach a much wider range of potential employees because unemployed people will sign up with a recruiter in order to find out about new jobs that become available...

> This answer is rooted in the context of Retro Homes. The candidate has considered issues within the business and attempted to apply these within their answer, i.e. referring to the high labour turnover and linking this to the question.

Human resource performance 1

Managers can use a number of calculations to interpret and analyse the performance of human resources within their business. Understanding human resource performance can help managers make decisions about job design, employee numbers, rewards and remuneration and human resource policies.

Labour productivity

This is a key measure of employee performance. Labour productivity interprets the output per worker over a given time period. Labour productivity directly effects profit margins and decisions around pricing.

It is calculated by:

$$\frac{\text{total output per time period}}{\text{number of employees at work}}$$

Interpreting labour productivity

Generally speaking the higher labour productivity the better the business is performing.

However:

- it does not take into account **wage rates** – a key factor in employees' performance.
- it does not take into account **technology** used in the production process.
- labour productivity may be affected by many **other factors** – such as internal disruptions to production, or the nature of the task or product being produced which will also influence this calculation.

Unit labour costs

This measures the labour costs per unit of output produced. The calculation takes into account non-wage costs such as national insurance and therefore considers the full cost of labour compared to output.

It is calculated by

$$\frac{\text{labour costs}}{\text{units of output}}$$

Interpreting unit labour costs

The lower the unit costs the better! Unit labour costs have an inverse relationship with labour productivity – they should go down as labour productivity rises.

However:

- labour costs will rise if employees receive training, but this should increase labour productivity in the long term
- lowering unit labour costs will be ineffective if other business costs rise.

Employee costs as a percentage of revenue

Directly compares employee costs against the business's revenue or turnover. This is a particularly important measure for businesses where labour costs are a high percentage of total costs – for example in service sector businesses.

It is calculated by:

$$\frac{\text{employee costs}}{\text{sales turnover}} \times 100$$

Interpreting employee costs as a percentage of revenue

Can be influenced by a number of factors:

- Higher labour productivity can lead to higher sales revenue, thus lowering the percentage of labour costs compared to revenue.
- Any increase in wages/salaries must have an impact on productivity otherwise the percentage labour costs will rise.
- Human resource capacity must be maximised in order to lower the percentage.

Now try this

1 Why is labour productivity important?

2 Why is there an inverse relationship between labour productivity and unit labour costs?

3 What factors can influence employee costs as a percentage of revenue?

Human resource performance 2

Labour turnover and labour retention

This is an important measure as the number of employees leaving a company can give an insight into a number of issues relating to happiness, motivation and the impact of this on overall labour costs.

Labour turnover is calculated by:

$$\frac{\text{number of staff leaving in a year}}{\text{average number of staff}}$$

Labour retention substitutes the average number leaving with the average number employed for one year (the year being measured).

Interpreting turnover and labour retention

- With labour turnover comes increased costs of recruitment and training.

- A higher turnover or low retention figure could indicate that employees are not happy with their jobs.

- This might be used as a key performance indicator as businesses try to retain the most talented workers within their company – having the best employees can be a competitive advantage.

- Some industries will expect high rates of labour turnover – for example holiday companies, due to contracts being seasonal.

- High rates of labour turnover may be encouraged as a business goes through a period of change.

Using data in human resource decision making

The measures considered in this unit will directly inform key human resource decisions.

> Organisation objectives and key information from other business functions

> Demand for labour
> - number of employees
> - skills required
> - new roles required
> - labour cost implication

> Supply of labour
> - review of existing workforce
> - forecast staff leaving in next year
> - changes required to current working practices

> Human plan
> - recruitment
> - training
> - reorganisation
> - redundancies
> - remuneration

1 What can a business interpret from a high labour turnover ratio?

2 Why might a business want high retention rates?

3 How might labour cost information be used by a manager?

Exam skills

The following exam-style questions use knowledge and skills you have already revised in Unit 3.6.2 and the final two questions refer to the Retro Homes case study on page 101.

Worked example

A small hair salon sees 370 customers come through its doors during a week for a range of services including cuts, colours and treatments. The salon employs seven stylists.

Which of the following best represents the salon's labour productivity per worker for one week of trading?

A   0.02   ○

B   53   ●

C   2   ○

D   47   ○

(1 mark)

On multiple-choice questions like this the distractors will often be answers where the calculations are back to front. In this case, A would be the answer if the student divided the number of employees by the number of customers per week.

Worked example

Analyse one way in which Retro Homes could lower its unit labour costs.   **(5 marks)**

One way that Retro Homes could reduce unit labour costs is to cut back on the number of employees. One way that the business could do this would be to not replace any members of staff who leave the company. This is known as natural wastage. This would reduce unit labour costs if the company is able to maintain output with one less worker. Retro Homes could ensure this happens by setting targets for the number of pieces of furniture produced each week.

Before answering the question the students must first ensure they understand what unit labour costs refers to – total output per time period / total labour costs.

There are a number of options the student might have chosen to answer this question. The student has explained how reducing employee numbers would reduce unit labour costs and gone on to say how the business could do this. They have also identified a condition – 'if'. However, the application of the context is relatively simple – the student makes reference to 'furniture'.

Worked example

To what extent is the workforce at the tea room performing well? Justify your answer.   **(16 marks)**

...Overall, the workforce is performing well because revenues are increasing. A key factor in a successful tea room will be the service provided by employees. Increasing revenues suggest that this must be true, although the success may also be due to the furniture showroom being next door and high quality food. High level of labour turnover will be a key factor contributing to the high labour costs as a percentage of revenue and if Louise is able to retain more of her workforce then these indicators of performance are likely to improve. The workforce is performing well but labour costs must fall if the tea room is to be profitable.

This is a good evaluation of the question. The student has identified what they believe to be the key factor (revenues increasing) and gone on to make a recommendation.

The first part of the answer will have discussed issues relating to different measures of labour performance.

Job design

Job design refers to the contents of a job in terms of its duties and responsibilities, the methods to be used in carrying out the job and the relationship between the job holder and their superior.

opportunity for flexible working practices (contracts and location)

focus on customer needs – especially important in job design for service sector workers

motivation of employees

Influences on job design

technology – new technology will influence how people work

legal requirements including health and safety

skills of the workforce – matching job design to utilise employees' skill sets

The Hackman and Oldman Job Characteristics Model

The model helps managers understand the different dimensions (core job dimensions) which contribute to the overall job design and how these impact the psychological state of their employees. Managers should design jobs so that they maximise these three psychological states in order to achieve the desired outcomes.

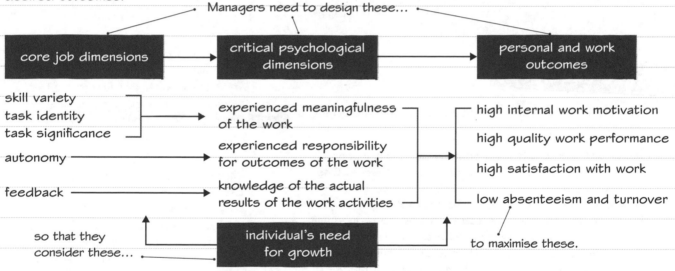

Managers need to design these...

| core job dimensions | → | critical psychological dimensions | → | personal and work outcomes |

skill variety
task identity
task significance

autonomy

feedback

experienced meaningfulness of the work

experienced responsibility for outcomes of the work

knowledge of the actual results of the work activities

high internal work motivation

high quality work performance

high satisfaction with work

low absenteeism and turnover

so that they consider these...

individual's need for growth

to maximise these.

Key aspects of job design

Job enlargement and rotation...	Job enrichment...	Empowerment...
• adds variety to a job • means employees understand more aspects of the organisation and how jobs fit together • means employees are able to cover for each other.	• adds more challenge and complexity to the job • promotes opportunities and skills for promotion • gives employees more responsibility • supports on the job training.	• gives employees more control over their working lives • means employees are able to make their own decisions on how best to achieve the necessary outcomes. • brings new ideas and innovation into the company • enables employees have autonomy to solve problems how they like.

Now try this

1 What is job design?

2 Identify two elements of the Job Characteristics Model.

3 How does job enrichment differ from job enlargement?

Organisation design 1

Organisational design is a key factor when managing a business as it determines how a business responds to external factors, how people within the business relate to one another and how the company adapts to change.

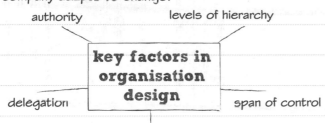

key factors in organisation design
- authority
- levels of hierarchy
- delegation
- span of control
- decision making process (centralisation vs decentralisation – see page 88)

Delegation

Delegation is the process of passing down authority through the organisation. Delegation can be used to lighten the workload of key personnel as the organisation grows and can be a key aspect of job design as it leads to job enrichment for junior members of staff. Delegation may not be suitable in certain situations where junior employees don't have the skills or in a crisis situation.

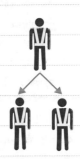

Organisation hierarchy

Chain of command
Refers to the levels in the hierarchy. Organisations with many levels are referred to as being 'tall' organisations. Organisations naturally increase the levels of the hierarchy as they grow.

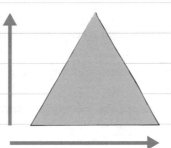

Span of control
Refers to the number of employees that a manager is directly responsible for. An organisation with a wide span of control will encourage delegation and is referred to as having a 'flat' hierarchy.

Types of organisation structure

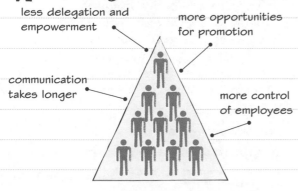

- less delegation and empowerment
- more opportunities for promotion
- communication takes longer
- more control of employees

Organisation A

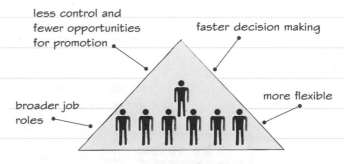

- less control and fewer opportunities for promotion
- faster decision making
- broader job roles
- more flexible

Organisation B

A 'tall' organisation structure will generally have many levels in the chain of command and there may be a narrow span of control. Organisations tend to add levels to their hierarchy as they grow.

A 'flat' organisation structure is characterised by few levels in the chain of command. There will be few middle managers but the span of control for managers at the top of the structure could be wide.

Now try this

1 What are the benefits of delegation?

2 When might a 'tall' organisation structure work best?

3 When might a 'flat' organisation structure work best?

Organisation design 2

Centralisation

Centralisation refers to a decision-making process whereby the majority of decisions are led by senior managers.

👍 works well where standardisation is required

👍 appropriate for situations where managers have the knowledge and workers are low skilled

👍 suited to authoritarian leadership styles

👍 more suitable in times of crisis

👍 effective at cost minimisation and achieving economies of scale.

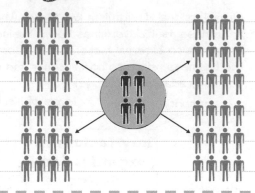

Decentralisation

Decentralisation refers to a decision-making process whereby the majority of decisions are delegated to managers in charge of regions, functions and product categories.

👍 effective where local teams are best placed to make decisions to meet the customer needs

👍 appropriate where business is spread over a wide geographic area and local trends/needs are important

👍 effective at reducing workload of senior managers and promoting autonomy and the skills of subordinates

👍 allows for flexible working conditions and supports job enrichment.

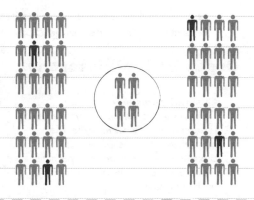

The value of change

customer needs – such as designing jobs that revolve around meeting customer expectations and excellent service

unit labour costs – such as making use of underutilised workers

The value of changing job design

employer brand – developing the reputation of the company as a good place to work

boost motivation and morale – happier workers leads to greater productivity and retention

The value of changing organisation design

delayering – removing unnecessary jobs to improve efficiency and communication

competitiveness – for example responding faster than competitors

---

📝 Exam focus — Job and organisation design

When discussing job and organisation design there are a few factors that you should consider when making any decisions or analysing the organisation. Consider how each of these relates to the business context and this should help you choose the right options such as whether to centralise or decentralise:

- financial position/strength
- skill of the workforce
- nature of the job/product
- morale/motivation of staff.

Now try this

1 When would centralisation be appropriate for a business?

2 What factors should a manager consider when thinking about organisation design?

3 Why might a business want to develop its 'employer brand'?

Human resource flow

Human resource flow refers to the movement of employees through an organisation. There are three specific areas of the flow that must be managed effectively for the business to achieve its human resource objectives.

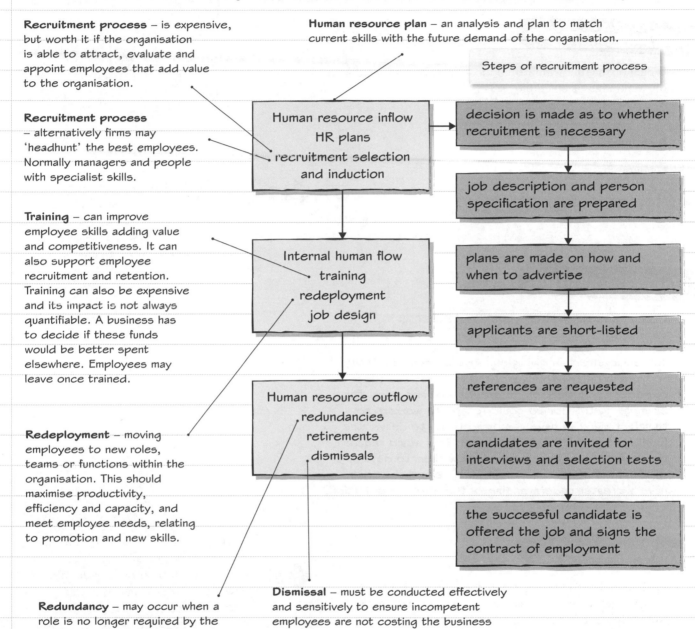

Recruitment process – is expensive, but worth it if the organisation is able to attract, evaluate and appoint employees that add value to the organisation.

Recruitment process – alternatively firms may 'headhunt' the best employees. Normally managers and people with specialist skills.

Training – can improve employee skills adding value and competitiveness. It can also support employee recruitment and retention. Training can also be expensive and its impact is not always quantifiable. A business has to decide if these funds would be better spent elsewhere. Employees may leave once trained.

Redeployment – moving employees to new roles, teams or functions within the organisation. This should maximise productivity, efficiency and capacity, and meet employee needs, relating to promotion and new skills.

Human resource plan – an analysis and plan to match current skills with the future demand of the organisation.

Steps of recruitment process

Human resource inflow
HR plans
recruitment selection and induction

Internal human flow
training
redeployment
job design

Human resource outflow
redundancies
retirements
dismissals

decision is made as to whether recruitment is necessary

job description and person specification are prepared

plans are made on how and when to advertise

applicants are short-listed

references are requested

candidates are invited for interviews and selection tests

the successful candidate is offered the job and signs the contract of employment

Redundancy – may occur when a role is no longer required by the organisation or in order to cut back on costs (downsize).

Dismissal – must be conducted effectively and sensitively to ensure incompetent employees are not costing the business financially and damaging its reputation.

Now try this

1 Identify the steps in the recruitment process.
2 Why is recruitment a key aspect of human resource management?
3 Why is the process of redeployment important within an organisation?

Exam skills 20

The following exam-style questions use knowledge and skills revised in Unit 3.6.3 and refer to the Retro Homes case study on page 101.

Worked example

Which of the following would most likely be associated with the job design of an employee?

A Recruitment ⬭

B Dismissal ⬭

C Hierarchy ⬭

D Empowerment ⬤

(1 mark)

> D is the correct answer because empowerment is associated with the level of autonomy a worker has. The other three options are all related to human resources, but not directly to job design.

Worked example

Explain how Retro Homes could make use of job enlargement. **(4 marks)**

Job enlargement is giving employees the opportunity to work in different areas of the business and the opportunity to work on different tasks and roles. For example, Retro Homes could rotate its workers so that factory staff have the opportunity to deliver the furniture or work in the showroom. This would reduce the monotony of their job and allow them to develop a wider range of skills. It would also mean that workers have a greater understanding of the whole organisation.

Worked example

With reference to the Hackman and Oldman Job Characteristics Model, analyse the possible benefits to Retro Homes of improving its employees' critical psychological status. **(9 marks)**

> This seems like quite a complicated question. However, all that the student needs to do is explain how Retro Homes could use the Job Characteristics Model to improve the jobs of its employees.

The Hackman and Oldman Job Characteristics Model identifies the different dimensions of a job and how these contribute to the psychological status of workers and therefore their performance. One dimension of a job is the way that an employee receives feedback. Retro Homes could use an appraisal system to give feedback to employees on their performance on a 6-monthly basis. This is likely to encourage praise and this will then boost morale and motivation because workers will know they are doing a good job.

> The student starts by explaining what the Job Characteristics Model is. They have then suggested how Retro Homes could use the model to improve the way it gives feedback to employees. The student has then analysed the benefits of this. In the second part of the answer the student could improve their application to the context by explaining how using the model could reduce labour turnover if employees are more satisfied at work.

Motivational theories 1

Motivation refers to the willingness to work and achieve a given target or goal. Employee engagement involves the contribution an employee makes towards their work, including intellectual effort and positive emotions. Both of these factors are desirable in a workforce.

the scientific management school

The extent to which employees are motivated by financial incentives or social interaction.

the human relations school

← ── →

employees driven by financial incentives

employees driven by the need to meet social needs

Frederick Taylor

- 👍 Focus on efficiency and improved competitiveness.
- 👍 People are motivated solely by money.
- 👍 Incentivise work with financial rewards.
- 👍 Improve efficiency through standardisation and the division of labour.
- 👍 Employees are given elementary training and clear instructions on how to complete a task.
- 👍 The application of Taylor's principles reduces the need for as many workers as productivity is raised.

Theory based on work study and improving productivity and efficiency of the workforce.

Elton Mayo

- 👍 Informal working groups are recognised as having a positive influence on productivity.
- 👍 Workers are not simply motivated by financial incentives.
- 👍 Social interactions outside of working hours are important.
- 👍 Efficiency can be achieved through teams and teamworking.
- 👍 Focus on the needs of the employees rather than the needs of the organisation.

Theory based on the fact that employees have social needs and these must be fulfilled through their work.

Abraham Maslow: Maslow's Hierarchy of Needs

self-actualization
morality, creativity, spontaneity, acceptance, experience, purpose, meaning and inner potential

self-esteem
confidence, achievement, respect of others, the need to be a unique individual

love and belonging
friendship, family, intimacy, sense of connection

safety and security
health, employment, property, family and social stability

physiological needs
breathing, food, water, shelter, clothing, sleep

- People are driven to achieve personal needs.
- Maslow identified five levels: people are motivated to achieve these in order starting with physiological needs.
- Basic needs (physiological and security) refer to those linked to survival.
- Higher order needs (social, esteem, self-actualisation) refer to the needs people have within a social environment.
- A person cannot move up the hierarchy without first fulfilling the needs below.
- Businesses can motivate workers by giving them the opportunity to satisfy these needs at work.

The Neo-human relations school focuses on the psychological aspects of motivation and the fact that motivation comes from within an individual. The role of managers is to unlock this motivation.

Now try this

1 What are two principles of scientific management?

2 How does Elton Mayo's theory contradict Frederick Taylor's?

3 What are Maslow's five human needs?

Motivational theories 2

Frederick Herzberg's theory identified that hygiene factors are important in so far as the satisfactory presence of them will not lead to the dissatisfaction of employees. However, hygiene factors do not motivate employees. Only those identified as motivators.

Frederick Herzberg's two-factor theory

employee dissatisfaction ⟵

- fulfillment
- commitment
- engagement

⟶ employee satisfaction

Factors leading to dissatisfaction:
- poor pay
- poor compensation
- poor work conditions
- lack of promotions
- poor benefits offering
- lack of job security.

When these factors are optimal, job dissatisfaction will be eliminated. However, these factors do not increase job satisfaction.

Factors leading to satisfaction:
- good leadership practices
- good manager relationship
- clear direction and support
- feedback and support
- personal growth
- advancement
- recognition.

When these factors are optimal, job satisfaction will be increased.

The value of motivation theory

Taylor	Mayo	Maslow	Herzberg
Although criticised as being against the well-being of the workforce, Taylor's focus on productivity and efficiency is still extremely important today.	Any job design and rewards package should consider the social dimension of work and ensure human interaction is designed to create the greatest benefit for the workers and the business.	Brings together other theories and encourages managers to provide the workforce with opportunities to fulfill their needs. It considers both financial and non-financial incentives of work.	Considers the dissatisfaction of the workforce and what employers must do to prevent this. Employers must secure the hygiene factors before they will be able to develop means of motivating employees.

Motivational theory

Motivational theory does not provide managers with the answers as to how they can motivate their employees. However, together they do provide a useful framework that managers can use to review and evaluate organisational policies, job design, pay, organisational structure and the way they communicate with employees.

 Exam focus **Motivation theory**

Unless specifically asked to explain a motivation theory it is not necessary to do so. However, when analysing workforce policies, it often useful to link your analysis to specific theories. For example, a good commission package on top of a basic salary might allow a worker to meet their physiological needs and prevent dissatisfaction as sufficient pay is a hygiene factor, but it may not help the worker achieve their higher order or social needs. (Motivation theories cross over and can be linked in your analysis.)

Now try this

1. Identify three hygiene factors.
2. What are the differences between Maslow's theory and Herzberg's theory?
3. How could a manager use motivational theory?

Financial methods of motivation

Financial methods are one way that a manager can motivate their workforce.

Benefits and drawbacks

Method	Benefits	Limitations
Salary schemes A set income based on the job role and calculated as an annual fee.	👍 Easily comparable – appropriate where nature of work is not time specific or hard to quantify.	👎 Not linked to performance. 👎 Little incentive to increase productivity.
Commission A bonus paid based on achieving a sales target.	👍 Appropriate for sales jobs. 👍 Incentive to increase sales revenue for the business.	👎 Focus taken away from other areas of the job such as customer service. 👎 Little attention to aspects of job that do not directly impact commission earned.
Piece rate Payment based on the number of units of output produced.	👍 Appropriate for production jobs. 👍 Incentive to increase output (units).	👎 Employees may ignore factors such as quality.
Performance-related pay (PRP) A salary or bonus scheme linked to job related targets. Targets and performance may be reviewed every 6 months or annually.	👍 Links pay to measurable targets specific to the nature of the job. 👍 Encourages review of employee performance.	👎 Can be expensive if large proportion of workforce achieve their targets; some areas of performance can also be very subjective. 👎 Difficult to ensure PRP is fair across the organisation.
Profit sharing/bonus schemes Distributing a percentage of net profit across the workforce.	👍 Reward linked to the overall success of the company.	👎 Depends on the profitability of the business.

What the experts say about financial methods of motivation

Financial reward will satisfy the basic needs and may boost self-esteem. It will not satisfy the higher order needs.

Maslow

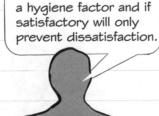

Financial incentives are a hygiene factor and if satisfactory will only prevent dissatisfaction.

Herzberg

The rational man is driven by financial reward.

Taylor

Financial incentives are irrelevant if an employee's social needs are not met.

Mayo

Now try this

1 When might a business use commission pay?
2 What are the benefits of profit-sharing?
3 What are the limitations of financial rewards?

Non-financial methods of motivation

There are also non-financial ways for managers to motivate their employees.

Benefits and drawbacks

Method	Benefits	Limitations
Job design Designing the role, tasks and responsibilities in a way that maximises employee motivation.	👍 Improving job design can create new challenges and give employees autonomy over their work.	🗨 Remedial / monotonous tasks are still required in most jobs. 🗨 There will always be aspects that employees don't like.
Appraisal system A system designed to review employee performance and recognise achievement – may be linked to PRP.	👍 Allows a business to recognise the achievements of employees and provides positive feedback when employees meet their targets. 👍 Appraisal may create opportunities for promotion and meeting the needs of employees.	🗨 Time devoted to appraisal takes employees away from doing their actual job.
Teamworking Organising the workforce into teams in order to benefit from the social aspects of motivation.	👍 Meets employees' social needs and encourages a sense of belonging. 👍 Helps employees develop a connection to the organisation through their colleagues.	🗨 Individual performance is harder to identify in a team situation. 🗨 Ineffective workers may not be identified.
Employee recognition (such as employee of the month).	👍 Recognises achievement, encourages positive competition and boosts self-esteem.	🗨 Only the best employees usually benefit.

What the experts say about non-financial methods of motivation

Non-financial incentives are linked to achieving the higher order needs of love and belonging, self-esteem and self-actualisation.

Maslow

Non-financial incentives are the key to motivating the workforce.

Herzberg

Non-financial incentives reduce productivity and create inefficiencies within the workforce.

Taylor

Non-financial incentives help employees achieve their social needs.

Mayo

Now try this

1 Why might employee training motivate the workforce?

2 What are the drawbacks of teamworking?

3 Why is it important to help employees achieve their 'higher order' needs?

Choosing motivational methods

The most suitable methods of motivation will depend on a number of factors including the nature of the job, the industry and the individuals involved.

Assessing methods of motivation

Costs – if profits are low a business will be unable to offer bonuses. Training and investment in job design may also have to be cut.

Attitudes – whether managers have a 'soft' or 'hard' approach to HRM will determine the methods used.

Financial and non-financial methods

Skill level of employees – a more skilled workforce may require more delegation and job enrichment.

Skill level of managers – the skill and training of managers will determine the variety and effectiveness of motivation methods. Managers trained in motivational theory may apply these concepts more effectively.

Nature of the organisation or work – creative industries may lean towards empowerment and enrichment in order to motivate their workforce. A competitive sales environment may only require an effective commission scheme.

Exam focus **Understanding the workforce**

Employees will not be fully motivated by one thing alone. It is always important to have a balance of financial and non-financial methods. Always look for clues in the case study to identify what factors are important to the workforce.

Benefits of a motivated workforce

- customer service
- labour productivity
- employee engagement
- product quality
- good relationships with managers

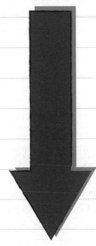

- absenteeism
- labour turnover
- labour cost per unit
- recruitment costs

Now try this

1 Identify two reasons why a manager might decide not to delegate decisions to their workforce.

2 Identify three benefits of a highly motivated workforce.

3 Why is the skill level of the workforce important when considering methods of motivation?

Exam skills

The following exam-style questions use knowledge and skills you have already revised in Unit 3.6.4 and refer to the Retro Homes case study on page 101.

Worked example

Explain why Retro Homes might pay its workers a wage with overtime. **(4 marks)**

Retro Homes may pay its workers a wage with overtime because the nature of the job is quantifiable and linked to the number of hours employees will work. Overtime will be appropriate because it will encourage employees to work for longer periods of time when the tea room or furniture showroom is busy. For example, they will be busier at the weekends and leading up to Christmas as people order furniture.

The student has shown an understanding of both concepts and linked them to the nature of the work being carried out at Retro Homes. An example is used at the end of the answer to apply the context.

Worked example

Any motivational theory will do. The student does not have to discuss them all!

With reference to relevant motivational theory, analyse the possible benefits to Retro Homes of 'creating a team spirit within the company'. **(9 marks)**

Achieving a team spirit will help employees achieve their 'love and belonging' needs as identified in the Hierarchy of Needs. This refers to employees' need to build social relationships with other colleagues in their working environment. If employees achieve this need they will feel motivated and this could lead to reduced absenteeism because they will enjoy their work. Furthermore, achieving these needs will improve employee engagement because they will care about their fellow workers and the overall success of the business.

The student has chosen to apply the theory of Maslow's Hierarchy of Needs. They have gone on to analyse how a team spirit could lead to greater levels of motivation. The student has shown limited application to the Retro Homes context.

In their answer the student must show an understanding of motivation and link it to the concept of profitability. They must also show an appreciation of the limitations of motivation.

Worked example

To what extent will developing a highly motivated workforce **increase profitability** at Retro Homes? **(16 marks)**

.... On the other hand, profitability cannot be achieved by motivation alone. If the fixed costs are too high then no matter how productive the workforce is, the business will find it difficult to break-even and then generate a profit....

This is part of the student's answer. This section of the answer shows that the student understands that motivation alone cannot create a profitable business. The first part of the answer will have explained the benefits of a highly motivated workforce, such as improved customer service and lower labour costs.

Employer–employee relations

Developing and improving good employer–employee relations through effective communication can lead to improved performance of an organisation and an enhanced reputation as an employer.

Employee representation

Employee representation involves collective representation of employees. There are three key ways that employees can find representation and have their voice heard.

Trade unions	Works councils	Employee committees
An organisation established to protect and improve the economic and working conditions of workers, for example the National Union of Teachers (NUT).	A forum within a business where workers and managers meet to discuss issues relating to conditions, pay and training.	A group of employees meeting together to focus on specific issues within the workforce. Unlike a works council, this may not be recognised or attended by managers.
<ul><li>focus on negotiations with employers through collective bargaining</li><li>focus on pay and working conditions</li><li>represent members at industrial tribunals and give workers advice on employment issues</li><li>prominent in public sector</li><li>substantial decline of trade union membership over past 20 years.</li></ul>	<ul><li>members elected from the workforce by the workforce</li><li>builds cooperation with managers</li><li>allows the voice of the workforce to be heard on a regular basis without trade union representation</li><li>involves employees in key business decisions such as restructuring or expansion.</li></ul>	<ul><li>informal groups set up by workers to focus on a certain aspect of work</li><li>typically focus on issues such as employee social events, safety and working conditions</li><li>employee committees may influence decisions made at works councils.</li></ul>

Influences on employee representation

The nature of the work carried out by employees – low skilled workers are less likely to have a significant input into decision making.

The history of the business – what has happened in the past?

Employment legislation, for example the European Union Information and Consultation of Employees (ICE) dictates that employees within EU countries must be consulted on certain aspects of work and employment.

Employee representation in decisions

The leadership and management style of the boss – autocratic managers may want to limit the input of employees.

The corporate objectives of the business and mission statement – a business in crisis may want to make quick decisions and avoid consultation with employees.

Disseminating information

Electronic mail can speed up communication and allow the whole workforce to be communicated with easily.

Social media has become very effective at sharing information on events, successes and building team spirit if used appropriately.

Intranets are effective at storing and organising important company information and helping employees access it.

Now try this

1 What is a trade union?

2 How is a works council different to a trade union?

3 How can technology improve employee communication?

Employee disputes

As with all stakeholder groups, there will be conflicts between managers/owners and the workforce. These disputes will often be linked to pay, rewards and working conditions. There are a number of ways employers can avoid or resolve employee disputes and these often involve channels of communication.

Employee communication

no opportunity for feedback (two-way communication)

ineffective meeting time – meetings are not purposeful or productive.

conflicting systems – when two businesses merge

Barriers to effective communication

misinterpretation – top down approach to communication

no time given to consult / inform employees

Managing employer–employee relations

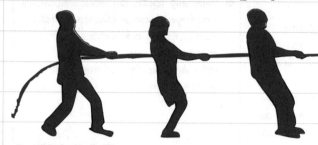

Avoiding conflict

- no strike and single union agreements
- advisory, conciliation and arbitration service (ACAS)
- effective employee communication
- developing a highly motivated workforce.

Resolving conflict

- arbitration – disputes resolution bound by the arbitrator's decision
- conciliation – negotiations facilitated by a third party
- employment tribunals.

Benefits of good employer-employee relations

- 👍 develops a strong employer brand – TGI Friday was reviewed in 2015 as the 'best big company to work for in the UK' through the Best Companies survey
- 👍 promotes employee engagement
- 👍 improves motivation and therefore labour productivity
- 👍 reduces costs such as legal fees
- 👍 improves competitiveness – employees are a key asset for the business.

📝 **Exam focus**

Employer–employee relations and motivation theory

Employer–employee relations are closely linked to theories of employee motivation. If an organisation takes effective measures to motivate its employees then this will go a long way to reducing the chance of disputes. Disputes are also less likely to occur in businesses where employees are involved in decision making and this relates to management styles and job design.

Now try this

1 Identify three benefits of effective employer–employee communication.
2 What is the difference between arbitration and conciliation?
3 Identify two barriers to effective communication.

Exam skills

The following exam-style questions use knowledge and skills covered in Unit 3.6.5 and the final two questions refer to the to the Retro Homes case study on page 101.

Worked example

AtoZ Delivery Ltd has experienced conflicts with its drivers, who are demanding better pay conditions when on long haul journeys to Europe. AtoZ Delivery Ltd is in negotiations with a **group of employees who have been elected to represent the workforce**.

Which of the following best describes this group of employees?

A Trade union   ○

B Arbitrators   ○

C Works council   ●

D Conciliators   ○

(1 mark)

> The bold text shows the key information in this question.

> The options in this question are all very similar. It is important to understand the key differences between different techniques or concepts.

Worked example

1 Analyse one way in which Retro Homes could improve communication with its employees.

(5 marks)

One way that Retro Homes could improve communication with its employees is to encourage an employee committee. As the organisation is growing it is important that the workers at Retro Homes have representation. An employee committee will help employees raise any issues and ideas on how to improve the company...

> There are a number of ways the student could have approached the question. They could have discussed email, intranets or the use of social media. However, it is always important to consider the nature of the business/situation and analyse a method that is appropriate. For example, email would work well in an office environment, but probably not in a restaurant or furniture factory.

2 To what extent is it important for Retro Homes to develop a strong employer brand? Justify your answer.

(16 marks)

A strong employer brand is the recognition that Retro Homes is a good place to work. Retro Homes has had a high rate of labour turnover and it needs to recruit new workers into the tea rooms. With a strong employer brand it is likely to attract the best employees. Not only will this improve the competitiveness of the business through having a better workforce than its competitors, but it will also mean its staff are less likely to leave the company if they are happy working for the company. As a result, Louise can start to build a cohesive team to run the tea rooms....

> On A level papers this style of question could be worth 20–24 marks.

> The answer starts by clarifying the concept outlined in the question 'employer brand'. The student then goes on to analyse the benefit in relation to Retro Homes. The answer should then go on to discuss any limitations of a strong employer brand and other factors that may be as/more important.

Exam-style practice

The following questions refer to the human resource function of a business. For these questions refer to the Retro Homes case study. There are answers on pages 198–199.

1 Which of the following motivational theorists is associated with the human relations movement?

A Taylor ○

B Maslow ○

C Mayo ○

D Herzberg ○

(1 mark)

> Think of a technique to help you relate each theorist to their theory.

2 Explain a suitable human resource objective that could be set by Louise. **(5 marks)**

> You could select any objective, but try to think about the context and identify an area of human resources that Retro Homes needs to focus on.

3 Calculate the change in labour costs as a percentage of revenue between Qtr 1 2014 and Qtr 4 2014. **(5 marks)**

4 Analyse how Paul could improve the job design of his employees. **(9 marks)**

> Start with the formula and remember to show your workings.

5 Paul has decided to introduce a number of fringe benefits for the employees at Retro Homes Ltd. These include:

• 35% off all furniture and accessories
• an extra 2 days' paid holiday per year.

To what extent are these measures likely to lead to a highly motivated workforce? Justify your answer. **(16 marks)**

> Note down the various aspects of job design and the benefits of effective job design before answering this question.

6 Figure 1 below shows the new organisation chart for Retro Homes Ltd in January 2015.

Evaluate the new organisational structure introduced by Paul in terms of its potential to improve performance at Retro Homes. **(20 marks)**

> How might these measures motivate employees? Are there any aspects of human needs that are not being met?

Figure 1. Retro Homes organisation chart as of January 2015

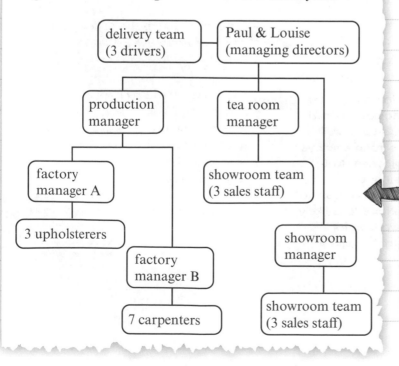

> Analyse the organisation chart and compare it to the previous version in Figure 1 of the case study on page 101. How has it changed? Consider the span of control and chain of command. How might these affect factors such as communication, control and flexibility?

Case study

Paul had run Retro Homes, a successful furniture store, for four years. The company produced furniture at two local factories and distributed nationwide. Retro Homes also had a large three storey showroom in Chesterfield. Paul employed a team of 20 within the business who worked across three areas of the company. The organisation chart for Retro Homes is shown in Figure 1.

Figure 1: Retro Homes organisation chart as of December 2014

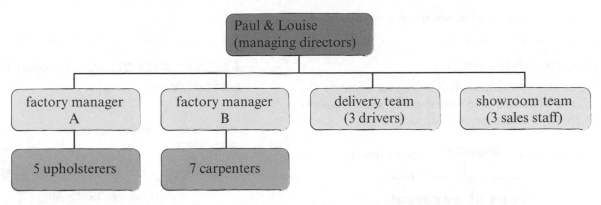

The showroom was always busy throughout the week and Paul's wife Louise saw the opportunity in 2014 to open a tea room on the ground floor of the showroom. The tea room was opened in January 2015 and soon became one of the most popular places to eat and drink in town. Louise managed the running of the tea room and the additional 10 employees. Despite its success, the tea room faced a number of human resource issues as key personnel left throughout the first 18 months of the tea room opening. Louise calculated that during this period there was a 70% turnover of staff. Furthermore, despite being extremely popular, the tea room was not generating the profits that Paul and Louise had hoped for.

	Qtr 1 2014	Qtr 2 2014	Qtr 3 2014	Qtr 4 2014
Total labour costs (£)	12 000	27 000	29 000	35 000
Tea room revenue (£)	20 000	51 000	55 000	72 000

Cost for four six-month periods + tea room revenue

In 2015 Paul and Louise decided to restructure the business in order to employ a manager of the tea room and a manager of the showroom. Paul and Louise hoped that the restructuring would allow them to concentrate on growing the business.

In order to bring the two sides of the business together Louise introduced a fortnightly meeting between the workers of the tea room and furniture business. The intention was to encourage employees to share their ideas about moving the business forward and create a team spirit within the company.

Mission and corporate objectives

The mission and corporate objectives of a business outline what the business aims to achieve. For this reason the mission and corporate objectives guide the actions and strategy of a business and act as the measures by which we can assess the overall success of the business.

Mission statements

A mission statement sets out the purpose of a business existing. The mission relates to all stakeholders and typically focuses on the following.

values of the business

scope of the business (the areas in which it operates)

To produce products that improve people's lives and delight our customers

long-term aim of the business

importance of different stakeholder groups

impact the business intends to have on society

Influences on missions

The mission of a business will be influenced by a range of factors, including:

- the values of the founder/s
- the industry the business is in
- the views of society
- the size of the business and type of ownership
- the culture of the business.

Corporate objectives

The corporate objectives of a business quantify the mission of a business and set specific and measurable targets for the whole organisation.

market standing   innovation   sustainability

profitability ⎯ **Focus of corporate objectives** ⎯ growth

social responsibility   shareholder value

Factors affecting corporate objectives

economic conditions

External factors

social change

Internal factors
- poor performance
- new leadership
- business ownership
- business culture
- business growth

actions of competitors

technological change

global prices

Short-termism is the pressure on achieving short-term gains over long-term success. Sometimes short-termism and the pressure for instant success can influence corporate objectives and decision making as much as any other internal or external factor.

Now try this

1 Why do businesses have mission statements?

2 What is the relationship between the mission and corporate objectives?

3 Identify three typical areas that corporate objectives focus on.

Strategy and tactics

Strategy

- A strategy is a long-term plan (A) or approach that a business will take to achieve its objectives (B).
- Strategies involve a major commitment to resources.
- Clear strategies guide tactical decisions. A business may have a strategy to become a market leader by having the widest range of innovative products on the market.
- However, a tactical decision to support this strategy might be to divert an extra £5 million into research and development and headhunt some of the most innovative designers in the industry.

Strategy

Current position → Tactics   Tactics   Tactics → Desired position

Tactics

- Tactics are the day-to-day decisions taken by middle managers.
- They are frequent and involve fewer resources but are taken to achieve the strategic direction of the business.

The objectives hierarchy

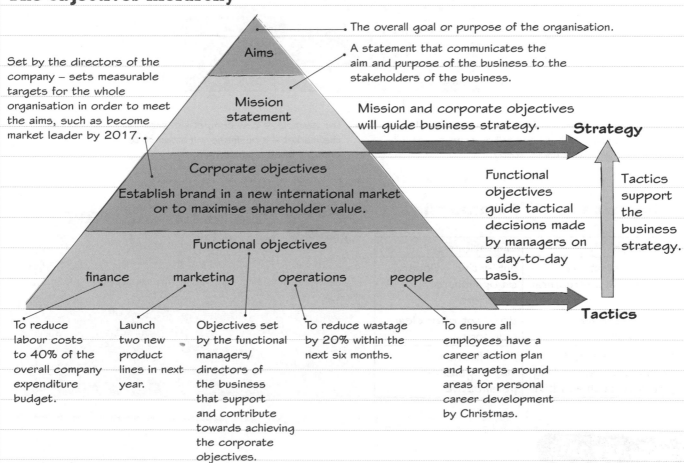

Set by the directors of the company – sets measurable targets for the whole organisation in order to meet the aims, such as become market leader by 2017.

Aims — The overall goal or purpose of the organisation.

Mission statement — A statement that communicates the aim and purpose of the business to the stakeholders of the business.

Mission and corporate objectives will guide business strategy. → **Strategy**

Corporate objectives — Establish brand in a new international market or to maximise shareholder value.

Functional objectives guide tactical decisions made by managers on a day-to-day basis.

Tactics support the business strategy.

Functional objectives

finance   marketing   operations   people → **Tactics**

To reduce labour costs to 40% of the overall company expenditure budget.

Launch two new product lines in next year.

Objectives set by the functional managers/ directors of the business that support and contribute towards achieving the corporate objectives.

To reduce wastage by 20% within the next six months.

To ensure all employees have a career action plan and targets around areas for personal career development by Christmas.

Now try this

1 How are strategic decisions different from tactical decisions?

2 Give three examples of functional objectives.

SWOT analysis

SWOT analysis is a strategic tool that a business can use to analyse its current position and the external factors that might affect it. SWOT stands for strengths, weaknesses, opportunities and threats.

For example, having a strong brand image or a highly skilled workforce. A business will develop a strategy around its strengths.

For example, poor cash flow – a business will try to eliminate these or avoid strategies that require the use of these.

	Helpful to achieving the objective	Harmful to achieving the objective
Internal origin (attributes of the organisation)	Strengths	Weaknesses
External origin (attributes of the environment)	Opportunities	Threats

For example, a fast growing geographical market. A business will attempt to exploit these with its strategy.

For example, a new competitor entering the market – a business will attempt to protect itself against these.

The value of SWOT analysis

Benefits	Limitations
assists strategic thinking in a structural way	subjective – depends on opinions of managers
low-cost, simple approach	does not offer clear solutions
can be combined with other decision-making models, such as PEST	classification may depend on perspective

Case study   Case studies and SWOT analysis

A simple SWOT analysis is an effective way to analyse case study information and identify key issues in an exam. It is always worth identifying a firm's objectives in any case study as this is often an effective way to justify decisions. For example, if an action can lead a business to achieving a certain objective then you can justify it.

Now try this

1 What does SWOT stand for?

2 Why might a business use SWOT analysis?

3 What are the limitations of SWOT analysis?

Exam skills

Questions 1 and 2 relate to the topics covered in Unit 3.7.1 and refer to the Sartorial Ltd case study on page 118. Question 3 is an essay question with a generic context.

Worked example

Explain one reason why Sartorial Ltd has set itself a target to increase the proportion of materials supplied from sustainable sources. **(5 marks)**

An increasing number of Sartorial Ltd's customers are valuing sustainable materials in the clothing that they buy. If Sartorial Ltd is able to achieve 90% of all materials being supplied from sustainable sources within 2 years then this will add value to its products and give it a competitive advantage over other bespoke tailors who do not achieve this. As a result, it will have a competitive advantage over these manufacturers and will possibly attract customers away from its competitors.

> The student has linked the target to information provided in the case study. They have then gone on to explain how achieving this target will benefit Sartorial Ltd in its market.

Worked example

Analyse how Sartorial Ltd's mission statement may contribute towards the success of the company. **(9 marks)**

Sartorial Ltd's mission statement will contribute towards the success of the company because it will act as a reminder to its employees of how they should treat every customer and ensure each transaction is a 'special experience'. The mission statement will therefore guide employees in their day-to-day decisions to ensure that everything they do contributes towards this aim. By doing this, employees will be giving excellent customer service and customers will be highly satisfied with the suit they receive...

> There are a number of ways the student could have approached the question. The student could go on to analyse how a mission statement would inform corporate objectives or communicate the aims of the business to other stakeholders such as investors and customers.

> The student has underlined the key information in the question. In particular, the context of an investment bank.

Worked example

To what extent is the use of SWOT analysis the **best tool** to analyse the current position of a large **investment bank that is the market leader**? **(25 marks)**

...However, SWOT analysis has its limitations. Although it can help a manager identify key issues, it can oversimplify complex issues. For example, the investment bank might identify a new technology as a potential opportunity to invest its customers' money. However, it will not provide an indication of the potential return or risks associated with the investment. Therefore, other tools such as investment appraisal may also be required to gain a full understanding of the opportunity...

> The extract from the student's answer provides a good example of how balance can be incorporated into an answer. The student explains a limitation of SWOT analysis in the context of an investment bank using an appropriate example. The candidate then goes on to identify another business tool that might be necessary to support SWOT analysis.

Financial accounts 1

A business will produce a range of financial information to support its stakeholders in decision making. Two key documents that all companies are required to produce are the **income statement** and the **balance sheet**.

The income statement

An income statement at its most basic will communicate the revenue generated by a business and then its profit at various levels following a series of expenses and exceptional incomes.

Cost of goods sold
The direct costs associated with the production and sale of the product or service.

Administration / Rent / Salaries
Operating costs (overheads) are then deducted from gross profit.

Operating profit
The profit left after other indirect operating costs (overheads) have been deducted.

Net profit
The bottom line – what a business has left to reinvest or return to shareholders/owners after tax has been deducted.

Income statement April 2014–March 2015	£m
Revenue	300
Cost of goods sold	(45)
Gross profit	255
Administration	(10)
Rent	(30)
Salaries	(25)
Operating profit	190
Exceptional expenses	(40)
Exceptional income	10
Profit before tax	160
Tax	(35)
Profit for the year (net profit)	125

Gross profit
The profit after direct costs have been deducted. Gives a broad indication of the success of a business's trading activity.

Exceptional expenses and income
These could be expenses or incomes not associated with the direct activity of the business. They may be one-off items. They are kept separate in order to give an indication of the **quality of profit**.

An income statement can be used to calculate profitability ratios such as gross profit margin, operating profit margin and return on capital employed (ROCE).

What we can find out from an income statement:

- Changes in sales revenue
- Changes in the direct costs of sales
- How well a business is managing its operating costs
- The profitability of a business
- Identify unusual incomes/expenses during the year

Now try this

1 What does an income statement show?

2 What is the difference between gross profit and operating profit?

3 What is an exceptional item?

Financial accounts 2

The balance sheet

A balance sheet is a financial document that records the assets and liabilities of a business. A balance sheet gives a snapshot of the value and financial strength of a business.

Non current assets
Also known as fixed assets, Non-current assets are used to operate the business and include land and machinery (tangible or fixed assets) and brands and patents (intangible).

Current assets
Assets that the business expects to use or sell within the year. These can be converted into cash to pay off liabilities.

Net current assets
Current assets − current liabilities = the working capital a business has available.

Balance sheet as at 31st March 2015		£m
Non-current assets		70
intangible non-current assets	10	
tangible non-current assets	60	
Current assets		55
inventories	30	
debtors	25	
Current liabilities		(35)
creditors	(30)	
interest	(5)	
Net current assets		20
Non-current liabilities		(50)
long-term loan	50	
Net assets		40
Total equity		40
Share capital	30	
Reserves	10	

Current liabilities
Payments due within 1 year.

Non-current liabilities
Debts that a business does not expect to pay within a year.

Total equity
Will always balance with net assets – it represents how a business has been financed.

Net assets
Total assets − total liabilities = the value of a business.

A balance sheet can be used to calculate financial ratios such as liquidity ratios, gearing ratios and efficiency ratios.

What we can find out from a balance sheet:

- The value of a business (equity)
- The current assets a business holds
- Short-term liabilities the business will need to pay within the year
- The liquidity of a business
- The long-term debts of a business
- How a business has been financed

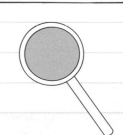

Now try this

1 What does a balance sheet show?

2 What is a current asset?

3 What are net assets?

Using financial ratios 1

A financial ratio compares two pieces of information. For example, profit as a percentage of revenue. For this reason, ratios give managers a more in-depth understanding of the financial performance of a business.

Financial ratios

Profitability ratio – provides a key measure of success for a business comparing profit to revenue and investment

Efficiency ratio – provides an indication of how well an aspect of a business has been managed

Types of financial ratios

Liquidity ratio – assesses the ability of a business to pay its debts

Gearing ratio – assesses the extent to which a business is based on borrowed finance

Profit margin ratios

Profit margin ratios compare a type of profit to the revenue that it was generated from over a trading period. The gross profit margin, operating profit margin and profit for the year (net profit) margin can be calculated.

They are calculated by:

$$\frac{\text{Gross profit}}{\text{Revenue}} \times 100$$

$$\frac{\text{Net profit}}{\text{Revenue}} \times 100$$

$$\frac{\text{Operating profit}}{\text{Revenue}} \times 100$$

Interpreting profit margin ratios

Business managers need to keep a close eye on profitability and performance to ensure a business's success.

Profitability is a key measure of success for most businesses and these ratios allow managers to compare performance over time. It is also useful to compare these ratios, as doing this will give an indication of the quality of profit and how well the business is managing various aspects of the business such as its direct and indirect costs.

Return on capital employed (ROCE) ratio

The ROCE ratio compares operating profit earned with the amount of capital employed by the business. Capital employed is its total equity plus any non-current liabilities.

It is calculated by:

$$\frac{\text{Operating profit}}{\text{Capital employed}}$$

Also known as the 'primary efficiency ratio', ROCE shows how effectively the business was able to generate a profit from the investment placed within the business. It can be compared to previous years and the general rate of interest.

A business can improve its ROCE by increasing operating profit or by reducing capital employed.

Now try this

1 What are the four categories of financial ratio?
2 State two profitability ratios.
3 What is capital employed?

Using financial ratios 2

Current ratio

The current ratio is a key liquidity ratio. It compares current assets with current liabilities. In doing so it assesses whether a business has sufficient working capital to pay its short-term debts.

It is calculated by:

$$\frac{\text{Current assets}}{\text{Current liabilities}}$$

Interpreting the current ratio

The current ratio is expressed as a ratio, such as 2:1. This suggests that the business has £2 of current assets for every £1 of current liabilities. If the ratio is less than 1, such as 0.5:1, then the business might struggle to pay its short-term debts.

➤ See Unit 3.5.4 on improving cash flow and profitability for strategies that a business could use to improve its current ratio.

Gearing ratio

Gearing analyses how a business has raised its long-term finance. The ratio represents the proportion of a firm's equity that is borrowed.

It is calculated by:

$$\frac{\text{Non-current liabilities}}{\text{Total equity + non-current liabilities}} \times 100$$

Interpreting the gearing ratio

A highly geared business has more than 50% of its capital in the form of loans. A highly geared business is vulnerable to increases in interest rates.

A low-geared business may have the opportunity to borrow funds in order to expand. Businesses with secure cash flow or considerable assets may be able to borrow more for this purpose.

 Do your sums!

Being highly geared is not always bad for a business. Some shareholders may prefer for a firm to be financed through loan capital as long-term borrowing can sometimes be cheaper than the annual return that shareholders require. For example, interest on a 10-year loan might only be 6%, whereas, shareholders might expect annual returns of 20%.

When the value of debt has been repaid, shareholders benefit as the value of that debt becomes their equity in the business.

Performance as a trend – financial information in isolation often holds little value. Understanding the trend might be more significant. Low profitability might be acceptable if it is improving gradually.

Using financial ratios

Benchmarks and industry average – manufacturers typically have lower operating profit margins than service businesses. Understanding the industry norm is important.

The economic environment – poor performance might be less significant if the business is operating in a tough economic climate.

Now try this

1 What is liquidity?

2 What does a current ratio of 0.8:1 suggest about a business?

3 What issues might a business face if it is highly geared?

Using financial ratios 3

Inventory turnover ratio

This ratio measures a company's success at converting inventories into revenue. It compares the value of inventories (at cost – cost of goods sold) with the sales achieved. The faster a business sells its inventories the faster it generates profit.

It is calculated by:

$$\frac{\text{Cost of goods sold}}{\text{Average inventories held}}$$

Interpreting inventory turnover

The lower the number, the more efficient the business is. This ratio is only really relevant for manufacturers. The turnover rate will be determined by the nature of the product. Perishable goods such as food will have a much faster turnover than manufactured goods such as Blu-ray players.

To determine average number of days an inventory is held, the number needs to be divided into 365.

Receivables days ratio

This ratio calculates the time it takes for a business to collect debts that it is owed. The shorter the period, the faster cash is flowing into the business.

It is calculated by:

$$\frac{\text{Receivables}}{\text{Revenues}} \times 365$$

This ratio is not pertinent to firms that deal in cash sales.

Interpreting receivables days ratio

The shorter the period the easier the firm will find it to meet its short-term cash needs. However, businesses that offer trade credit to customers will experience long payment periods. Businesses can use a range of techniques to reduce the length of time debtors take to pay.

Trade credit can mean a business will wait quite some time before payment is received and this can cause cash flow problems.

Payables days ratio

This ratio calculates the time it takes for a business to pay its creditors. The longer the period, the longer the business is retaining cash within the business.

It is calculated by:

$$\frac{\text{Payables}}{\text{Cost of sales}} \times 365$$

This ratio is not pertinent to firms that deal in cash sales.

Interpreting payables days ratio

The longer the period the easier the firm will find it to meet its short-term cash needs. However, businesses that delay payments to suppliers or creditors may damage the business relationship and this may cause problems when making future deals.

Now try this

1 When might a business calculate its inventory turnover?

2 What are receivables and payables?

3 What is the link between receivables and the liquidity of a firm?

The value of financial accounts and financial ratios

Managers – to assess the performance of the business and whether resources are being used efficiently

Potential investors and lenders – to assess the security and liquidity of the business

How financial accounts are used

Shareholders – to assess the return they may receive on their investment

Government – to calculate the tax liability of the business (HM Revenue and Customs)

The value of ratio analysis

Allows a business to calculate and compare trends over time.
Shows greater insight than financial accounts on their own.
Information can be used against benchmark data – such as an industry average.
Can be used to assess the performance of other functional areas of the business – operations and human resources.

Does not take into account qualitative issues such as brand image or customer service performance.
Does not take into account the impact of long-term decisions, such as investments today may lower profitability but boost it in the long term.
Economic climate – ratios do not take into account economic conditions or the performance of other businesses.

Using given information in answers

 Exam focus

Wherever financial information is available, you should do your best to use it within your answer. If a relevant financial ratio can be calculated then this should also be applied within the context of your response.

Window dressing

Window dressing involves a business manipulating its financial accounts to make them look more favourable to stakeholders. For example, delaying payments to a later financial period in order to boost short-term profit. Window dressing can limit the value and validity of information interpreted from financial accounts.

Any aspect of a business can be made to look more attractive – even the financial accounts!

Exam skills

The following exam-style questions relate to the topics covered in Unit 3.7.2 and refer to the Sartorial Ltd case study on page 118.

Worked example

Using the extracts from the financial accounts of Sartorial Ltd, calculate the operating profit margin for the 2 years 2014 and 2015. Comment on the performance of the company.

(5 marks)

$$2014 = \frac{412}{1240} \times 100 = 33.2\%$$

$$2015 = \frac{195}{1390} \times 100 = 14\%$$

The operating profit margin has also halved between 2014 and 2015. The reduction is mainly due to a significant increase in operating costs.

The student has clearly laid out their calculations. The student has also commented on the ratios and identified the main cause of the fall in profitability based on information from the financial accounts.

Worked example

Using the extracts from the financial accounts of Sartorial Ltd and a relevant calculation, comment on the liquidity of the company.

(5 marks)

$$\text{Current ratio} = \frac{252}{219} = 1.15$$

Sartorial Ltd has a relatively secure liquidity position as it has sufficient current assets to cover current liabilities. However, it may struggle to pay debts if it is looking to expand.

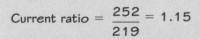

In this second question the student has not been told which ratio to use. You may be asked to analyse profitability, liquidity or efficiency using financial information. If so, you will need to choose the most appropriate ratio to use given the information available to you.

Worked example

Using the data in Figure 1 and Figure 2 on page 118, evaluate whether Sartorial Ltd is in a position to become the market leader within the next 5 years. **(16 marks)**

The income statement of Sartorial Ltd indicates that revenue has increased from £1.24 million in 2014 to £1.39 million in 2015. This increased revenue will be as a result of increasing the number of bespoke suits they sold or maximising the value on each suit sold. Revenue is a key indication that consumers are buying the products and this shows potential for future growth. Furthermore, growth in sales revenue indicates a potential growth in market share if similar businesses have not grown at the same rate. This will therefore support Sartorial Ltd in moving towards the position of market leader in the next 5 years...

The student has presented a clear argument using the financial information presented in the income statement. The second paragraph should go on to discuss some of the weaknesses from the data to give a balanced answer, for example, the fall in profitability.

Analysing the internal position

There are a variety of internal measures other than financial analysis that a business can use to measure success. These additional measures are related to the other three functions of a business – marketing, operations and human resources.

Measuring performance

Data from all three functions may be used in conjunction to analyse the performance of the business over time or in comparison with other businesses.

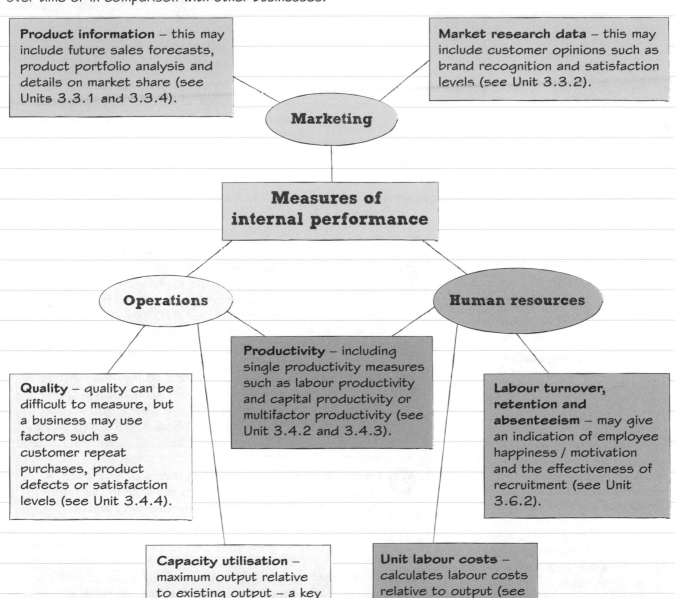

Product information – this may include future sales forecasts, product portfolio analysis and details on market share (see Units 3.3.1 and 3.3.4).

Market research data – this may include customer opinions such as brand recognition and satisfaction levels (see Unit 3.3.2).

Marketing

Measures of internal performance

Operations

Human resources

Quality – quality can be difficult to measure, but a business may use factors such as customer repeat purchases, product defects or satisfaction levels (see Unit 3.4.4).

Productivity – including single productivity measures such as labour productivity and capital productivity or multifactor productivity (see Unit 3.4.2 and 3.4.3).

Labour turnover, retention and absenteeism – may give an indication of employee happiness / motivation and the effectiveness of recruitment (see Unit 3.6.2).

Capacity utilisation – maximum output relative to existing output – a key measure of efficiency (see Unit 3.4.3).

Unit labour costs – calculates labour costs relative to output (see Unit 3.6.2).

Now try this

1 Identify two measures of marketing performance.
2 Identify two measures of operational performance.
3 Identify two measures of human resource performance.

Core competencies

Core competencies are the unique abilities that a business possesses that provide it with a competitive advantage. Core competencies are developed over a period of time through the learning and skills developed within a business relating to the production of its goods and services.

Benefits of core competencies

👍 Core competencies give a business uniqueness.

👍 Core competencies add value to a business's product.

👍 Core competencies are difficult for competitors to imitate.

👍 Core competencies allow a business to enter a variety of markets.

👍 By focusing on its core competencies a business will develop key efficiencies.

👍 Aspects of a business that are not a core competence could be outsourced to a third party so the business can focus on its strengths.

Criticisms of core competencies

👎 As markets and environments evolve, businesses must be able to develop new skills and strengths – they cannot rely on core competencies.

👎 Outsourcing areas of the business can lead to a fragmented workforce.

👎 Core competencies take time to develop and nurture – not all businesses have core competencies or they might not have the right ones!

Long and short term performance

These measures help give a business perspective on its long-term performance.

Some businesses might be criticised for focusing their attention on short-term measures such as profitability and productivity.

Short-term measures of performance include:
• cash position
• revenue
• productivity
• profit.

1 **Research and development (R&D)** – investment in R&D might give an indication of the likely impact of product development and innovation in the future. However, there is no direct link between R&D spending and the level of innovation within a business.

2 **Profit quality** – firms may choose to focus on profits that they believe they will be able to sustain in the future. Net profit does not always give a good indication of this where exceptional items are included.

3 **Employee engagement** – high levels of employee engagement are likely to return rewards in the future and lead to greater levels of productivity and innovation.

4 **Sustainability** – a sustainable approach to business is one that can be conducted in the long term. A business can measure its sustainability through a Corporate Social Responsibility audit or report.

Now try this

1 What is a core competency?

2 Why can a core competency lead to competitive advantage?

3 How might a business assess its long-term performance?

Analysing human resource performance

Below are two business tools to help managers gain a rounded understanding of their business's performance. Each takes into account a variety of factors other than financial measures.

Kaplan and Norton's Balanced Scorecard

This is a planning and management tool used to match a business's activities to its vision and strategy. It aims to improve internal and external communications, and monitor organisation performance against strategic goals.

1 Financial
'To succeed financially, how should we appear to shareholders?'

Vision and strategy

2 Internal business processes
'To satisfy our shareholders and customers, what business processes must we excel at?'

3 Learning and growth
'To achieve our vision, how will we sustain our ability to change and improve?'

4 Customer
'To achieve our vision, how should we appear to our customers?'

Measures that may be included in a balanced scorecard

1	• revenues • profits • ROCE • cash flow (working capital)
2	• productivity • quality • efficiency
3	• effectiveness of training • employee engagement • R&D investment • number of new products developed
4	• customer loyalty • satisfaction levels • meeting customer needs

Elkington's Triple Bottom Line (TBL)

The Triple Bottom Line looks at the impact of a business against three key areas.

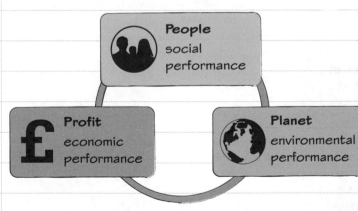

People social performance

Profit economic performance

Planet environmental performance

Profit	• monitoring the financial performance over time • this might typically involve using information from financial accounts and financial ratios
People	• measures how socially responsible the business is to all involved • measures might include health and safety figures, fair pay, fair trade and customer satisfaction
Planet	• covers the impact the business has on the environment • this will include reducing carbon emissions, waste and use of non-renewable sources of energy

The value of alternative measures

The value of the Balanced Scorecard and the Triple Bottom Line comes from the fact that they consider all stakeholders and not just the shareholders/owners of the business. For this reason they encourage businesses to approach internal analysis of performance from a long-term perspective, considering the impact they have on the community, environment and economy.

📝 Exam focus · Balancing your response

Using tools such as the Triple Bottom Line or Balanced Scorecard can allow you to add balance to your answers when analysing the financial performance of a business.

Now try this

1 What is Elkington's Triple Bottom Line?
2 What is the value of tools such as the Balanced Scorecard and the Triple Bottom Line?

Exam skills

The following question relates to the topics covered in Unit 3.7.3 and refers to the Sartorial Ltd case study on page 118. The answer below is a complete model answer for an essay question.

Worked example

Using Elkington's Triple Bottom Line, evaluate the performance of Sartorial Ltd.   **(24 marks)**

The Triple Bottom Line (TBL) is a business tool used to measure the performance of a business against three key areas – profit, people and planet.

Between 2014 and 2015 gross profit margin fell from 55% to 49%. Furthermore operating profits also fell considerably. This could suggest that the business is facing some inefficiencies and struggling to manage cost of sales and operating expenses. However, we can also see that revenue has increased between 2014 and 2015 and this gives an indication that the suits are still attractive and the business is able to maximise sales. The fall in profit may only be a short-term issue, especially if Sartorial Ltd is looking to expand its operations in order to achieve its objective of being market leader within the next 5 years. It is likely that expansion will drain the cash reserves of the business, but the company is currently in a healthy position with a current ratio of 1.15:1.

Although there is little information to analyse the environmental impact of Sartorial Ltd, the managers have set clear targets to move production to the UK and achieve 90% of materials from sustainable suppliers. If Sartorial Ltd is able to achieve these targets it will not only increase satisfaction of its environmentally conscious customers, but it will be a far more sustainable business in the long term. One drawback of moving production to the UK is that this may result in redundancies in the Czech Republic. Sartorial Ltd has a responsibility to its employees and this could have a negative impact on 'people' if redundancies are not handled effectively.

Overall, 'profit' might be the most important factor for Sartorial Ltd in the short term. Especially if it aims to achieve its objectives of becoming market leader in the next 5 years. For this reason, Sartorial Ltd should have some concerns about profitability as profit is a key source of capital for an expanding business. The extent to which this is a concern may depend on whether profits have fallen as a result of capital investment. If so, the managers may consider the falling profits to be less of a concern. Ultimately, all aspects of the TBL are important to Sartorial Ltd if it is to be successful in the long term. If it is able to manage the transition of production to the UK effectively it will be able to improve its overall performance against the TBL and achieve the mission statement of the organisation.

Use the checklist below to evaluate the essay.

☐ Key terms defined and used
☐ Key issues from case study applied
☐ All points clearly explained
☐ Financial data applied and interpreted
☐ Analysis is well developed
☐ Balance shown by considering benefits and limitations
☐ Alternative perspectives and/or approaches considered
☐ Evaluation answers the question
☐ Clear justification using the key issues in the case
☐ Use of the 'depends on' rule
☐ Recommendations given where appropriate

Exam-style practice

Have a go at the exam-style questions below that apply to the concepts covered in Units 3.7.1 to 3.7.3 and the strategic position of a business. Refer to the case study on page 118. There are answers on page 199–200.

1 Analyse how reducing the lead time on each suit will help Sartorial Ltd meet the needs of its customers. **(12 marks)**

> Lead time is an operational issue. Consider how a shorter lead time could increase flexibility and help Sartorial Ltd provide a better service. Tie your answer in with the objectives of the business.

2 Analyse the value of Sartorial Ltd, measuring its performance based on the quality of its suits. **(12 marks)**

> Consider how quality might add value to performance beyond simply using financial measures. You may also consider the difficulties in measuring quality.

3 Between 2014 and 2015 Sartorial Ltd's gross profit margin fell from 55% to 49%. To what extent is financial performance a key indicator of business success? **(16 marks)**

> Remember to apply your answer to Sartorial Ltd. Bring additional performance measures into your answer.

4 To what extent will Sartorial Ltd's functional targets help it achieve the vision laid out in its mission statement? **(20 marks)**

> In your answer you will need to show an understanding of the objectives hierarchy and how functional objectives support the aims of the organisation.

Case study

Sartorial Ltd provides a bespoke tailoring service for men. The company runs a network of trained tailors operating from temporary offices around the country. Customers visit their 'Sartorial Expert' at a local office where they can be measured, consulted and advised in order to design a completely bespoke suit considering every detail.

The board of directors have set the corporate objective to be the UK's market leader in bespoke tailoring within the next 5 years. Their mission statement is:

To give every customer a special experience and a suit they are proud to wear.

A Sartorial suit is designed in the UK but made in the Czech Republic. The lead time on a suit being ready for first fitting is 6 weeks. However, the operations director believes that the company will be able to reduce this lead time to 2 weeks if production was moved to the UK. Reducing the distance a suit travels and the use of sustainable materials is very important for the business and something customers value in a bespoke suit. In order to achieve the corporate objectives several functional targets have been set, including:

- 100% customer satisfaction rating of good or better
- zero defects or complaints
- 90% of all materials supplied from sustainable sources within 2 years.

Figure 1: Extracts from income statement 2014–2015

Income statement	2015 £(000)	2014 £(000)
Revenue	1390	1240
Cost of sales	(698)	(558)
Gross profit	692	682
Other expenses	(497)	(270)
Operating profit	195	412

Figure 2: Extracts from balance sheet as at 31 May 2015

Balance sheet	£(000)
Fixed assets	**3001**
total current assets	252
less current liabilities	(219)
less long-term liabilities	(1734)
Net assets	**1300**
Financed by	
capital	450
reserves and retained profit	850
Capital employed	**1300**

Political

The political environment covers the actions taken by national and international authorities. Their actions are designed to maximise economic activity, whilst protecting businesses, individuals and the environment.

regulating markets   enterprise   environmental issue

Factors influenced by the political environment

national infrastructure   international trade

Encouraging enterprise

UK and EU political decisions are aimed at encouraging an enterprise friendly environment for businesses. This includes:

👍 making finance accessible for small businesses

👍 providing funding for research and development

👍 support on establishing new businesses

👍 guidance on running a new business.

Specific policies and schemes include: Enterprise Allowance, Funding for Lending, and Enterprise Finance Guarantee (EFG).

Developing infrastructure

Infrastructure includes transportation, utilities, communication and energy. Government spending on infrastructure may benefit businesses by:

👍 speeding up communication

👍 making transportation of goods faster and cheaper

👍 allowing access to new markets

👍 attracting new business to the UK – potential customers and suppliers.

Recent infrastructure plans in the UK include the investment in a high-speed rail line connecting the south and north (HS2).

Regulators

The UK and EU have established a range of regulators. Their aim is to support businesses with compliance and conducting business in an appropriate way. In particular regulators focus on:

• promoting free competition between businesses

• regulation of specific industries, such as the Financial Conduct Authority (FCA)

• regulators of privatised monopolies (such as British Gas)

• self-regulation – businesses agreeing and operating a code of conduct.

Regulation can sometimes limit the actions of a business and slow down the speed at which strategies can be implemented. However, regulation also creates a stable environment for businesses to operate in.

Environment opportunities

Similar to regulation, the government may develop policies to protect the environment. This can create a number of opportunities for businesses that specialise in environmental products, for example, renewable energies, recycling and developers of old 'brownfield' sites.

International trade

The UK government implements a number of policies to support UK exporters. Increased exports bring revenue and employment opportunities. International trade initiatives include:

• 'Open to Export' initiative

• UK Trade and Investment (UKTI)

• the World Trade Organization (WTO).

Increased international trade makes it easier for UK businesses to sell their products, particularly high-quality specialist products.

Now try this

1 Why does the UK government encourage enterprise?

2 How does investment in infrastructure benefit businesses?

3 What is self-regulation?

Legal

The legal environment covers the laws that govern how our society operates. Businesses must abide by legislation set out by the UK government and the EU.

environment

Factors influenced by the legal environment

labour   competition

Competition

Competition legislation is put in place to protect the interests of consumers and businesses. In particular, legislation aims to control:

👍 cartel activity – businesses working together to manipulate the market and limit competition

👍 abuse of market power – such as imposing unfair conditions on small suppliers

👍 anti-competitive practices – such as anti-competitive mergers and acquisitions.

Examples of UK legislation governing competition include the Competition Act 1998, the Enterprise Act 2002 and the Enterprise and Regulatory Reform Act 2013.

Labour market

Labour laws aim to prevent exploitation of workers at an individual level and at a collective level. They legislate for issues such as pay, working conditions and grievances. Legislation also governs the powers of trade unions and has diminished those powers over the past 30 years. Consequently, trade union membership has fallen considerably.

Individual labour laws include:
• Working Time Directive Regulations 1998
• the National Minimum Wage Act 1998
• Equality Act 2010.

Collective labour laws include:
• Trade Union Act 1984
• Employment Relations Act 1999.

Environment

Environmental legislation aims to internalise any negative externalities associated with business activity. Therefore, businesses are made to pay for the full cost of production, such as the cost to clean up or repair damage caused by pollution. Much of the UK environmental legislation comes from EU directives.

Specific environmental legislation includes:
• the Environmental Protection Act 1990
• the Environment Act 1995.

The political and legal impact on business decision making

Political and legal change can impose costly change on businesses which might have to adapt their products and processes in order to meet legal standards. Where a business fails to implement the necessary changes, this could limit competitiveness, damage the business's reputation or worse. For example, it could lead to bad publicity and loss of trust in a business that has been fined for breaking the law.

Ultimately, businesses prefer a stable political and legal environment so that they can carry out business activity. However, political and legal change can create new opportunities for some businesses.

 Exam focus

Demonstrate your understanding

It is not necessary to understand a range of Acts or political policies. Instead, understand how a changing political and legal environment might impact on a business at a functional level and the threats and opportunities it could create.

Now try this

1 What is the drawback of legislation for a business?

2 How can new legislation create opportunities for a business?

3 How can legislation make a business pay for the full cost of production?

Exam skills

The following questions relate to Extracts A, B and C on pages 140–1 and relate to the topics covered in Unit 3.7.4.

Worked example

The following question refers to Extract A.

Explain the potential legal implications of Uber's alliance with Facebook. **(5 marks)**

Uber's alliance with Facebook could be deemed as anti-competitive. This means that it might not be in the best interests of consumers and the market. Many countries have legislation in place to prevent anti-competitive actions of businesses. For example, the Competition Act 1998. As a result, the alliance between these two companies could be stopped and a case taken to court.

The student has shown an understanding of legislation around competition and clearly explained how this could affect Uber. Relevant examples of legislation have been given in the answer.

Worked example

The following question refers to Extract B.

Analyse the potential impact of the government's fiscal policy relating to transport. **(9 marks)**

There has been a dip in government spending on public sector transport since 2009 but this has increased in 2013/14. The increase in spending will improve the infrastructure of the UK. As a result, this could make it easier for people to travel to work and increase mobility of the workforce. As a result of this and new jobs being created in the transport sector, unemployment in the UK could fall...

The student has started by interpreting data from the extract. They have then gone on to make a link between this data and the impact it could have on the UK economy. The student could now go on to discuss the implications of rising transport costs as represented in the first graph.

Worked example

The following question refers to Extract C.

To what extent should the UK and EU impose new legislation to cover the technological advancement of car technology? **(16 marks)**

Extract C suggests that there will be a number of technological advancements and innovations in car technology over the next 5 years. A number of these technologies will create opportunities for businesses. For example, in-car advertising. As there are a number of safety issues with such technology it is important that legislation is in place to protect consumers who might use the new technology. Without legislation such as the Consumer Protection Act 1987, consumers could get injured due to the distractions of in-car advertising. As a consequence, this will create negative externalities such as pressure on A&E and roadside recovery services...

The student has selected relevant information from Extract C to help contextualise their answer. The need for legislation is well developed and appropriate examples have been used. The student could now go on to explain the limitations of legislation, such as its potential to restrict innovation and increase business costs.

121

Economic change

The economic environment includes a range of economic variables such as GDP, inflation, unemployment and consumer confidence. Governments use a range of policies to influence economic activity and economic change creates a number of opportunities and threats for businesses that will have an impact on strategic and functional decisions.

Gross domestic product

Gross domestic product (GDP) is a measure of a country's total output of goods and services over a period of time. GDP changes over time are represented by the business cycle.

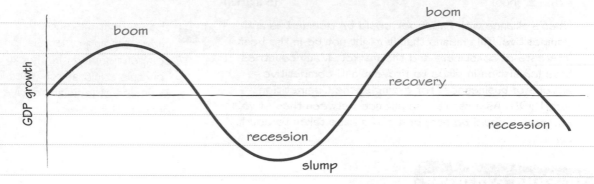

	Boom	Recession	Slump	Recovery
	High rates of economic growth and production	Output starts to fall, growth declines	Prolonged period of economic decline	Economy starts to pick up after a period of decline
Features	• high profits • low unemployment • high inflation • shortages in supply.	• production declines as demand falls • governments use policies to stimulate growth • consumer/business confidence starts to fall.	• high levels of unemployment • high rates of business failure/closure • low interest rates • low levels of spending and investment.	• increasing consumer confidence • businesses start to invest/take on new employees • spare capacity is used up.
Impact on strategic and functional decisions	• Firms make strategic decision to expand into new markets through market development. • Functional decision to expand workforce/increase recruitment. • Businesses seek opportunities for efficiencies and cost reductions as a result of economies of scale.	• Expansion plans are 'shelved'. • Market penetration strategies become more attractive as they are low risk. • Businesses stockpile products. • Functions try to increase efficiency and cut costs – such as flexible working implemented.	• Businesses adopt a strategy of rationalisation. • Functional decisions may include redundancies, scale down of production and reduction in capacity. • Businesses reduce prices and focus on their most profitable product lines. • Businesses may decide to cease trading or leave certain markets.	• New business start-ups emerge. • Business investment rises – product development strategy. • Businesses take on new employees and increase contracts to meet growth in demand. • Functional decisions focus on ways to increase productivity – training, growth in production, increased marketing activity.

Now try this

1 Identify two features of a boom.

2 Identify two features of a slump.

3 Identify two features of a recovery.

Economic factors

The exchange rate is the price of one currency expressed in terms of another. A UK business will purchase a foreign currency in order to buy products and services from overseas. The exchange rates change due to fluctuations in demand for a currency, economic growth and interest rates.

£1.00 = €1.20

If the pound increases in value against other currencies it is said to STRENGTHEN. The pound can buy more euros, or fewer pounds are needed to buy one euro.

£1.00 = €1.10

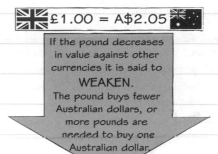

£1.00 = A$2.05

If the pound decreases in value against other currencies it is said to WEAKEN. The pound buys fewer Australian dollars, or more pounds are needed to buy one Australian dollar.

£1.00 = A$1.46

Exchange rates and decision making

- Businesses will try to avoid uncertainty when exchange rates are volatile. Businesses may set an agreed rate for future transactions.
- A business may choose to target a specific international market (or economy) when the exchange rate is favourable.

Importers

👍 may switch international suppliers when the exchange rate is less favourable

👍 stockpile raw material and products when currency is strong.

Exporters

👍 lower prices to limit the impact of a strong currency

👍 increase promotion in foreign markets when currency is weak.

Inflation

Inflation is the general rise in prices over time. Inflation is measured by the consumer price index (CPI). A low rate of inflation can be managed by businesses but a high rate of inflation will increase costs and reduce demand.

Deflation

Deflation is a fall in prices as measured by CPI. Deflation is relatively rare in the UK. Short-term falls can boost sales for businesses. Prolonged deflation can have severe consequences for businesses as consumers postpone purchases whilst waiting for prices to fall further.

| 7 | 6 | 5 | 4 | 3 | 2 | 1 | 0 | −1 | −2 | −3 | −4 | −5 |

High inflation
- Businesses may increase prices to pass costs on to consumers or may decide to absorb the cost rises.
- Businesses will look to reduce internal costs to protect profits.
- Price rises may fuel further inflation.

Low inflation
- Businesses feel confident in a stable economic environment.
- Businesses may look to invest and grow.

Deflation
- Businesses may struggle to pay debts – assets may have to be sold to pay off debts if deflation persists.
- Low demand may lead to redundancies and rationalisation.

Now try this

1 How does the exchange rate affect importers and exporters?
2 Why do businesses want a steady rate of inflation?

Fiscal and monetary policy

A government will use fiscal and monetary policy to influence economic activity in order to maintain growth and limit negative factors such as high levels of inflation, unemployment and the negative externalities of growth.

Monetary policy

This is the policy to adjust the amount of money in circulation and therefore influence spending and economic activity. The main form of monetary policy is interest rates – the cost of borrowing money and the reward for saving.

Monetary policy generally includes:

• manipulating interest rates

• influencing the exchange rate

• quantitative easing

• forward guidance.

The impact of the interest rate on business activity

High %

Interest rate

• consumer and business spending falls
• inflation falls
• stronger £

• consumer and business spending rises
• inflation may rise
• weaker £

Low %

Fiscal policy

Fiscal policy involves government spending and taxation as a means of controlling economic activity. The difference between government income (mainly taxes) and expenditure in a fiscal year is known as the budget balance.

Expansionary fiscal	Contractionary fiscal
Reduces direct and indirect tax to increase disposable income. Increases borrowing (PSNCR).	Reduces spending in areas such as health and education. Pressure on inflation slows. Budget deficit may fall or reach a surplus.
Increases spending in areas such as health and education. Spending stimulates demand for businesses and creates jobs. Budget deficit may rise.	Increases direct and indirect taxes to slow down growth and reduce the budget deficit.

Taxation – income tax, national insurance payments, VAT, corporation tax, customs and excise duties
Government expenditure – infrastructure, human capital, goods, services

Now try this

1 What is monetary policy?

2 What is fiscal policy?

Trade and protectionism

Supply-side policies

A range of measures intended to improve the efficiency and effectiveness of free markets. Policies include:

- **manipulating the labour market** – training, free movement of labour, tax cuts for low incomes
- **privatisation** – transferring organisations (or part) to state ownership to encourage competition
- **reducing 'red tape' and regulations** – making it easier for businesses to operate.

Protectionism

Protectionism involves protecting domestic business and home industries against foreign competition and limiting the number of imports into a country.

Open trade can benefit all countries by creating opportunities for growth and economic prosperity. Free trade encourages specialism, leading to greater efficiencies and lower prices. It is also a key factor in reducing poverty in many countries. For this reason protectionism is sometimes criticised and may provoke a retaliation from trading partners. Some of these practices are outlined below.

Protectionism in practice

Factors affecting exports

Soft loans – generous loan agreements offered to exporting businesses to help them compete in foreign markets.

Subsidies – grants given to support exporting businesses so that they can lower their prices in order to compete internationally.

State procurement – favouring domestic businesses as suppliers over foreign competition.

Factors affecting imports

Technical barriers – such as rules and regulations governing the standard of products entering the country.

Quotas – physical limit set on the number of units that can be imported into a country.

Tariffs – tax on imports increases price of imported goods. Raises government income and makes domestic businesses more competitive.

Risks – protectionism may force businesses to use more expensive domestic suppliers, therefore making them less competitive. It may also encourage businesses to move abroad to avoid trading barriers.

Now try this

1 Why might a government impose protectionist strategies?

2 Identify three protectionist strategies a government might use.

Globalisation

Globalisation is the process by which the world is becoming increasingly interconnected as a result of massively increased trade and cultural exchange. Globalisation involves the movement towards worldwide markets.

Reasons for greater globalisation

The process of globalisation allows businesses to enter new markets, access new skills, resources and the expertise, technology and experience of international businesses and industries. The benefits of greater globalisation are:

- support/encouragement by governments and businesses

- lower costs of transportation and better infrastructure
- improved communications technology
- society becoming more culturally aware
- reduction in trading barriers
- growth in international trading blocs.

Multinational companies

Globalisation has also been driven by large multinationals such as Toyota, McDonalds and HSBC. Not only do they standardise their products and make them available all over the world, they also influence governments and make the process of globalisation more possible. Globalised corporations also encourage the movement of labour between countries.

Emerging markets

Emerging markets are low income countries that are experiencing high rates of growth, e.g. the BRIC countries. Emerging markets hold significant potential for UK and European businesses in terms of resources, labour and market growth. For example, 80% of growth in the airline industry over the next 30 years is expected to come from BRIC nations. There are also a number of risks involved when operating in emerging markets.

Globalisation: opportunities and threats

Opportunities

👍 new markets – opportunity for businesses to move into new markets or operate on a global scale

👍 cheaper resources – access to raw materials

👍 labour – cheaper labour and access to skills

👍 economies of scale – growth of business leads to an advantage of size.

Threats

🔨 competition – home markets can be targeted by foreign competitors

🔨 downward pressure on prices – cheaper materials and labour may force prices down and therefore potential profits

🔨 threat of takeovers – some businesses will face takeover pressure from foreign competitors looking to enter the market

🔨 economic risks – inflation and recession in other countries

🔨 political risks – developing countries have less stable political systems and government.

Effective use of CSR – avoid damaging local cultures and traditions.

Global vs. local – standardise the product to gain economies of scale or make slight tweaks to meet the specific needs of a local market – this is a 'glocal' approach.

Strategies for global markets

Strategic alliances – look for partnerships with international businesses that have experience operating in foreign markets.

Strategic takeovers – acquire brands and businesses that international customers trust.

Now try this

1 Identify two risks associated with operating in international markets.

2 Identify two potential opportunities for businesses operating in international markets.

Exam skills

The following questions relate to Extracts A and D on pages 140–1 and relate to the topics covered in Unit 3.7.5.

Worked example

Using Extract D, analyse the long-term impact of interest rates on UK businesses. **(9 marks)**

The extract suggests that UK interest rates are likely to rise by 0.5% in the first quarter of 2016. Although this is only a small increase it will increase the costs for some businesses that have borrowed money. This is likely to directly impact profits of a business unless it decides to pass the increased costs on to customers...

The student has interpreted the graph from Extract D and used the information to suggest how rising interest rates might affect UK businesses directly. The student could then go on to explain how a rising interest rates could have an indirect impact – through the actions of customers.

Worked example

Evaluate the impact a slowdown in economic growth in China is likely to have on UK businesses. **(16 marks)**

...On the other hand, UK importers may find that it is easier and cheaper for them to import products from China. This is because there will be less pressure on prices and fewer shortages in supply. Furthermore, as China's growth slows, it is likely that the value of the Yuan will fall. This will increase the buying power of UK importers and in turn reduce their costs...

This is an extract from a student's answer. In this short paragraph they have analysed one benefit to UK importers. The rest of the answer should contain an analysis of the threats of declining growth in China. For example, a fall in demand for UK exports from Chinese consumers and businesses.

Worked example

Using Extract A, to what extent is the globalisation of firms such as Uber likely to benefit society? **(20 marks)**

...The key issue is that Uber is encouraging competition in local markets and improving market efficiencies by introducing new technologies. Although Uber may disrupt domestic taxi firms and disturb local traditions, such as London black cabs, competition lowers prices and improves service quality. However, this will depend on the ability of traditional taxi firms to lower their prices and adopt similar technology. Providing Uber does not move to a position where it has a monopoly in the taxi market, the service it provides will benefit society. In order to avoid a monopoly it is important for legislation to be put in place along with guidance from regulators to prevent this from happening.

This is the student's evaluation. The student has included a number of features that make a good evaluation:

- answering the question!
- making a decision based on the context
- identifying the key issue/most significant factor
- using the 'depends on' rule
- giving a recommendation to limit any negatives.

Social change

Social change relates to the changing demands of society for different goods and services. It also includes the way society spends money (such as increased spending on luxury products) and accesses products and services (such as the subscription box trend). All businesses must keep up with the changing demands of society if they are to remain competitive.

Demographic change

Demography is the study of the human population (such as profiling postcodes by the demographic make-up of its residents). There are a number of demographic trends that businesses are having to adapt to. These create new changes and opportunities for businesses.

Age – the general population is getting older as people live longer. Increasing demand in the 'grey' market.

Growth – the population in many countries is growing at a considerable rate, increasing the demand for products and services.

Key demographic factors

Migration – migration varies from country to country, but a significant and growing proportion of the UK and EU are migrants.

Urbanisation – a growing trend in developed countries of people moving from rural areas to towns and cities.

Lifestyle changes

Consumers' lifestyles affect their buying behaviour, including what, when and how they buy products and services. Key lifestyle changes in recent years include:

Technology – consumers are increasingly using technology to access products and services, such as growth in online shopping and consuming services via mobile devices.

Health and well-being – consumers are more health conscious than they have ever been.

Single occupancy – more people are living on their own than ever before.

Luxuries – people spend a greater proportion of their income on luxury items.

Time – in a busy world, consumers' time is precious. Consumers want products and services that save time.

On-demand culture – consumers are accessing products and services instantly or when it suits them, including TV and online shopping.

1 Identify three changing demographic factors that may affect a business.

2 What opportunities might arise through changing consumer lifestyles?

Technological change

Developments in technology not only create opportunities for new products and services, but also advancements in the way in which businesses produce products and deliver them to the consumer. Technology can completely reshape a market (for example Uber) and businesses can be left behind if they don't keep up with technological advances (for example Kodak).

Online business

Online business has grown considerably in the last 10–15 years as bandwidth speeds have increased along with the sophistication of e-commerce websites and the security of online payments. Online business creates a number of opportunities and drawbacks for businesses.

Opportunities for small business start-ups – little capital is required to start up an online business.

Cutting out retail – online businesses offer lower prices for consumers, but this can cause retailers to close and add to the declining state of the UK's high streets.

Reducing business overheads – online businesses have lower overheads if expensive premises are not important.

Access to a global market – the internet allows businesses to reach a global market.

Growth of direct delivery – online businesses require fast and effective delivery services to get products to their customers.

Fraud – a considerable amount of business fraud takes place through bogus ecommerce sites, costing businesses and consumers millions of pounds each year.

Key technological changes

A number of advancements in technology are changing the way businesses operate and will create a number of opportunities in the future. Some of these emerging technologies include:

- 3D printing
- wearable technology
- smartphone/mobile technology
- renewable energies
- virtual reality
- the 'internet of me' (personalisation) of online experience
- cloud computing.

Opportunities and risks of technology

Technological advancements create many opportunities for business in terms of:

- innovating products
- access to new markets
- improving internal efficiencies
- streamlining operations.

However, technological advancement can also be a risk for businesses:

- At times, technological advancement can become a threshold resource that businesses have to keep up with if they are to remain in a market and compete.
- New technologies also make some products and services obsolete.

When Apple updated the power source on its devices to the thunderbolt cable, many third party products that supported old 30 pin chargers became obsolete.

Now try this

1 How has online business changed the way businesses operate?

2 Identify two key technological advancements in recent years.

3 What are the business risks involved with developing new technologies?

Corporate social responsibility 1

Social and technological change may have an impact on strategic and functional decisions.

Strategic decisions

Constant social and technological change means business models cannot stay static. The strategic direction of businesses will shift to meet these needs, and businesses will have to develop different core competencies. As the needs of society change, businesses will inevitably have to change their position in the market.

Functional decisions

Marketing

As society changes market research must keep up with these trends to ensure the business understands the needs of its customers. Technology also gives a business new ways of communicating and interacting with its customers.

Finance

As technology grows exponentially businesses must think very carefully about where they want to invest their money. Online retail also offers businesses the opportunity to reduce their investment in expensive capital such as retail premises.

Operations

The growing trend for instant access to products and services means businesses have to find ways to get their products to customers in a faster, more efficient and simple way.

Human resources

Flexible working conditions mean employees no longer need to operate from a single place of work. Human resources face the challenge of managing this and the impact nomadic working can have on teamwork and motivation.

Corporate Social Responsibility

Corporate Social Responsibility (CSR) is the belief that a business should act responsibly and protect the interests of all its stakeholders. Going beyond following rules and regulations, CSR dictates that a business should operate in a way that actually benefits society and the environment, not just to behave as a 'good citizen' but for the long-term sustainability and prosperity of the business. CSR shapes the ethics that guide most modern-day businesses.

CSR may involve businesses doing the following for each of their stakeholder groups.

CSR in practice

Customers	👍 fair prices 👍 transparency 👍 honesty 👍 reliable after-sales service 👍 safe products
Employees	👍 fair pay 👍 good working conditions 👍 job security
Suppliers	👍 fair prices 👍 frequent and regular orders
Local community	👍 employment opportunities 👍 investment in infrastructure 👍 minimal negative externalities

Now try this

1 Explain two ways in which changes in society and technology can affect functional decisions.

2 What is CSR?

3 What are the forces against a focus on CSR?

Corporate social responsibility 2

Stakeholder vs shareholder concept

Shareholder concept – the belief that a business's prime function should be to satisfy its shareholders. This means maximising profitability. Profits will support the long-term success of the business and economic prosperity.

Stakeholder concept – where businesses cater for the needs of all stakeholders, not just shareholders. In doing so businesses create long-term prosperity and avoid unsustainable business practices.

Enlightened shareholder value – many businesses now adopt the principles of enlightened shareholder value (ESV). ESV involves focusing on shareholder value with a long-term perspective, not just for short-term profitability gains. As businesses adopt a long-term perspective, consideration of other stakeholders becomes more agreeable – such as the investment in training to improve the skills of the workforce.

Corporate Social Responsibility Pyramid

Philanthropic responsibility
Be a good corporate citizen.
Contribute resources to the community; improve quality of life.

Ethical responsibility
Be ethical.
Obligation to do what is right, just and fair. Avoid harm.

Legal responsibility
Obey the law.
Law is society's codification of right and wrong. Play by the rules of the game.

Economic responsibility
Be profitable.
The foundation upon which all others rest.

Carroll's CSR pyramid

This business model sets out four responsibilities that all businesses should meet in order to be socially responsible. The responsibilities are hierarchical, with economic responsibility at the base. Without first meeting this responsibility a business will fail and will therefore be unable to meet its other responsibilities.

The problem with CSR

There is sometimes a short-term contradiction between the first step of the pyramid and the following three. The pressures for a business to be legally, ethically and philanthropically responsible can require significant financial investment, therefore, having an impact on short-term profitability.

The pressures for effective CSR

Appropriate CSR practices can have a significant impact on the competitiveness of a business:

- Bad publicity can be shared easily through social media, damaging its reputation.
- Ethically orientated customers may choose a business based on its CSR record.
- Good CSR will help attract the best employees.
- Supporting developing countries through effective CSR policies supports long-term sustainability and growth in these markets.

📝 Exam focus — Evaluating in an exam

CSR can provide you with an effective 'depends on' argument when evaluating. For example, when evaluating the decision of a business to enter a new international market, you can consider the impact this might have on its social responsibility; for example how might this affect its employees in terms of relocation and job security? Is it exploiting cheap labour?

Now try this

1 What is the shareholder concept?
2 Why is CSR important for all businesses?
3 Identify the four responsibilities in Carroll's CSR pyramid.

Exam skills

The following questions relate to Extracts A, B and C on pages 140–141 and relate to the topics covered in Unit 3.7.6.

Worked example

1 Using Extract C, analyse the long-term impact of technological change on car manufacturers. **(9 marks)**

The extract outlines a number of innovations that are likely to be developed in the next 5 years within the car market. For manufacturers this will give them the chance to add value to their products and improve competitiveness. For example, comprehensive vehicle tracking could make cars safer and less likely to be stolen. This would be attractive to many customers who own valuable cars or live in areas of high risk. Furthermore, developing these technologies could become a competitive advantage for businesses if they are able to protect their innovation and make it a USP...

2 UK consumers are becoming increasingly conscious of the impact they have on the environment. In particular, a growing proportion of society actively seeks ways to conserve energy in their homes, recycle and minimise their carbon footprint.

Using Extract B, analyse the impact this social trend is likely to have on businesses providing public transport in the UK. **(9 marks)**

With UK consumers becoming more environmentally conscious it is likely that more people will look for transport methods that are green and limit the impact on the environment. This may include purchasing electric cars, but also switching to public transport and cycling.

As the costs of public transport rise it is important for businesses to absorb these costs and improve internal efficiencies if they are to attract customers. As costs rise, people may be more tempted to walk or cycle to work and this could reduce trade and revenues for public transport providers such as bus and coach companies. In order to remain competitive they will have to find ways to reduce costs and ensure that the price of public transport is competitive against other alternatives...

3 To what extent is Uber failing to meet its Corporate Social Responsibility? **(16 marks)**

...Overall, Uber has not broken any laws and its customers are likely to appreciate the services it provides in order to make hailing a taxi more convenient. For this reason, Uber is certainly meeting its economical and philanthropic responsibilities as outlined by Carroll's CSR pyramid.

However, a key aspect of CSR is ensuring no stakeholders are affected in a negative way. As Uber currently has a number of lawsuits going through the courts it is yet to be seen if it is meeting its legal and ethical responsibilities. Uber is meeting the needs of its shareholders and some businesses will set this as a key objective. Therefore, the extent to which Uber is meeting its Corporate Social Responsibility may depend on its corporate objectives and long-term goals.

The student has explained how technological advancement could create an opportunity for some businesses and has used the extract to provide an example. The student could also look at some of the threats or pressures that the changes could place on manufacturers, such as the pressure to adopt these technologies in order to remain competitive.

The student has used the extract well and identified that public transport costs are rising. They have then used this information along with the question stem to identify the threats these changes could have on public transport providers and how they may have to react. The student could go on to discuss the pressure for public transport providers to offer environmentally friendly transport, such as low carbon emissions.

This is a student's evaluation for this question. See how the last paragraph is clearly focused on answering the question. The student has used some good techniques in their evaluation, including the 'depends on' rule and using appropriate management theory.

The competitive environment 1

The competitive environment refers to the factors within a market that determine how businesses operate and compete in that market. A business must respond and make functional and strategic decisions based on these factors. Michael Porter's Five Forces model presents a framework for analysing the competitive environment.

The Five Forces model

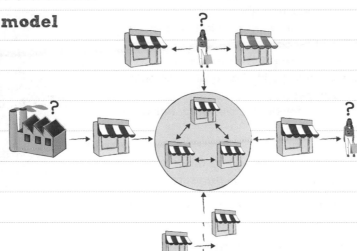

The five competitive forces are:
- competitive rivalry
- bargaining power of suppliers
- bargaining power of buyers
- threat of substitutes
- threat of new entrants.

Porter's five forces model can be used alongside other popular models such as SWOT and PEST-C in order to analyse the key issues facing a business and how that business might respond to these competitive forces.

Rivalry within the market

This is the level of competition and aggressive rivalry between businesses within the market. As markets grow and become more attractive, new businesses may enter the market, increasing the competitive rivalry.

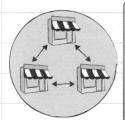

Competition is fierce if:
- easy entry to market
- easy for customers to switch
- little differentiation of products
- little growth or decline in the market

Key problem:
- profit margins are squeezed

Options for businesses to consider:
- lower costs of production and prices to compete
- develop a basis for differentiation
- takeover, merger or strategic alliance

Bargaining power of suppliers

This is the power suppliers have to negotiate terms and prices. The bargaining power of a supplier may change if the supply of a commodity, such as wheat or copper, fluctuates.

Supplier power is high if:
- few suppliers
- supplier's product is essential for production
- the supplier is able to integrate vertically forward and sell direct to the business's customers
- low availability of viable substitutes.

Key problem:
- high production costs and unfavourable terms of supply

Options for businesses to consider:
- build strong relationships with suppliers
- agree long-term contract of supply with favourable conditions
- backward vertical integration

Now try this

1 What are Porter's five competitive forces?

2 What might determine the rivalry within a market?

3 What decisions might a business take where suppliers are powerful?

The competitive environment 2

Buyer power

This is the power buyers have to negotiate terms and prices. This might change as consumers gain greater access to information and greater choice between rival businesses.

Buyer power is high if:
- there is little difference between products offered by competitors
- products are price sensitive
- customers buy in large quantities on a regular basis
- it is easy for buyers to switch between competitors.

Key problem:
- prices forced low and credit terms demanded so there is pressure on cash flow

Options for businesses to consider:
- develop a USP
- build switching costs into agreements
- lower prices to attract customers
- forward vertical integration (if buyer is another business)

Threat of substitutes

A substitute is an alternative product that may deliver the same benefits to the customer. The threat of substitutes may change with social trends. For example, the health trend for consumers to use coconut oil as a healthier alternative to sunflower oil or olive oil when cooking.

Threat of substitutes is high if:
- alternative products exist
- alternative prices fall
- customers can easily switch to a substitute.

Key problem:
- Buyers have high bargaining power. Competition exists outside of the market.

Options for businesses to consider:
- develop a USP
- build switching costs into agreements
- lower prices to attract / keep customers
- promote benefits in comparison to substitute products

Barriers to entry

A barrier to entry is a physical, technological and intellectual factor that makes it difficult for a rival business to enter the market. The existence of large companies can create barriers to entry as they dominate resources and networks. However, disruptive technology and innovation can give small businesses leverage to enter a market.

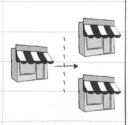

Barriers exist when:
- capital investment to enter the market is very high
- customers are brand loyal to existing businesses
- levels of specialist knowledge and expertise in the industry are very high.

Key problem:
- If few barriers exist it is easy for new competitors to enter the market and increase competitive rivalry.

Options for businesses to consider:
- innovation – continuous development of new products can keep the business ahead of any new competition
- build strong relationships with buyers, making it difficult for new entrants
- growth – economies of scale can keep prices low and make it difficult for small businesses to enter the market

Now try this

1 What are two factors that may give buyers power in a market?

2 What is a substitute product?

3 How might a business compete with new entrants in a market?

Exam skills

The following questions relate to the topics covered in Unit 3.7.7. Question 3 refers to Extract A on page 140.

Worked example

With reference to Porter's Five Forces model, which of the following relates to the ability of a new business to set up in a market?

A Threat of substitutes ⬭

B The bargaining power of buyers ⬭

C Barriers to entry ⬤

D The competitive rivalry within the market ⬭

(1 mark)

Barriers to entry refers to the factors that may determine how easy it is for a business to set up or enter a market. If the barrier to entry is high, it might be very expensive to enter the market or require unique technical expertise.

Worked example

With reference to Porter's Five Forces model, which of the following is not likely to result in prices falling?

A Increased number of substitutes ⬭

B Increased bargaining power of buyers ⬭

C Increased rivalry within the market ⬭

D Increased bargaining power of suppliers ⬤

(1 mark)

The only option that would not put pressure on businesses to lower their prices is **D**. If suppliers have greater bargaining power it is likely that business costs will rise. This may put pressure on businesses to increase prices to maintain profit margins – not lower their prices.

Worked example

To what extent will Uber's partnership with Facebook affect the competitive environment within the taxi market?

(16 marks)

One way in which Uber's partnership with Facebook will affect the market is that it is likely to reduce the competitive rivalry within the market. Uber's partnership gives it another way to reach its customers and makes it easy for them to hail/book a taxi. Uber already has a unique app that allows customers to book taxis and normal taxi firms are finding it difficult to compete. This additional feature will make it even harder for local firms to compete in terms of convenience, especially in large cities. As a result, some taxi firms may close down and this will reduce competitive rivalry and the incentive for Uber to keep prices low...

The student has used the theory of Porter's Five Forces model to help them answer this question. The candidate could now go on to discuss other features of the taxi industry that could be affected by Uber's partnership with Facebook.

Investment appraisal 1

Investment appraisal is a series of techniques designed to assist businesses in judging the desirability of investing in particular projects. Investment appraisal may use a range of techniques, including financial and non-financial methods.

What businesses invest in

Investment appraisal may be used to aid businesses in making decisions when investing in:

- non-current assets
- launching new products
- new technology
- expansion
- infrastructure.

Financial methods

Financial methods for investment appraisal include:

- **payback** – calculates the length of time it takes for an investment to recoup its original cost
- **average rate of return** – calculates the annual average return over the life of an investment in order to compare the investment with other alternatives
- **net present value** – can be used alongside other techniques and considers the future value of an investment by discounting the decreased future value of money.

Payback

Payback is a quick and simple investment appraisal tool. It simply focuses on the time taken to recoup the initial investment and considers the cash inflows over a number of years. It is useful for firms who need a quick return and may be facing liquidity problems.

Payback can be calculated by using a table.

In this example payback is achieved after 2 years.

Year	Cash outflow	Cash inflow
0	100,000	40,000
1		30,000
2		30,000
3		30,000

If payback point falls between two years use:

$$\frac{\text{Amount remaining to recover}}{\text{Amount recovered in following year}}$$

Average rate of return

The ARR is useful because it measures the profit achieved on an investment over time, which can then be compared to other investments or the zero risk strategy of leaving money in a bank account. However, profits may fluctuate considerably over the life of a project and this is not taken into account.

ARR is calculated by:

$$\frac{\text{Average annual profit}}{\text{Asset's initial cost}}$$

There are three steps to calculating ARR:

1 Total income from investment − cost of investment = total profit from investment

2 $\dfrac{\text{Total profit from investment}}{\text{expected lifespan of asset}} = \text{average annual profit}$

3 $\dfrac{\text{Average annual profit}}{\text{cost of investment}} \times 100\% = \text{ARR}$

Now try this

1 Why might a business use investment appraisal?

2 Why might a business calculate payback?

3 Why is ARR useful when making investment decisions?

Investment appraisal 2

Net present value

Net present value (NPV) takes into account the future value of money by discounting cash flows. NPV considers time in an investment and follows the principle that the value of money depreciates over time. For example, 2 years from now, £1 will buy less than it does today. NPV is good for considering opportunity cost of an investment, but identifying the appropriate discount factor can be difficult.

Year	Investment A	Investment B
1	40,000	10,000
2	20,000	20,000
3	10,000	40,000

Investment A is preferable as a higher proportion of the return is received towards the start of the investment – year 1.

Year	Discount factor at 10%
1	0.909
2	0.826
3	0.751
4	0.683

Cash flows are discounted using a discount factor for each year, such as 5%, 7% or 10%.

Investment decisions

A business might consider the following factors and use them to form criteria when making investment decisions.

Financial
- the rate of interest – using current rate of interest as a benchmark to judge investments against
- ROCE – is there an expected minimum % return on the investment?
- cost – can the firm finance the investment?

Investment criteria

Non-financial
- corporate objectives – does the investment support business strategy?
- ethics – does the investment support CSR policy?
- industrial relations – what will be the impact on employees?

Risk and uncertainty

Risk is the chance of an adverse outcome and the impact it might have. The following might determine the level of risk associated with a particular investment:

1 timescale of the investment

2 knowledge / expertise of the business in the investment

3 if the investment is in a new market

4 stability of the external environment (legal, political, social, etc.).

A business can reduce the impact of any negative outcome by agreeing prices in advance, providing allowances for revenue and costs, ensuring the firm has sufficient financial assets and developing contingency plans.

Sensitivity analysis

Sensitivity analysis involves using variations in forecasting to allow for a range of outcomes. It allows a business to ask 'what if' questions and put in place plans to deal with these scenarios.

Examples might include:

- comparing NPV using a variety of discount factors
- allowing for a 20% fluctuation in sales and costs
- building in contingency for unforeseen expenses.

Sensitivity analysis is useful for identifying the possible risks involved in an investment if only a few variables are considered. The value of it depends on the accuracy of the data on which it is based.

Now try this

1 What two non-financial factors might a business use to evaluate a potential investment?

2 Identify two factors that may determine the risk associated with an investment.

3 How might a business use sensitivity analysis?

Exam skills

The following questions relate to the topics covered in Unit 3.7.8 and provide examples of how you might be expected to calculate investment appraisal in an examination.

Worked example

1 Use the information in Table 1 to calculate the payback period for Investment Project A. **(3 marks)**

Table 1: Cash flows for Project A

Year	Net cash flow	Cumulative cash flow
0	(500)	(500)
1	100	(400)
2	125	(275)
3	175	(100)
4	200	100

3 Years +

$\frac{100}{200} \times 12 = 6$ months... Payback = 3 years 6 months

The student has completed the cumulative cash flow table to show that payback falls between years 3 and 4. The calculation shows this to be 6 months by dividing the amount left to recover the investment after the third year (100) divided by the cash flow for year 4 (200) = 0.5. This is then multiplied by 12 (months) to get 6.

2 Use the information in Table 2 to calculate the average rate of return for Investment Project B. **(5 marks)**

Table 2: Cash flows for Project B

	Project B
Initial cost	£50,000
Return yr 1	£10,000
Yr 2	£10,000
Yr 3	£15,000
Yr 4	£15,000
Y5 5	£20,000
Total net cash flow	£70,000

Profit = £70,000 − £50,000 = £20,000

Average annual profit = $\frac{£20,000}{5}$ = £4,000

ARR = $\frac{£4,000}{£50,000} \times 100 = 8\%$

First the student works out the average annual cost by taking the profit from the investment initial cost. This is then divided by the lifespan of the project (5 years). The average annual profit is then divided by the initial investment to give an ARR of 8%.

3 Use a discount factor of 5% to calculate the net present value for Project C. **(5 marks)**

Year	5% Discount factor	Cash flows Project C
0	1.00	(100,000)
1	0.95	0
2	0.91	0
3	0.86	80,000
4	0.82	70,000
5	0.78	50,000

NPV = 80,000 × 0.86 = 68,800
+ 70,000 × 0.82 = 57,400
+ 50,000 × 0.78 = 39,000
= 165,200 − 100,000 = NPV £65,200

The student has been given a discount table to use in this question. There are three cash inflows after year 2 and the student has discounted each using the relevant discount factor from the table. These have then been totalled and the initial investment cost has been deducted to reach the NPV.

Exam-style practice

Use Extracts A to D on pages 140–1 to answer the exam-style questions in this section covering the topics from Units 3.7.4 to 3.7.8. There are answers on pages 200–201.

1 Using Extract B, explain the impact of changes in transport costs for the UK population.

(5 marks)

Make sure that you actually use the data from Extract B to explain the impact of an increase in transportation costs.

2 Using Extract B, analyse how public sector spending could impact the competitive environment within the transport industry.

(9 marks)

What could public sector spending involve? Could it be spending on infrastructure? Or perhaps subsidies for public transport? For this question consider how government spending could link to the prosperity of transport-related businesses.

3 With reference to Extract C, to what extent will technological advancement lead to growth in the automobile industry?

(16 marks)

4 Using the information in Extract A and the information in the table below, evaluate whether Uber should continue with their partnership with Facebook.

(16 marks)

Consider the technological developments in Extract C and consider the impact these may have on the automobile and related industries. Will it lead to growth opportunities? What might be some of the limitations?

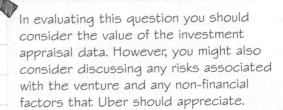

Uber Facebook Messenger investment	
Payback	approx. 5 years
ARR	4%

5 Using the information in Extract D, evaluate the impact on UK businesses of economic growth in the UK if it were to 'remain above 2% between 2017 and 2020'.

(20 marks)

In evaluating this question you should consider the value of the investment appraisal data. However, you might also consider discussing any risks associated with the venture and any non-financial factors that Uber should appreciate.

In your answer consider the benefits of economic growth and discuss relevant economic factors such as employment, consumer/business confidence and standard of living. In your answer you might also consider the extent to which 2% is good. How might this compare to other nations? Are there any drawbacks of economic growth? What will be the key issue that you use to evaluate your answer?

Case study 1

Extract A: Uber's expansion

Uber, the Californian taxi network company that operates the Uber app linking customers to Uber taxi drivers, has agreed an alliance with Facebook Messenger that will allow users to order a ride from within Facebook's Messenger chat app. The agreement gives Uber access to millions of potential new users and marks the first time that Messenger – for which Facebook has ambitions ranging from retail to concierge services – has ventured into transport.

Uber is the biggest ride-hailing company in the world in terms of funding, with about $12bn raised so far – even as lawsuits relating to its treatment of drivers and compliance with local laws work their way through courts in many countries.

Its Facebook Messenger service, initially released in 10 cities on Wednesday, will be rolled out across the US before Christmas, with the goal of expanding internationally in 2016. Uber would not disclose whether there was a revenue-sharing agreement with Facebook as part of the deal.

Extract B: UK transport costs

UK transport report
- The total cost of motoring has risen around the same as the cost of living (RPI).
- Rail and bus fares have increased faster than the cost of living (RPI).

Retail Prices Index, transport components: 1987–2013

UK public sector expenditure on transport

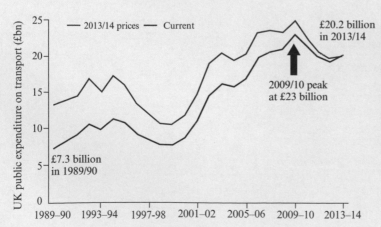

£ The peak in expenditure on transport was £23 billion in 2009/10, three times the £7.3 billion in 1989/90.

↓ In 2013/14, prices expenditure nearly doubled from 1989/90–2009/10.

Case study 2

Extract C: Cars of the future

A recent Forbes article outlined the following emerging technologies as some that will change the automobile industry in the next 5 years.

1 **Comprehensive vehicle tracking** – insurance companies, and some state governments, are already talking about fees based on how many miles a person drives. By 2020 insurance companies will offer a reduced rate for drivers who agree to full tracking of their behaviour.

2 **Active health monitoring** – for example, seatbelt or steering wheel sensors that track vital statistics. Combine this with basic autonomous technology and you've got a car that can pull over and call paramedics when the driver has a heart attack.

3 **Smart/personalised in-car marketing** – by 2020 the average car will be fully connected to the internet, meaning your vehicle will provide marketers with a powerful set of metrics to customise their message. Hopefully these will manifest as an opt-in feature, but get ready for personalised, location-based ads in your car's display.

Extract D: UK Economic Forecast

The Bank of England is likely to keep interest rates on hold until the middle of next year rather than raising them sooner, following a gloomier outlook for the global economy, according to the economic forecaster CEBR.

The Centre for Economics and Business Research now believes a rise in May or August 2016 to around 1% is likely. Signs of a global economic slowdown have been growing in recent weeks, especially in the world's second-largest economy China and emerging markets. The UK's performance may not be sustainable if economies elsewhere continue to struggle. However, the Office for Budget Responsibility expects growth to remain above 2% between 2017 and 2020.

Choosing strategic direction 1

Strategic direction will involve a business choosing which markets it will operate in and which products it will provide. Strategic direction is important because the external environment is constantly changing and businesses must develop and compete in areas that make the best use of their strengths and core competencies.

The Ansoff matrix

The Ansoff matrix is a strategic tool that businesses can use to help choose the market they wish to operate in and the products they will sell within that market. The model offers four distinct strategies based on the products' degree of newness and the firm's understanding/ experience of the market.

The Ansoff matrix provides a useful framework, but there are always degrees of newness, and a decision might not fit nicely into one strategic option.

	Existing products	New products
Existing markets	marketing penetration	product development
New markets	marketing development	diversification

Market penetration

Market penetration involves a business increasing its market share in an existing market without the need for significant investment or risk.

A strategy to boost sales of current products in the current market. →

Possible approaches
- increase promotional activities
- change pricing model if product is price sensitive
- build brand image
- focus on increasing repeat purchase by developing customer loyalty
- incentivise customer affiliations

→

Benefits
👍 low risk
👍 product and market are familiar to the business
👍 limited investment required

Limitations
👎 possibly limited growth potential
👎 business becomes vulnerable if it does not innovate

Product development

Product development allows a business to introduce new products to a market to improve competitiveness, encourage repeat purchase and, therefore, customer loyalty.

Develop new products for existing customers. →

Possible approaches
- conduct market research with existing customers to identify areas for improvement / innovation
- use product portfolio tools to manage product range, e.g. Boston Consulting Group Matrix
- divert funds into R&D and product development

→

Benefits
👍 familiar with customers
👍 builds on / innovates current products

Limitations
👎 product development takes time and can be expensive
👎 product cannibalisation

Now try this

1 What are the four strategic options presented by the Ansoff matrix?

2 Why is market penetration low risk?

3 What are the benefits of a product development strategy?

Choosing strategic direction 2

Market development

Market development allows a business to enter new customer markets with an existing product or slightly modified product, increasing sales potential.

Take existing products into new market segments (demographic or geographic). →

Possible approaches
- use of penetration pricing to enter new market
- heavy promotion targeting new customers
- strategic alliance or takeover of a business already operating in the market
- develop new channels of distribution to reach new customers, such as an international agent

→

Benefits
- 👍 potential for considerable growth
- 👍 no need for expensive product development

Limitations
- 🚩 limited understanding of new customers' needs
- 🚩 competing against established businesses

Diversification

Diversification allows a business to utilise its core competencies to move into totally new areas of business, often by leveraging the value of its brand.

Offer new products to new customers in a new market. →

Possible approaches
- This strategy often applies to conglomerates with considerable financial power and economies of scale. This power might allow them to adopt such a strategy.
- Business may have a particular asset (such as a patent) that allows them to be competitive without having particular expertise.
- This strategy could be achieved through external growth – merger or a takeover.

→

Benefits
- 👍 spreads the business risk by engaging in different markets
- 👍 business can utilise some of its core competencies and apply them to a new context

Limitations
- 🚩 can be extremely high risk
- 🚩 no reputation or expertise in the market

Choosing a strategy

The expected cost – product development and diversification are likely to be considerably more expensive than the other strategies.

Stakeholders – apart from financial returns a business will consider the impact of its strategy on its stakeholders.

Anticipated returns – a business will conduct investment appraisal in order to consider the potential reward of the strategy.

Factors to consider

Risk aversion – the willingness of the owners/managers to take risks.

Core competencies – a business will look to choose a strategy that makes use of the strengths and advantages possessed by the business.

External environment – could new legislation in a market make a strategy less attractive?

Now try this

1 When might diversification be a suitable strategic option?
2 Identify three factors a business may consider when choosing a strategic direction.

Exam skills

The following exam-style questions relate to the topics covered in Unit 3.8.1 and refer to the Right Plumbing Ltd case study on page 151.

Worked example

Explain the benefits of Right Plumbing Ltd using a market penetration strategy to expand the business. **(5 marks)**

A market penetration strategy involves targeting the same customers with the same products and services with the intention of increasing the number and value of sales. Right Plumbing Ltd may be able to do this through offering a loyalty programme to its customers. This might involve an upfront fee to cover future callouts and maintenance. The benefits of this approach are that it is a low risk strategy and it involves minimal investment. A market penetration strategy would help Right Plumbing Ltd become market leaders in the North Yorkshire region.

The student starts by defining what a market penetration strategy involves. They then go on to give an example of how this might apply to the Right Plumbing Ltd context and then explain the advantages of this strategy for the company.

Worked example

Analyse the benefits of Right Plumbing Ltd expanding its services into Lancashire. **(9 marks)**

If Right Plumbing Ltd were to expand into Lancashire this would be an example of market development. This is because it would be offering the same service in a different geographical location.

One benefit of this approach is that Jeremy has built up a very good reputation for having excellent service and fast response times. This is very important in the plumbing industry and something that he could heavily promote to potential new customers. However, as his business is not already established in the county, it is likely that he will face stiff competition who will try to make it difficult for Right Plumbing Ltd to enter the market.

Another benefit is that expanding into Lancashire would avoid the very expensive investment in renewable energy. Recruiting a further 10 plumbers will take time and money, but it will be much cheaper than a £110,000 investment in an area in which he has little experience.

Note that this question does not require the student to evaluate and make a choice. However, the student has explained that expansion into Lancashire would be an example of market development. They have then applied this concept by explaining the benefits for Right Plumbing Ltd using this approach. Context is present throughout and the student has shown balance by identifying the limitations too.

Porter's strategies 1

Strategic positioning will involve a business choosing how it intends to compete within a market. Strategic positioning involves deciding on the right mix of product features/benefits and matching this against price. The aim of a business will be to strategically position itself differently from its competition.

Porter's strategies

Michael Porter suggested that a business should follow one of three positioning strategies in order to compete within its market. Essentially, Porter maintained that companies compete either on:

- price (cost leadership) or
- perceived value (differentiation) or
- by focusing on a very specific customer (market segmentation).

These strategies are identified in the diagram to the right and explained below. Porter believed that a business must have a distinguishable focus in order to compete with rivals. The strategies are based around the source of the competitive advantage and the scope within the market.

	Strategic advantage	
	uniqueness perceived by the customer	low cost position
Strategic target — particular industrywide	differentiation	overall cost leadership
segment only	focus	

Cost leadership strategy

Achieve an advantage by being the lowest cost operator in the market.

Ways to achieve the strategy
- operate at a scale that keeps average costs low
- achieve economies of scale through growth
- have unique access to technology
- have unique access to skills or raw materials
- control the supply of a product

Benefits
- 👍 Cost leadership strategy can help to achieve high profit margins as cost per unit is kept low.
- 👍 It can maintain market price and gain higher profit margins (parity).
- 👍 It can lower price and acquire market share (proximity).

Limitations
- 👎 Few businesses can operate as the cost-leader within a market as multiple businesses cannot directly compete on cost.

Differentiation strategy

Compete by offering a unique product or service to the market or a niche.

Basis for differentiation might include:
- quality
- customer service
- brand personality
- customer experience
- after sales service
- speed and efficiency
- meeting the unique needs of a specific market niche.

Benefits
- 👍 It can make the business stand out.
- 👍 Differentiation helps develop a unique brand image.
- 👍 Differentiation adds value (special or unique) and therefore higher prices can be charged.

Limitations
- 👎 Other businesses may be able to copy the strategy if it is not sustainable or defensible, e.g. a product is defensible if it is under copyright.

Now try this

1 How can a business achieve cost leadership?

2 How might a business differentiate its product?

Porter's strategies 2

Segmentation strategy

Segmentation can be achieved through either cost leadership or differentiation. It involves targeting a specific group of customers (niche) and not the whole market.

→ Both cost leadership and differentiation can be achieved through targeting the whole market or a specific segment or niche. The basis of the segment could be its unique needs, geographic or demographic characteristics or a specialist product or service.

→ **Benefits**
👍 It is easier to target a narrow segment of the market as communications and marketing can be focused.
👍 It is possible to develop a better understanding of customer needs as the segment has narrower interests, needs and characteristics.

Limitations
👎 Customer loyalty is vital if sales are to be maintained – every customer counts.
👎 The market may disappear (or no longer be a viable option) if it shrinks in size.

 **Walmart**

Walmart is the USA's largest retail chain and is one example of a company that adopts a cost leadership strategy. The company targets a broad market with everyday low prices. Walmart sells brands targeted at a mass market where customers are price sensitive. The scale on which Walmart operates allows it to achieve economies of scale that few other businesses can compete with. Walmart's subsidiary in the UK is ASDA..

 Whole Foods Market

Whole Foods Market is another supermarket chain in the USA that focuses on selling natural and organic products. A sizable number of customers in the USA are willing to pay a premium in order to feel better about the foods they are buying. Whole Foods adopts a differentiation strategy as it targets a mass market, but utilises organic high-quality produce as a factor to distinguish it from other supermarket retailers.

📝 **Exam focus** **Applying Porter's strategies**

Applying Porter's strategies to a case study can help you demonstrate business knowledge and provide structure to your analysis. For example, understanding the size of a business, its core competencies (or strengths) and the market it operates in can allow you to identify the strategy it is using and the value of adopting that strategy. For example, it would be inappropriate for a business to adopt a cost-leadership strategy (competing on price) if it operates on a small scale and is unable to achieve economies of scale.

Now try this

1 Why is customer loyalty important with a segmentation strategy?
2 What is a niche market?

Bowman's strategic clock

Bowman's strategic clock

Similar to Porter's strategies is the strategic clock developed by Bowman. The model considers a wider variety of strategic positions based on the value of a product compared to its price. Bowman's strategic clock also identifies strategies (those in the bottom right hand corner of the clock) that are only competitive in certain situations.

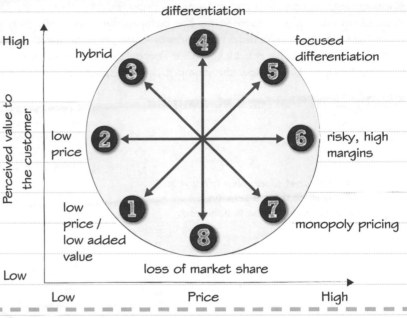

Bowman's eight strategic positions

1 Budget or 'no frills' products – for example, Poundland sell low value products at a low price.

2 Excellent value (similar to cost leadership with proximity). Businesses compete through economies of scale – for example, Walmart operates on a large scale and achieves low costs through economies of scale.

3 Hybrid – companies offer fair prices for reasonable products (middle of the road operators). For example, Ford cars are good quality with a range of features, but priced for the mass market.

4 Differentiation – without price premium. High perceived value possibly through effective branding – for example, Hollister targets a teenage market with a desirable brand, allowing it to charge a higher price.

5 Focused differentiation – premium products where customers may expect to pay high prices for status. For example, Rolex watches differentiate themselves on quality, but target the top end of the market.

6 High margins – short-term strategy to achieve high margins without justified value. For example, selling a product to an uninformed customer or buying a Bluetooth music speaker without understanding the features associated with audio quality.

7 Monopoly pricing – a captive market where customers have no choice or alternative. For example, motorway services where customers have limited or no choice.

8 A non-competitive product – value/benefits do not justify the price. These products may still sell if customers have no choice or are unable to experience/test the product first.

Now try this

1 What is Bowman's strategic clock?

2 How does Bowman's strategic clock differ from Porter's strategies?

3 Why are some of the strategies Bowman identified risky?

Comparing strategic positions

Another way to compare the strategies proposed by Porter and Bowman is to use the graph below. The line dissecting each graph represents the competitive threshold. Any position below the competitive threshold represents a strategy where the price or cost position for the business does not justify the benefits or perceived value of the product. Unlike Porter, Bowman's strategic clock identifies strategies that may be successful operating below the competitive threshold in certain circumstances.

Analysis of Porter's strategies

Costs may be higher than the average competitor but the perceived value and unique features add considerable value to achieve a desirable profit margin. This can be achieved in a mass market or niche market.

Similar to cost leadership (parity) in that lower costs are achieved. However, higher value is achieved.

Perceived value may be the same as the average competitor, but by being able to achieve lower costs the business achieves higher profit margins.

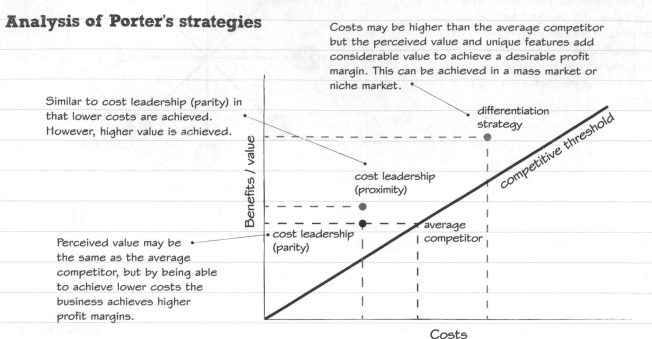

Bowman's strategic clock analysis

Companies successfully positioning themselves here are likely to gain market share, but this might not be sustainable in the long term.

Some products can achieve a very high price point through perceived value and the prestige of the brand.

Strategies used by a business to enter a market or by those able to keep costs low through a competitive advantage or economies of scale.

The diagrams represent the similarities between Porter's strategies and Bowman's strategic clock. The key differences being that Porter identified a relatively narrow range of options, whereas Bowman believed businesses could hold a wider range of strategic positions. The theories also differ in that Porter focused on costs whereas Bowman considers a price point.

These strategies are not viable in a competitive market where customers are educated and have access to information about products.

Benefits / value

- differentiation (no price premium)
- differentiation (focused)
- hybrid strategy
- penetration strategy
- risky high margins
- low value / low price
- monopoly pricing
- loss of market share
- competitive threshold

Price

The value of strategic positioning

There are a number of factors that may influence the position a business chooses within its market.

External environment – for example, commodity prices (an increase in price may limit a business's ability to be cost-leader) and social trends (if a clothing company focuses on a certain fashion style, this can quickly lose popularity) may determine whether certain positions are attractive or feasible.

The position of competitors – the principle of positioning is that businesses should aim for a unique position so that they are not competing 'head on' with a rival, for example Next Home will avoid direct competition with Ikea.

Influences on strategic position

Core competencies – a business will base its position on its relative strengths, for example, a business that has developed a strong brand image for high quality.

Strategic positioning over time

The business environment is constantly changing. Customer needs change as do economic conditions along with the competitive environment. Over the past few years the growth of budget supermarkets such as Lidl and Aldi have made market leaders like Tesco reconsider their strategy of cost leader by being able to offer fewer but cheaper prices along with customers' desire for value for money. Sometimes a business will have to change its strategic position, (for example from cost leadership to differentiation) but this is not easy as businesses build a reputation and brand for offering a certain type of product at a certain price.

The value of strategic positioning

Strategic positioning helps businesses develop a USP and basis for differentiation. Without strategic positioning  the only way that a business can compete is on a price basis. We see this in generic markets where there is no difference between products. Therefore, strategic positioning also helps businesses to maximise profitability and avoid direct competition. The value of various strategic positions has been discussed in this topic.

When Dyson first entered the market with its bagless vacuum cleaners, this helped it differentiate its product against other vacuum cleaners, giving it a unique strategic position within the market.

Competitive advantage

Competitive advantage exists where a business creates value for its customers that is greater than the costs of supplying those benefits and that is greater than that offered by competitors. A sustainable competitive advantage can only be achieved through three areas of practice:

1 **Innovation** – the ability of a business to create new and unique processes and products. These can sometimes be legally protected through a patent.

2 **Architecture** – this refers to the relationships within a business that create synergy and understanding between suppliers, customers and the employees of a business.

3 **Reputation** – brand values are hard to replicate and may take years to develop.

Each factor can lead to a **sustainable competitive advantage** because they are all unique, not easily copied and may take a long time to achieve. Competitive advantage gives a business a basis for competition and a way of adding value that other businesses cannot imitate – a reason for customers to choose the business over its rivals. However, over time each of the factors above can gradually erode, such as relationships in a business as the workforce changes over time or as a valuable patent expires.

Now try this

1 Identify two factors that may influence the strategic position a business takes.

2 Why might the strategic position of a business change over time?

3 How can a business achieve a sustainable competitive advantage?

Exam skills

The following exam-style questions relate to the topics covered in Unit 3.8.2 and refer to the Right Plumbing Ltd case study on page 151.

Worked example

Explain the benefits of Right Plumbing Ltd using a differentiation strategy to compete in the market.

(5 marks)

A differentiation strategy involves a business identifying a unique feature of the business or product to develop and promote. For Right Plumbing Ltd, this might be its fast response times. By promoting itself as the business with the fastest response times, customers will value this and as a result Right Plumbing Ltd could charge a higher price for this benefit.

> The student has started by explaining what a differentiation strategy is. They have not explained that the theory belongs to Michael Porter, but this does not matter as they have shown good understanding and explained the benefits in context of Right Plumbing Ltd.

Worked example

Analyse the reasons why Right Plumbing Ltd might want to set a price point somewhere in the middle of the market.

(9 marks)

Right Plumbing Ltd might set its prices in the middle of the market because it feels that this price range is justified given its target market and the service it provides. If the price set is appropriate to the service then customers will feel as though they are receiving suitable value for their money. Furthermore, this price might meet the needs of the customers in the local area in terms of their household incomes.

Another reason why Right Plumbing Ltd might set a 'middle of the road' price is to gain market share from its competitors. Right Plumbing Ltd has a very good reputation for providing fast response times. Customers value this in a plumber and they might be willing to pay a premium for this service. However, using Bowman's strategic clock we can see that a differentiation strategy without a price premium is a competitive positioning strategy that a business might use. If Right Plumbing Ltd adopts this strategy it could place itself in a unique position within its local plumbing market.

> In your business exams it is important to think about the theories and concepts you have studied and how these can be used to help you answer a question. The student could have approached this question from a number of angles, such as referring to Porter or Ansoff, but they have decided to use the concept of the strategic clock to analyse pricing decisions for Right Plumbing Ltd. This is appropriate, as it allows the student to analyse the issues in the question. It is not always feasible to discuss every theory in an answer, so it is important to select the most relevant concepts that are applicable to the question and the context.

Exam-style practice

The following exam-style questions relate to the topics covered in Unit 3.8 and refer to the Right Plumbing Ltd case study below. There are answers on page 201.

1 Explain one factor that may influence the strategy of Right Plumbing Ltd.

(5 marks)

> Think PEST.

2 Analyse the value of Right Plumbing Ltd using a strategic positioning strategy.

(9 marks)

> Or, what are the benefits of Right Plumbing Ltd positioning itself in a different position to its competitors?

3 To what extent is diversification an appropriate strategic direction for Right Plumbing Ltd?

(16 marks)

> Remember that diversification is a high-risk strategy.

4 Evaluate the factors that may contribute to Right Plumbing Ltd gaining a sustainable competitive advantage.

(20 marks)

> For this question you could consider the three principles of sustainable competitive advantage: 1. architecture 2. innovation 3. reputation.

🔍 **Case study**

Right Plumbing Ltd

Right Plumbing Ltd is a successful domestic plumbing business that has been established for 5 years. The company has grown in the North Yorkshire region and now employs over 25 full time independent contractors.

In 2015 Right Plumbing Ltd won a local business award for excellence in customer service. The company has also built up a reputation for having the best response rates for emergency callouts and this has been documented in a number of local press articles.

Jeremy Stokes, the managing director, is looking to expand the business and has considered a number of options. The first is to expand across the Pennines into parts of Lancashire. Jeremy anticipates that this will require recruitment of at least another 10 employees, who he would personally recruit. The initial workforce of 20 plumbers had been contacts he had made during his 15 years in the industry and the new venture would require him to look further afield.

The second option for Jeremy is to move into installing renewable energy systems such as solar panels and wind turbines into homes around North Yorkshire. Jeremy has little experience with this technology but believes it will be a key market 5 years down the line, with considerable growth potential. Jeremy anticipates that this second option will require an investment of £110,000.

Assessing a change in scale 1

Growth is an important objective for many businesses. Business growth can create greater wealth for the owners. It can also leverage a number of benefits and opportunities for the business that may not be available to smaller organisations.

Ways a business can grow

A business has a number of options when it is looking to grow.

Organic growth is steady and gradual, whereas **external growth** is very sudden and can bring about significant change in an organisation. For this reason organic growth is a lower risk option, but external growth offers the opportunity for fast expansion but with the risk of clashes in the way the two businesses that have been joined together operate.

Synergies – when 2 + 2 = 5. External growth can bring businesses together that complement one another's strengths. For example, one business could be extremely innovative whilst another might have the financial power to support investment in R&D. Synergies may not occur where there is a clash of cultures.

Economies of scope – operating with a wide variety of products in a number of markets creates benefits through reduced costs which are shared across the different product lines and spreading the risk of any one product failing. Nevertheless, widening a business's scope may lead to a loss of focus on any particular product or market and potentially poor performance.

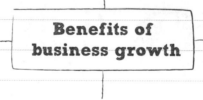

Benefits of business growth

Economies of scale (see below)

The experience curve – big businesses typically have more experience than smaller businesses. They have made mistakes and have gained knowledge and experience that smaller businesses simply don't have. However, big businesses can sometimes become complacent – this happened to M&S in the mid 1990s and more recently Blackberry.

> See Units 3.10.1 and 3.10.2 for issues a business may face as it grows and factors it will have to consider when managing growth – change management.

Economies of scale

Economies of scale occur when unit costs fall as a business expands – these are the advantages of size. There are a number of specific benefits a business gains as it grows in size:

- 👍 **purchasing economies** – bulk buying
- 👍 **technological economies** – larger businesses can invest in the best technology
- 👍 **financial** – larger businesses have more collateral and can raise more capital (especially if Plc)
- 👍 **managerial** – larger business can employ specialists to manage a particular aspect of the business.

Now try this

1 What is the difference between organic and external growth?
2 What are economies of scope?
3 What are financial economies of scale?

Assessing a change in scale 2

The benefits and drawbacks of growth

Economies of scale result in unit costs falling as the business grows in size. However, at a certain point the business will start to experience diseconomies of scale. Here unit costs will start to rise as the business starts to lose some of the efficiencies it gained from growth.

For many businesses there is an optimal size where they are able to operate efficiently. Furthermore, large businesses can lose some of the advantages they had when they were smaller.

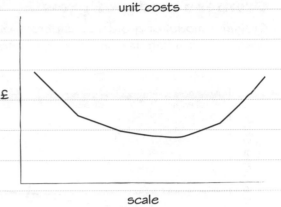

Diseconomies of scale

Diseconomies of scale occur when unit costs rise as a business expands – these are the disadvantages of size. There are a number of specific problems a business might face as it grows:

- **Communication problems** – it becomes harder to communicate a clear message across the organisation.

- **Control** – in order to control the organisation layers of management are added. This slows down decision making and quality becomes harder to monitor.

- **Flexibility** – due to the issues of communication and control the business may be less flexible in its ability to adapt to the changing business environment.

- **Motivation** – workers in large organisations find it difficult to see the impact they have and feel less significant.

Overtrading

Overtrading occurs when businesses grow too fast and overstretch their financial resources, such as cash. A business may also face logistical problems if it cannot manage operations. Overtrading can lead to business failure.

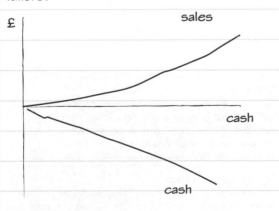

Retrenchment

There may be times when a business needs to reduce its scale. This may be to counteract the problems of diseconomies of scale or to improve efficiency and reduce costs as demand falls, perhaps as a result of a downturn in the economic climate.

Retrenchment may involve:

- redundancies
- closure of branches
- discontinuing product lines
- pulling out of international markets
- delayering
- reallocating business resources
- cancelling expansion plans
- outsourcing aspects of the business's operations.

Now try this

1 Identify two diseconomies of scale.

2 What are the problems associated with overtrading?

Managing growth

Greiner's model of growth

Greiner's model of growth considers some of the issues a business might face as it grows in scale. The model can help managers predict and plan for different issues as the business grows.

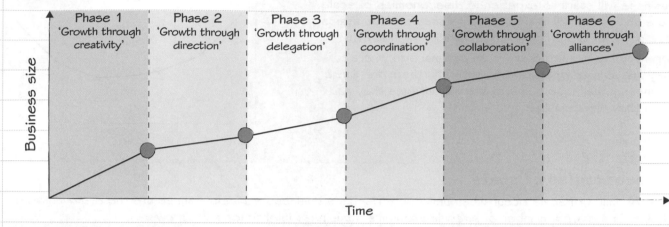

Phase 1	Phase 2	Phase 3	Phase 4	Phase 5	Phase 6
Informal business practices. Business driven by creativity and all employees understand the impact they have on the business. Rules are not clear.	**Leadership crisis** – as the business grows some tasks may get missed or jobs will be duplicated. At some point, clear direction is needed along with leadership.	**Autonomy crisis** – as the business grows, there is a need for more delegation as managers desire autonomy to make their own decisions and respond to localised issues.	**Crisis of control** – as the business continues to grow, directors may feel that they are losing control of some aspects of the business and they worry about strategic direction.	**Red tape crisis** – as the leaders put in place systems and mechanisms of control, bureaucracy leads to inefficiencies and a distraction from the core business activities.	**Growth crisis** – as the business reaches its potential for internal growth it may look for growth through external collaboration. This brings with it a new set of dilemmas.

The model demonstrates the conflicting forces managers will face as a business grows. Mainly there are fluctuations between controlling the business and providing autonomy to maximise employee potential and adapt to specific needs.

Impact on business functions

Marketing
As businesses grow they will launch new products and move into new markets. Marketing must ensure that the business understands the needs of its new customers and effectively promotes the new ventures.

Finance
As businesses grow cash flow is essential. Furthermore, Finance should identify the capital investment required to finance growth and find suitable sources of financing.

Operations
Operations will look to maximise capacity and put in place systems to manage increased production and sales. Operations may also need to find additional capacity to cope with expansion.

Human resources
As businesses grow, so will the workforce. Human resources will recruit and train the new employees.

Now try this

1 How might Greiner's growth model help a manager plan for expansion?

2 How might growth affect the operation function of a business?

Types and methods of growth

Takeover – also known as acquisition, which may be hostile or voluntary. One business will acquire another along with its assets. If hostile, the takeover is riskier for the acquiring business.

Methods of external growth

Franchise – growth through selling the rights of the business (name, product, assets) to a third party (franchisee) who will run the business independently following the business model. The franchisee will pay a percentage of revenue. Requires little effort or investment but requires close monitoring.

Joint venture – two businesses come together to work on a particular project such as a product launch. Information and expertise will be shared but the businesses will remain separate, removing the problems of integrating two businesses.

Merger – two businesses come together for mutual benefit. This may be to share strengths or with the purpose of business survival. The business will seek synergies through the merger.

Method of growth and level of control

Where growth occurs through a takeover/acquisition there is more likely to be resistance from employees, customers and shareholders if they believe their own interests may be damaged – such as loss of jobs.

takeover	franchise	merger	joint venture

High control / influence   Low control / influence

Types of growth

A number of options are available to a business looking to externally grow through a takeover, merger or joint venture.

Backwards vertical
taking over a supplier such as a tree farm

Horizontal
merging with a business at the same level of the supply chain such as another Christmas tree wholesaler

Conglomerate
taking over an unused business in a different market such as a jewellery retailer

Christmas tree wholesaler

Forwards vertical
taking over a customer such as a retailer that sells Christmas trees

---

Now try this

1 Why might a business choose a joint venture over an acquisition?

2 Why is franchising a popular means of external growth for a business?

3 Why might a business choose to take over a supplier?

Exam skills

The following exam-style questions relate to the topics covered in Unit 3.9.1 and refer to the Cloudburst Plc case study on page 167.

Worked example

Which of the following is an example of forwards vertical integration?

A A consumer electronics company acquiring a clothing company ◯

B A clothing manufacturer taking over a supplier of fabric ◯

C A consumer electronics company merging with another electronics company ◯

D A clothing manufacturer taking over a clothing retailer ⬤

(1 mark)

> Option D is the only answer where the business is involved with a business further along the supply chain.

Worked example

Analyse the benefits for Cloudburst Plc of expanding into new markets. **(9 marks)**

...As Cloudburst Plc enters new markets it will be increasing its scale by creating more computer games, apps and software. As the business grows it will experience economies of scale. For example, technological economies. As the business is a technology company it will be able to invest in the latest gaming technology, which it may not have been able to do if it was a smaller company. This may give it a competitive advantage over other software developers through developing innovative games in the future...

> This is a rather open question and the student could consider the answer from a number of perspectives. In this extract the student has discussed economies of scale and applied this to the Cloudburst Plc context. The student could also discuss some of the benefits of external growth relating to the plans Cloudburst Plc has to merge/take over associated businesses.

Worked example

To what extent will Cloudburst Plc experience synergies through the acquisition of Interact Gaming Ltd?

(16 marks)

...As Interact Gaming Ltd is in a different market to Cloudburst Plc it is possible that its expertise might complement that of Cloudburst Plc. Cloudburst Plc is also looking to use a product development strategy and Interact may provide it with fresh ideas and the experience to develop apps for mobile devices. The two businesses will experience synergies if their core competencies complement one another and the two companies can easily integrate their processes and systems. For example, the way decisions are made within each business...

> This question requires the student to use the case study to explain the synergies a business might experience through joining with another company. The student has understood the issues in the case study well and applied them to the concept of synergy. The student might now go on to explain the problems associated with external growth and how this could limit the potential synergies.

Assessing innovation 1

Innovation involves a business developing new products and processes to create products or distribute them to customers. Innovation through product development creates benefits for customers. Process innovation can also help a business become more efficient. Both types of innovation increase competitiveness and this is why many businesses have to continually innovate.

The pressures of innovation

There are significant pressures for a business to continually innovate. We can explore these reasons using the PEST-C model:

- **Political change** – may alter regulations around products which open up new opportunities or force businesses to amend current products to meet the new requirements.
- **Economic change** – in an economic downturn there is pressure for businesses to improve efficiency and lower costs.
- **Social change** – trends and tastes are continually developing, meaning businesses have to keep up with consumer expectations.
- **Technological change** – as new technologies are developed, businesses face the challenge of keeping up to date in order to compete.
- **Competitive change** – as competitors innovate, businesses must be able to match this innovation if they are going to maintain market share.

Innovative organisations

A business might adopt a number of techniques or policies in order to encourage innovative practices.

The leadership within a business must set innovation as a priority, link innovation to the corporate objectives and make resources available to support it.

A business must have a culture of innovation. These issues must be accepted and encouraged within the company.

Culture — acceptance of failure, innovation is rewarded, listening to all shareholders, sharing is commonplace

Leadership supports innovation

Kaizen
(continuous improvement) – Kaizen groups meet regularly to discuss and develop incremental improvements that can be applied across the organisation. Kaizen brings together workers from across the organisation to work together on improvement.

Research and development
In innovative organisations a considerable amount of money will be invested in research and development. Indeed, research and development may be built into an employee's working week. For example, Google once were claimed to give employees 20% of their working time to work on creative projects.

Intrapreneurship
Individuals are given time within their working week to develop their own ideas and work on innovative projects. 'Intrapreneurs' are then given support and authority to implement their ideas. This encourages the development of intellectual property.

Benchmarking
Managers may set a target based on best practice or a shining example from a similar business. This is then set as the standard that the business must aim to achieve. Benchmarking works well where there is collaboration between businesses or within an industry.

Now try this

1 Why is there pressure on businesses to keep innovating?
2 What factors might contribute towards an innovative business culture?

Assessing innovation 2

The value of innovation

A business may improve competitiveness through better quality, faster delivery, lower costs or improved service. Innovation can directly influence each of these. Furthermore, without innovation a business will lose ground on its competitors, leading to a loss of market share and possible failure.

Innovation may provide a business with a competitive advantage, but may also be a threshold requirement for it simply to maintain its place.

Problem with innovation

It is possible for a business to spend too much time focused on innovation. Potential issues include:

- Innovation is constant change – sometimes a business might need to get good at what it does instead of going through a constant cycle of change.

- Innovation is no guarantee of success – time and resources can be wasted if innovation is not successful.

- First mover advantage – innovation can be expensive and other businesses can sometimes copy and reap similar benefits.

Protecting innovation

A number of options are open to a business when trying to protect its innovations such as designs, inventions, intellectual property and creative content.

1. **patent** – protects inventions and products if registration is successful

2. **copyright** – literary work and creative content – no need for registration

3. **trademark** – product name, logo and jingles – registration required

4. **design rights** – on styles, shapes and objects – no need for registration.

Disruptive innovation

Disruptive innovation occurs where innovation considerably alters a market. For example, digital photography or music downloads.

Disruptive innovation can cause significant problems for businesses as they have to make the choice between adopting new technology, processes and products or sticking with what they know. At these times disruptive innovation can result in some big questions being asked and major change within businesses.

What impact do you think Ebook readers have had on the strategic decisions of bookshops?

The impact on business functions

Marketing
Marketing must provide the drive for innovation within a business by identifying the needs of customers.

Finance
Finance must make a long-term commitment to innovation through investment in R&D. Profits may also need to be retained in order to finance growth through innovation.

Operations
Operations managers may be responsible for developing new products or implementing process innovation to improve efficiency and reduce costs.

Human resources
Job design and working practices must encourage employees to be innovative. For example, giving employees the opportunity for job enrichment and rewarding innovative ideas put forward by employees.

Now try this

1 Why might disruptive innovation cause concerns for a business?

2 Why should all businesses try to innovate?

3 How might a business protect the design of a new product?

Exam skills

The following exam-style questions relate to the topics covered in Unit 3.9.2 and refer to the Cloudburst Plc case study on page 167.

Worked example

1 Cloudburst Plc is looking into taking out a patent on a piece of coding it used to write its latest computer game.

The main purpose of a patent is to:

A make it easier for Cloudburst Plc to innovate in the future ⦿

B ensure that Cloudburst Plc gets repeat purchases ⦿

C limit the number of people who can copy the computer game ⦿

D register a new invention so that Cloudburst Plc has sole rights to its use. ⬤

(1 mark)

> Option D is the only answer which involves registering a product or invention in order to prevent other businesses from copying it.

2 To what extent is it important for Cloudburst Plc to continuously innovate in the computer games industry?

(20 marks)

> The word 'continuously' in this question is significant. It might be important for a business to innovate, but should it continuously innovate? The student might discuss some of the limitations and risks associated with innovation in their answer.

Innovation in the computer gaming industry may involve bringing out new games on a regular basis or developing technology to improve the processes by which Cloudburst Plc makes its games.

The computer game market is very competitive and new games are brought out each year. Furthermore, customers do not stick with one game for long, so products have a relatively short life-cycle. For this reason Cloudburst Plc must develop new games in order to keep up with the demands of customers. Computer games are also developing all the time and Cloudburst Plc must also innovate in order to improve the experience of customers when playing its games.

However, Cloudburst Plc became successful through a very popular product. This is a cash cow for the business and may continue to make it significant revenue. There is also no guarantee that investment in new games and technology will be successful. Indeed, innovation is very expensive and a high-risk strategy for a business that already has a number of very successful products.

The key issue in the case of Cloudburst Plc is that it operates in a technology based industry where innovation is constantly pushing game design forward. For this reason Cloudburst Plc would be naïve not to invest in innovation, but it must also maximise the potential of current products. The need for innovation might depend on the competitive environment, such as a new console being launched or a competitor launching a desirable new game. Overall, the merger with Interact Gaming Ltd might be the best way to remain competitive as this company already has a strong track record for innovation.

> This is a complete student response to this question. The student has used business concepts very well in their answer. The analysis is also well developed and it is rooted in the Cloudburst Plc context.
>
> The evaluation is effective and finishes with a recommendation linked to the case study.

Checklist for a good essay:

☐ Key terms defined and used

☐ Key issues from case study applied

☐ All points clearly explained

☐ Financial data applied and interpreted

☐ Analysis is well developed

☐ Balance shown by considering benefits and limitations

☐ Alternative perspectives and / or approaches considered

☐ Evaluation answers the question

☐ Clear justification using the key issues in the case

☐ Use of the 'depends on' rule

☐ Recommendations given where appropriate

Assessing internationalisation 1

The world is a shrinking place and it is not only large businesses that are now able to operate on an international scale as operating in international markets becomes easier and cheaper. Internationalisation brings with it many opportunities for businesses as well as a number of threats.

The forces for and against internationalisation

There are a number of incentives and risks for businesses operating in international markets.

For

- improvements in transportation
- Improvements in communication
- trade agreements including customs unions such as EU, NAFTA, ASEAN
- opportunity to target a larger population and enter new geographical markets
- the need to counteract foreign competition

internationalisation

Against

- reliability when dealing with some international businesses and shipping companies
- existence of trade barriers such as quotas and tariffs between some countries
- issues of dealing with local trends and customs
- language barriers

A tariff is a tax placed on foreign goods and services. A quota is a limit on the number of imported goods and services.

Methods of entering international markets

Exporting
Produces domestically but ships products abroad. Lowest risk strategy but may have to deal with protectionist measures imposed by foreign countries.

Direct investment (set-up abroad)
Involves investing overseas into production facilities, retail and distribution facilities. Can be highly profitable but capital intensive – firm becomes a **multinational**.

Licensing
Giving the rights to a foreign country to produce goods / services for a foreign market. This gains an insight into new markets as a test, but responsibility for sales passes to another business.

Alliances
Partnership with a foreign firm. Risk is shared as well as expertise of operating in the foreign market. Profits are shared with partner.

Benefits of MNCs
- better access to local markets
- may receive tax incentives from local government
- costs of production (e.g. labour costs) can be lower
- operating in multiple countries spreads the risk.

Multinational companies (MNCs)
A business with production in more than one country. MNCs are often welcomed by foreign governments (including the UK) because they create jobs, bringing investment to the country and increase tax revenue.

Drawbacks of MNCs
- harder to manage business across countries – time zones, legislation, consistency
- attention taken away from home markets
- some multinationals are criticised for damaging local traditions and taking trade away from local businesses.

Now try this

1 Why do some firms choose to operate in international markets?

2 How does internationalisation relate to the Ansoff matrix?

3 What options are open to a business looking to expand abroad?

Assessing internationalisation 2

Assessing the attractiveness of international markets

Some businesses might consider the following when choosing which international markets are viable options.

size and growth potential   barriers to entry

alignment with the business's corporate strategy

Which international market?

similarities to / differences from home market

competitive rivalry within the market   PEST-C factors

Pressures for internationalisation

There are considerable pressures for a business to expand internationally. These include:

- The pressure for growth – growth leads to greater profitability, a key driver of shareholder value.

- The pressure to lower costs – manufacturing abroad can be cheaper, mainly due to the lower labour costs.

- Location – businesses may need to have close proximity to resources and skilled labour. This can speed up transportation and lower transport costs.

- Declining domestic markets – to continue growth businesses may seek opportunities in international markets.

Reasons for outsourcing and re-shoring

Outsourcing is where businesses move production overseas and re-shoring is where production is moved back to the domestic country. See below for reasons for moving production abroad and reasons for moving production back to the UK.

- lower costs
- closer to resources
- lower distribution costs
- avoids barriers to trade

- pressure to support local employment
- better quality can be achieved domestically

The Bartlett and Ghoshal matrix

The Bartlett and Ghoshal matrix considers the different approaches a business might take towards internationalisation. The matrix considers two variables: the level of responsiveness to local markets and the drive for a standardised global product.

Global – a standardised product sold around the world.

International – products produced for the domestic market with some slight alterations for international markets – perhaps to meet national standards.

National responsiveness

	low	high
Global integration — high	global strategy	transnational strategy
Global integration — low	international strategy	multi-domestic strategy

Transnational – highly responsive to local markets but business is highly integrated sharing knowledge and expertise.

Multi-domestic – products and services tailored for local markets; subsidies may operate independently of one another affiliated to the brand.

Now try this

1 Identify three factors a business might consider when choosing international markets.

2 Why might a business choose to re-shore production?

3 What is the difference between a global strategy and a multi-domestic international strategy?

Assessing internationalisation 3

The issues of different international strategies

Global
Business maximises the benefits of economies of scale and efficiencies but will struggle in markets where localised needs exist.

Transnational
Business operates as one entity and there is lots of sharing and learning together. Very hard to implement effectively, but successful transnational businesses benefit from economies of scale but remain responsive to demands of local markets.

International
Business focusses on domestic markets but through slight modifications with a product to export. Gains benefits of economies but makes slight tweaks to satisfy localised needs.

Multi-domestic
A true MNC – the business is completely focused on meeting local needs through decentralisation. Highly adaptive but difficult to manage and control strategic direction of the business.

The risks of running international businesses

Anti-globalisation – anti-global pressure groups and a growing distaste for international firms in some industries can draw negative publicity for MNCs.

Ethical standards – moral codes in business are not the same across countries. Neither are legal systems to protect businesses and consumers.

Risks of internationalisation?

Cultural differences – often very subtle and form barriers to entry. In particular marketing can be very difficult in foreign markets.

Differing styles of business – often linked to cultural norms, nations negotiate and make decisions differently. This can make partnerships and trade more complicated.

The impact on business functions

Marketing
Marketing must be able to understand cultural differences and communicate effectively with customers in foreign markets. Understanding needs of foreign customers can be very challenging and may require localised expertise.

Finance
Exporting may require limited financial investment, but becoming an MNC will require significant capital investment and long-term finance.

Operations
Distribution and transportation will become a significant operational issue. The business may also have to learn to manage multiple product varieties in order to meet local needs. Maintaining economies of scale will be a key challenge.

Human resources
As with marketing, localised skills may be required to recruit and train staff. It may be necessary for managers and specialists to relocate in order to establish international production.

Now try this

1 What is the benefit of running a transnational business?
2 What are the risks of running an international business?

Exam skills

The following exam-style questions relate to the topics covered in Unit 3.9.3 and refer to the Cloudburst Plc case study on page 167.

Worked example

Explain why Cloudburst Plc might face pressure to grow internationally? **(5 marks)**

Cloudburst Plc may face pressure to grow internationally because the business is a Plc. This means that the business is owned by shareholders who may be external to the organisation. Shareholders invest in companies in order to gain a return on their investment. In order to keep shareholders happy and maintain a strong share price it will be important for Cloudburst Plc to grow and one way it can do this is to move into international markets where there is significant opportunity for market growth.

The student has applied their answer by using the ownership of the business and used this to discuss the interests of shareholders – a public limited company. This is a good way to apply your answer to the case study.

Worked example

Analyse why Cloudburst Plc may choose to outsource aspects of its production. **(9 marks)**

Outsourcing involves moving production of your business to another country. One reason that Cloudburst Plc might do this is to utilise the expertise of computer game designers abroad. For example, there may be lots of highly skilled designers in Japan. Moving production to Japan would make it easier for Cloudburst Plc to employ a specialist team of highly skilled designers and be close to other computer game production companies. This would allow it to gain external economies of scale...

The student has defined outsourcing at the start of the answer. They have then gone on to explain one of the benefits of this approach and tied this in with the Cloudburst Plc context. The second paragraph may go on to explain other benefits, such as reduced costs of production.

Worked example

To what extent is it important for Cloudburst Plc to adapt its products to meet the needs of international markets? **(16 marks)**

...However, If Cloudburst Plc is able to produce standardised games then it will be able to maximise economies of scale. This is because it will not need to make multiple versions of a game, produce and repackage them for different markets. If it was able to avoid this, it would maximise profitability by reducing average unit costs. It would also make it easier for the business to market a standardised game...

This extract provides balance to the answer. The student has already discussed the argument for adapting its products for different markets. This part of the answer provides the counter argument explaining why a 'global' strategy might also be effective.

Assessing the use of digital technology 1

Over the past 15 years digital technology has had a huge impact on the way businesses operate. Digital technology includes a range of technologies that affect all functions of a business and can be used to develop the strategic direction of a business.

Digital technologies

There are several digital technologies that are shaping strategic direction for many businesses.

 E-commerce
Continues to grow as delivery networks and collection lockers become more effective and accessible.

Benefits:
- 👍 The growth of mobile devices means online purchasing can happen anywhere and at any time.
- 👍 Prices are transparent.
- 👍 There is greater access to suppliers.
- 👍 Start-up costs are low.

Drawbacks:
- 👎 It is not suitable for all products where customers need to touch and experience the product.
- 👎 Delivery costs can be expensive.
- 👎 Lots of fraud is committed through e-commerce.

 Data mining
Data mining is a process of analysing business data to identify patterns and relationships between a number of variables. For example, demographics and buying behaviour in supermarkets.

Benefits:
- 👍 Businesses are able to profile customers and better understand their needs.
- 👍 It uses analytics to effectively target customers with offers and products that they will want.
- 👍 It accurately forecasts sales numbers based on a wide variety of data, including economic and social trends.

Drawbacks:
- 👎 It may only be valuable to large firms where a large quantity of data is available.
- 👎 Correlation of data does not necessarily mean there is a relationship.

 Big data
Closely linked to data mining, big data refers to the vast quantities of information that businesses are now able to collect through sources such as GPS data, bar code readers and social media. These huge datasets give businesses vast amounts of information to help them make decisions.

 **Enterprise resource planning**
Enterprise resource planning (ERP) is the data management software that links the functional areas of a business together such as stock ordering, customer relationship management, human resource management and financial management.

Benefits:
- 👍 ERP improves flexibility and efficiency by coordinating the functions of a business.
- 👍 It provides managers and employees with useful information on a number of business processes.
- 👍 ERP improves customer service.

Drawbacks:
- 👎 There is the cost of developing the system for businesses' specific needs (not an 'off-the-shelf' package).
- 👎 There has to be investment in training staff to effectively use the system.

Now try this

1 What is data mining?
2 Why is e-commerce not suitable for all forms of business?
3 What business processes might be integrated with ERP?

Assessing the use of digital technology 2

The impact of digital technology

When used effectively, digital technology can improve the competitiveness of a business.

faster access to information

offers new ways of doing business (paperless transactions, crowdfunding, virtual reality)

Benefits of digital technology?

knowledge management systems can replace the need for a moderate level of expertise – e.g. computer diagnosis of illnesses

better communication between employees and functions

The pressures of digital technology

Digital technology also creates a number of pressures for businesses:

- Technology can remove barriers to entry increasing the level of competition in markets.
- Technology creates transparency in markets – customers can easily compare prices and find online reviews.
- Constant change – the pace of technology is extremely fast and it can be very difficult for businesses to keep up with these advancements.
- Disruptive technology – as discussed in Unit 3.9.2, disruptive technology is a threat for many businesses should their current technologies become obsolete.

 Exam focus ## Use your knowledge of change management

The topics covered in Unit 3.9, including innovation, growth, internationalisation and digital technology are all issues that lead to considerable change within businesses. In the next unit you will learn about managing change and organisational culture. You can use your understanding of change management when assessing and evaluating the value and implementation of any of the topics covered in Unit 3.9. For example, you could use your understanding of change management to suggest why some employees might be opposed to the introduction of new technology within the business.

The impact on business functions of digital technology

Marketing
Big data gives businesses access to vast amounts of information on their customers. Effective use of this information in order to understand customer needs can improve products and customer service.

Finance
Digital technology provides businesses with the ability to monitor financial transactions and closely monitor business costs. Thus, leading to greater efficiency and control over budgets.

Operations
ERP systems can integrate all aspects of production, leading to greater efficiency and reduced waste. For example, just-in-time stock control systems will reduce inventory levels and free up cash.

Human resources
A modern day workforce must be computer literate and have the skills to work with data management software. Technology can also replace some of the decision-making processes formerly made by humans.

Now try this

1 How can digital technology benefit a business?

2 What are some of the risks when investing in digital technology?

Exam skills

The following exam-style questions relate to the topics covered in Unit 3.9.4 and refer to the Cloudburst Plc case study on page 167.

Worked example

1 Which of the following digital technologies would involve the integration of management of the functions within a business?

A E-commerce ⬭

B Enterprise resource planning ⬤

C Data mining ⬭

D Social media ⬭

(1 mark)

 Enterprise resource planning is management software that links business information and processes to improve efficiency and access to information.

2 Analyse the pressures for Cloudburst Plc to adopt new digital technologies.

(9 marks)

One of the pressures Cloudburst Plc might face to adopt new digital technologies is the extent to which its competitors also use this technology. If a competitor has adopted technology which gives it a significant advantage over Cloudburst Plc, then it may be necessary to invest in the technology in order to maintain its position in the market. For example, if competitors adopt a new e-commerce platform that makes it easy for customers to download their games, then Cloudburst Plc may have to launch its own platform...

 The student has identified a relevant pressure and suggested why Cloudburst Plc might have to adopt new digital technology in order to keep up with competition. However, this is still a little vague. The student then goes on to use an appropriate example. This gives clarity to the answer along with context to the computer gaming industry. The student may then go on to analyse a second pressure in the context of Cloudburst Plc.

3 To what extent is the use of 'big data' likely to have a significant impact on Cloudburst Plc's ability to maintain market leadership in the MMORPG gaming segment?

(16 marks)

This is a complicated question as it requires the student to show their understanding of 'big data' and then make a link between the use of big data and Cloudburst Plc's competitiveness in the MMORPG segment.

Big data refers to the vast amounts of information that businesses are able to collect on their customers from multiple sources, allowing them to 'mine' the data in order to identify trends, links and relationships.

 A good start. The student starts by defining what big data is.

The use of big data may allow Cloudburst Plc to gain a better understanding of its customers by monitoring which game features are the most popular within its MMORPG. This would allow it to design future content based on these features, and in doing so, better meet the needs of its customers. Computer games typically have a life-cycle of 18 months and customers could easily lose interest in Cloudburst Plc's leading MMORPG game. Big data is one way that Cloudburst Plc can evolve and continue to provide features that customers are looking for and that differentiate the game from other MMORPGs on the market. In effect, big data can help Cloudburst Plc launch extension strategies to extend the product life-cycle...

The student has successfully linked two business concepts together in their answer: the ability of big data to help a business understand its customers and how understanding its customers may lead to better games being developed – extending the product life-cycle. The rest of the answer could go on to explain the limitations of big data and other factors that may help Cloudburst Plc maintain its position in the market.

Exam-style practice

The following exam-style questions relate to the topics covered in Unit 3.9.4 and refer to the Cloudburst Plc case study below. There are answers on pages 201–202.

1 Explain how digital technology could help improve efficiency within Cloudburst Plc.

(5 marks)

When answering this question try to identify a specific digital technology relevant to Cloudburst Plc.

2 Explain one diseconomy of scale that Cloudburst Plc might experience as it grows.

(5 marks)

After identifying an appropriate diseconomy, remember to explain the impact this may have on Cloudburst Plc.

3 Analyse the factors that could contribute to Cloudburst Plc's ability to innovate.

(9 marks)

Think carefully about how you can apply the case study to this answer.

4 Analyse how Cloudburst Plc could use the Bartlett and Ghoshal matrix to inform its business strategy.

(9 marks)

Start by explaining what the Bartlett and Ghoshal matrix is. It might be worth discussing particular strategies and how these might apply to Cloudburst Plc.

5 To what extent is disruptive innovation likely to affect the success of Cloudburst Plc?

(16 marks)

6 Evaluate which of Cloudburst Plc's growth strategies is most likely to lead to the long-term success of the company.

A a merger with Interact Gaming Ltd

B a joint venture with a leading game console manufacturer

(20 marks)

Remember, disruptive innovation could bring significant advantages to a business if it is the one leading an innovation, but could also cause a number of problems if it gets left behind.

The case study offers two alternative options as to how Cloudburst Plc could grow externally. Which of these could provide the company with the greatest opportunity for long-term success? You should also consider the risks involved with each approach.

 Case study

CLOUDBURST PLC

Cloudburst Plc is a large computer software company that makes computer games for platforms such as Xbox 1, PlayStation 4, PC and Mac computers. The company's most successful product is a Massively Multiplayer Online Role Playing Game (MMORPG), which is market leader in the MMORPG gaming segment. Subscribers pay a monthly fee to play alongside other players from Europe and North America in a fantasy world completing quests and challenges. In addition to regular updates to its MMORPG, Cloudburst Plc also releases one to two new games each year. Nevertheless, Cloudburst Plc's popular MMORPG still brings in around 70% of the firm's revenue.

Cloudburst Plc is looking to expand into new sectors of the industry. Recently the board have been negotiating terms for a merger with a Chinese gaming company, Interact Gaming Ltd, which specialises in developing apps for smartphones. Interact Gaming Ltd is considered to be a very innovative company which could benefit from the considerable cash reserves held by Cloudburst Plc. Even with its extremely successful MMORPG, Cloudburst Plc knows that computer games have a life-cycle of around 3 years and a merger with Interact Gaming Ltd would not only add the expertise of its game designers, but allow it to acquire a number of successful app brands into its product portfolio.

Cloudburst Plc has also been in negotiations with a popular console manufacturer to integrate its MMORPG with the new version of its gaming console. This would give players free access to content updates and exclusive access to in-game features. Cloudburst Plc believes this joint venture could increase the reach of its popular game.

Managing change 1

Change in a business can be driven from within (internal) or from the external environment. Change is a process that has to be managed carefully by managers in order for new practices, processes and products to be successful.

The value of change

Change can create a number of opportunities for businesses, such as creating new markets. Change is also an opportunity for businesses to re-evaluate what they do in order to improve productivity, efficiency, quality and perhaps profitability.

However, many stakeholders will see change as a threat. If businesses do not foresee some changes, or manage change poorly, this can result in business failure.

Types of change

Change can take a number of forms. Each will need to be managed in a different way.

- **internal or external** – change driven by internal factors, such as management and strategic direction, or change driven by external forces, such as economic conditions
- **rapid and unexpected** (such as in response to a disaster)
- **long-term** – steady, planned, and gradual
- **incremental** – broken down into steps, gradual improvements over time
- **disruptive** – adapting to external forces that change the nature of the industry (see disruptive innovation).

Lewin's force field analysis

This model presents a business with the opportunity to determine the forces driving change vs those resisting change. Change may be deemed necessary, but it will not happen if the resisting forces are greater than the driving forces. Managers can use this model to identify resistance and develop strategies to remove them. These forces can be internal or external.

Forces for change | Current state | Forces resisting change

Forces for change	Forces resisting change
high number of customer complaints	lack of funding
productivity falling	limited understanding or appreciation that change is needed
significant investment in new technology by a leading competitor	no strategic direction to drive the change

The value of flexible organisations

Rigid organisations may find it more difficult to adapt to a changing environment or the internal pressures for change. The more agile a business is, the easier and faster it will be able to manage the change process. There are a number of approaches businesses can use to add flexibility:

Restructuring – for a reminder see Unit 3.6.3 on organisation design.

Delayering – remove unnecessary levels of hierarchy.

Flexible contracts and flexible teams (matrix structures).

Flexible business practices

Organic structures – organisational structure where teams evolve depending on the needs of the task. Teams based around projects not functions.

Information and knowledge management – through technology, vast amounts of information are available to managers. How they use and share this information is key to flexibility by identifying changes before they happen and evaluating strategies.

Now try this

1 How might external forces lead to change within a business?

2 How might a manager use Lewin's force field analysis?

Managing change 2

There are a number of reasons why people resist change in an organisation and a number of approaches that a manager can adopt in order to remove these barriers and ensure the process of change runs smoothly. These barriers and approaches to overcoming them were put forward by Kotter and Schlesinger.

Reasons for resistance to change

Self-interest	Prefer present state	Different assessment	Misunderstanding
Individuals may lose out in terms of pay, status or anticipating harder work.	Some employees may be very comfortable with the current situation. Change will take them outside their comfort zone.	Some employees may simply disagree and believe that change is not necessary or that a different approach would be more successful.	Employees may not see the need for change or may not understand what the change process will involve – fear of uncertainty.

Change
This may include:
- new technology
- new ways of working
- new products
- new structures
- new processes and regulations
- new members of staff (leadership).

Approaches used to overcome resistance to change

Education and communication	Facilitate and support	Participation and involvement
Clearly share the reasons and logic behind the change and provide necessary training in new approaches.	Give employees what they need to accomplish the change along with encouragement and support.	Involve employees in the decision making so that they have ownership of the change.
Manipulation and co-option	**Negotiation and bargaining**	**Explicit / implicit coercion**
Involve and influence key people. Get individuals with influence on board and use them to drive the change.	Compromise may involve employees receiving higher wages or better working conditions.	Force change through using authority. Threats may be involved – openly or applied. Long-term success may be more important than short-term agreement.

The factors that may determine which are the most appropriate tactics to deal with the change process include the reason for resistance, the level of that resistance the time available and the leadership style of the managers involved.

Managing information and knowledge

Businesses have far greater access to information than they have ever had before, through technology such as store/loyalty cards, social media and data mining. The effective use of this information can give a business an insight into likely changes ahead. If businesses use this information wisely they are better placed to foresee and manage change within the organisation. The same is true of knowledge. Expertise must be managed, shared and retained in the business, for example, the experience of managers who have successfully gone through significant change.

 Using Kotter and Schlesinger's findings

Most case study material in your exams will involve a business going through some form of change. This model is useful when analysing and evaluating the situation and providing recommendations on how the change could be managed. Try to make a link between the reason for any resistance and the best way to remove the barrier from the six options above.

Now try this

1 What might change within a business that will need planning and managing?

2 Identify two reasons why employees might resist change.

3 Identify two ways that a manager might ensure the process of change runs smoothly.

Exam skills

The following exam-style questions relate to the topics covered in Unit 3.10.1 and refer to the Cloudburst Plc–Interact Gaming Ltd merger case study on page 183.

Worked example

Which of the following best describes Lewin's force field analysis model?

A A model used to analyse the life-cycle of products ⬭

B A model used to analyse the position of a business within its market ⬭

C A model used to analyse the factors driving and resisting change within a business ⬤

D A model used to analyse a business's strategy in terms of the products it offers and the markets it operates in ⬭

(1 mark)

> The correct answer is C.
> A = the product life-cycle
> B = market map
> D = Ansoff matrix

Worked example

Analyse the benefits of Cloudburst Plc introducing measures to increase the flexibility of the organisation.

(9 marks)

One way that Cloudburst Plc could create a flexible organisation would be to introduce flexible contract conditions. This would allow it to employ game designers as and when it needs them. This would mean that it would be able to reduce costs when it were not developing a new game or app. This would also allow it to increase the size of the workforce if it wanted to expand or start a number of new projects quickly, as it would not have to go through a long process of recruitment...

> The student has given one method Cloudburst Plc could use to run a flexible organisation and has then gone on to explain some of the advantages of this approach. The student could now go on to discuss a second technique and make the link between this and change management. Appropriate examples could also be used.

Worked example

Evaluate how Cloudburst Plc could ensure that implementation of new working practices within the company runs smoothly.

(16 marks)

...Another issue that Cloudburst Plc has experienced is difficulties between the two sets of employees who seem to have different approaches to game design and decision making. One way that it could overcome this problem is to negotiate terms with Interact Gaming Ltd's designers. This could lead to a compromise that permits employees to make their own decisions within the design process. This could help the two sets of employees get along better and therefore ensure that the app is developed in time. However, as the two companies have now merged into a larger organisation it is important that structures and procedures are in place to control processes and ensure games are produced to the standard Cloudburst Plc wants. In order for this to happen employees will need support and training to ensure they know how to do this...

> In this extract the student has made reference to techniques for managing change as suggested by Kotter and Schlesinger – negotiation and bargaining and facilitation and support. The student then explains how these approaches might solve some of the problems outlined in the case study.
>
> The student could have made it explicit that they were using this theory to help answer the question.

Managing organisational culture 1

There are a number of reasons why people resist change in an organisation and a number of approaches that a manager can adopt in order to remove these barriers and ensure the process of change runs smoothly. These barriers and approaches to overcoming them were put forward by Kotter and Schlesinger.

Organisational culture

Many things contribute towards the culture of a business. These factors determine the way the business operates and may respond to the external environment and changes within the business.

physical environment — rituals – significant events or ways of doing things

stories – things that have happened, good or bad, in the past

Forming a business culture

key personalities – leaders and employees who influence others

rewards – what the business recognises as success and the way it rewards this

Charles Handy's model of culture

Charles Handy's models of culture outline four distinct organisational culture types.

power culture

A few people, or one person, drive the organisation and decisions. The culture is determined by a few individuals. Common in small businesses.

role culture

People associate with a team or function. Very clear structure and cultures may differ across these functions. May develop out of a power culture as a business grows.

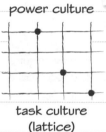

task culture (lattice)

Employees associate with a task or project. New groups are formed regularly and cultural norms will frequently change as new groups are formed.

person culture (cluster)

Employees have a great deal of independence and may not be strongly affiliated with a specific group.

Geert Hofstede's model of culture

Geert Hofstede also categorised cultures based on a number of factors. Hofstede suggests that these categories can be seen on a national level with different countries/societies exhibiting characteristics somewhere on each of these scales.

small power distance	big power distance	the relationship between line managers and subordinates; low power distance may accept each other as friends
individualism	collectivism	the degree that employees see themselves as a team or an individual
masculinity	femininity	the extent to which employees demonstrate aggressive or competitive tendencies
weak uncertainty avoidance	strong uncertainty avoidance	uncertainty avoidance – the extent to which the business will take risks
long-term orientation	short-term orientation	the focus on short-term gains or long-term investment
indulgence	restraint	the extent to which society indulges gratification of human needs in comparison to regulation of these needs through strict social norms

Now try this

1 How do business cultures differ across nations?

2 How can organisational culture be classified?

Managing organisational culture 2

Organisational culture can change over time and a number of factors can influence these changes. The nature of culture in a business may be influenced more or less by a number of factors.

The factors below are likely to influence the culture of a business. These factors overlap and merge with one another, but they will vary in significance across different businesses. For example, in Business A the leader of the organisation is the most significant factor in forming the culture within the organisation. However, in Business B the values and norms (traditions and ways of doing things) are more important.

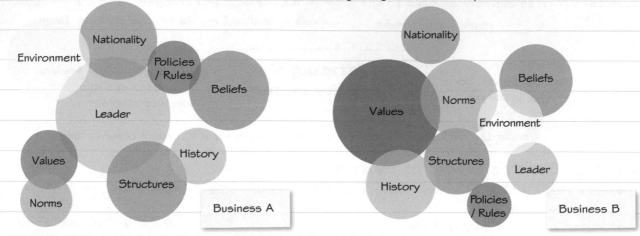

Reasons for changing organisational culture

There are a number of reasons why changing organisational culture might be desirable.

👍 A new leader – who may want to impose their own way of doing things.

👍 Poor performance – a negative culture may have contributed to this.

👍 Corporate objectives – a change in direction and strategy may require a different approach.

👍 Customer needs – expectations of customers or society in general may call for change.

Problems changing organisational culture

Although a change in culture may be desirable, it is not always easy to impose cultural change. Reasons are outlined below.

👍 Changing culture is a long process. It may require significant education and training of the workforce.

👍 Large organisations may have more than one culture across different functions or regions.

👍 Culture is deep set – it extends from people's attitudes and beliefs. These are not easy to change.

Kruger's Change Iceberg

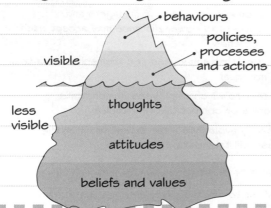

Attitudes and beliefs are part of an organisations culture. But like the iceberg below the surface, they are hard to see, let alone change.

 Key points

A strong culture – one that exhibits desirable characteristics – can lead to a competitive advantage for a business. For example, it can lead to a creative, innovative, cohesive or highly motivated organisation. However, changing an organisational culture is very difficult and can take a long time as certain aspects of human behaviour are driven by attitudes and beliefs. This is a key point of evaluation that you might use when answering questions on this topic. A strong culture might be desirable, but it will be difficult to change if it is not working.

Now try this

1 What factors might influence organisational culture?

2 Why might a business choose to change its culture?

3 Why is changing organisational culture difficult?

Exam skills

The following exam-style questions relate to the topics covered in Unit 3.10.2 and refer to the Cloudburst Plc–Interact Gaming Ltd merger case study on page 183.

Worked example

Which of the following factors is most likely to influence the culture of a business?

A Corporate objectives ●

B Competitors ○

C Inflation ○

D Recruitment policy ○

(1 mark)

Note that the question asks for the 'most likely' influence – the corporate objectives of a business may influence its culture because this will determine what the business sees as important. For example, a business that is focused on customer satisfaction may develop different norms and rituals to a business that is driven to maximise profit.

Worked example

Explain why Cloudburst Plc may find it difficult to change the way that the former employees of Interact Gaming Ltd work.

(5 marks)

Cloudburst Plc will find it difficult to change the way that the designers from Interact Gaming Ltd work because their previous practices such as making many of their own decisions is part of their culture. Organisation culture is formed, amongst others things, by norms, rituals and beliefs. People do not change their beliefs easily and the former Interact Gaming Ltd designers may believe that they should have the authority to make key decisions without the supervision of line managers.

The student has used the information in the case study to answer the question. They have also shown an understanding of organisational culture and the role it can play in the way employees may act or react to different situations.

Worked example

To what extent will the organisational culture be a barrier to the successful merger between Cloudburst Plc and Interact Gaming Ltd?

(16 marks)

...On the other hand, organisational culture can be changed and influenced. For example, setting clear objectives will give employees the same targets to achieve. This will mean they will be striving to achieve the same things and this will encourage them to cooperate. Clear leadership is another way that the culture within a business can be changed. If the directors of Cloudburst Plc are demonstrating the characteristics that they want their employees to have then in time this is likely to influence the behaviour of the workforce. Nevertheless, Cloudburst Plc is now a multinational organisation and it needs to appreciate that different societies have different cultural norms, as highlighted by Hofstede's cultural dimensions. For example, the former Interact Gaming Ltd employees may be used to greater power distance between themselves and their line managers...

This extract from the student's answer analyses how the culture of the two companies could be aligned. Appropriate examples have been used to put the response in context. The student has also gone on to use relevant theory – Hofstede's cultural dimensions – to explain that there are likely to be inevitable differences now that Cloudburst Plc is a multinational organisation.

Managing strategic implementation

Choosing the right strategy in business is extremely important. However, just as important is how the business implements that strategy. The business will have to consider a number of factors in order to realise and execute its strategy effectively.

The strategic planning process

The diagram below represents the stages a business will go through to plan, implement and evaluate its strategy. You have covered each stage of this process whilst studying your A Level Business course.

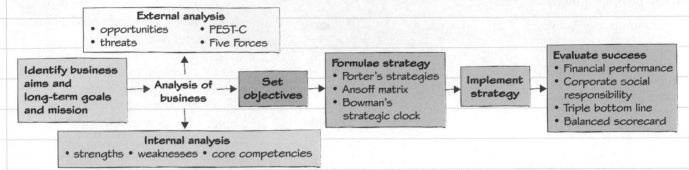

The importance of leadership

Leadership at all levels is extremely important in implementing business strategy. Leaders will:

- 👍 set the vision
- 👍 motivate the workforce to implement the strategy
- 👍 keep the business on course to achieve the strategy and realign tactics if it drifts from the strategy
- 👍 assess progress and performance
- 👍 ensure success is recognised
- 👍 adjust the strategy or implementation if it is not working.

Implementing strategy

The stages in implementing a strategy effectively might include the following.

1 Communicate the strategy to employees.

2 Identify key personnel to implement the strategy and delegate responsibility.

3 Ensure resources are made available to implement the strategy – for example, budgets allocated, training given.

4 Set measurable steps with appropriate deadlines.

5 Put in place systems key performance indicators (KPIs) to measure progress.

6 Identify and celebrate quick wins along the way.

7 Regroup, assess and if necessary adjust strategy.

The importance of communication

Communication is vital if business strategy is to be implemented successfully. Effective communication will ensure that all employees understand what they should be doing and why they are doing it. If employees share the vision for the business they are more likely to be successful. It is important that employees understand the part they play in strategic implementation and where they are at along the process of implementation.

 Exam focus ## Analysing problems / making recommendations

Whenever analysing a business that has failed or where things are not going to plan, you can use the principles on this page to analyse what might have gone wrong and make recommendations on how the business can improve. The strategy might be right, but the business might not have implemented the strategy effectively.

Now try this

1 What is strategic implementation?

2 How can a business ensure that its strategy is implemented effectively?

3 Why is communication important in strategic implementation?

The role of organisational structure in strategic implementation

When implementing strategy a business must ensure that the organisation is set up in a way that will accomplish the strategy. This might include having the right teams and personnel working together with the appropriate authority and leadership in place.

Factors to consider when designing an organisation structure to implement a strategy

- What span of control is appropriate?
- How many levels of management are appropriate?
- What specialist roles will be required – for example, are specific managers with specific remits required?
- Should decisions be centralised or decentralised?
- What teams and mix of skills will be required to implement the strategy?

Organisational structures

Functional structure

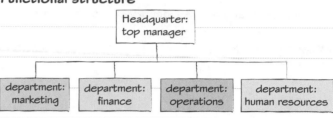

Clear focus on roles and shared expertise. Employees can identify with function rather than the business as a whole.

Product structure

product A, product B, product C, product D
marketing
finance
operations
HR

A structure based around specific products and therefore specific customer needs. Cross function teams are deployed who have specific skills and knowledge of operating in one product area.

Regional structure

Chief executive
region A, region B, region C, region D
marketing
finance
operations
HR

Appropriate for global businesses where regional conditions vary such as language, social trends and attitudes, economic climate and political systems.

Matrix structure

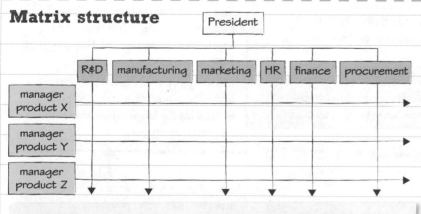

Employees are line managed by two managers from different areas, such as function and product/region. Frequent movement between teams and flexible working practices.

Choosing the right structure

There are a number of factors to consider when identifying the most appropriate structure. These include:

- formality and control
- the variety and complexity of the product range
- the global regions the business operates in.

In some circumstances it might not be appropriate for a formal structure to be imposed, for example, where creativity and flexibility are paramount or where the business is starting up.

Now try this

1 Identify two organisational structures a business might adopt in order to implement its strategy.

2 Why might a business decide to decentralise decision making?

Network analysis 1

Network analysis involves using a network diagram to manage the various tasks required to complete a project. The use of network analysis can help a manager to complete a project in the shortest space of time possible and identify critical activities.

Information required to carry out network analysis

- identification of all the tasks necessary to implement the strategy
- the length of time each task takes to complete it to a satisfactory level
- the order in which tasks must be completed – the dependent activities
- activities that can be completed at the same time – parallel activities.

Interpreting network analysis diagrams

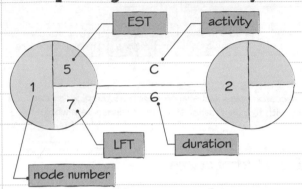

- Each circle (node) is numbered and represents the start and end of an activity.
- A straight line represents the activity. Activity number above the line, duration below the line, for example, 8 weeks.
- The earliest start time (EST) of an activity is shown in the top right of the left side node; for example, Activity C EST is week 5.
- The latest finish time (LFT) of an activity is shown in the bottom right of the right-side node.

The steps in constructing a network diagram

1 If required, construct the network diagram from an activities table showing the activity, what each activity is preceded by and the duration of each activity.

2 All activities start as soon as possible; for example, if three activities can start immediately, three separate lines will be drawn from the first node.

3 Add the earliest start times for each activity. Left to right. EST = EST of previous activity + duration of the activity.

4 Add the latest finish time to each activity working right to left. LFT = previous LFT − activity duration. If there is a choice of numbers, choose the largest to deduct.

5 Calculate the float time for each activity. Float time = LFT − duration − EST.

6 Identify the critical path by hatching the lines of the activities on the critical path (///).

Float and critical path

The float time of an activity is any slack by which an activity can overrun. Float time is important for identifying which activities have flexibility.

The critical path is the route through the network diagram where there is no float time. These activities are critical because, if they overrun, the expected duration of the project will be extended.

Identifying the float time on activities and the critical path is the last stage of completing network analysis.

Carrying out network analysis can help managers to identify key activities, improve efficiency and manage resources effectively.

Now try this

1 What are the EST and LFT on a network diagram?

2 What is the 'float' on an activity?

3 What is meant by the 'critical path'?

Network analysis 2

Example of a completed network analysis diagram

Use the notes below to interpret the information shown in this network diagram.

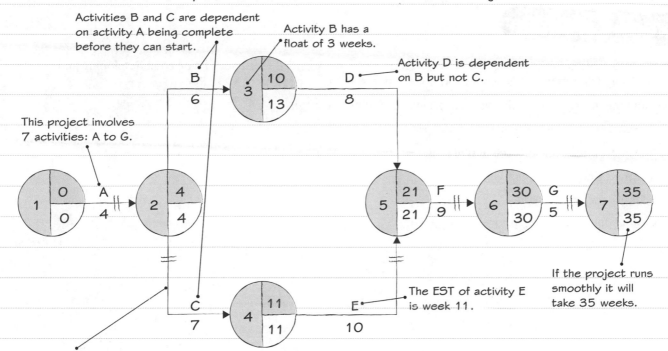

Activities B and C are dependent on activity A being complete before they can start.

Activity B has a float of 3 weeks.

Activity D is dependent on B but not C.

This project involves 7 activities: A to G.

The EST of activity E is week 11.

If the project runs smoothly it will take 35 weeks.

The critical path for the project is ACEFG.

The benefits of network analysis

A manager can use network analysis to:

👍 identify the exact activities involved in implementing a strategy

👍 effectively plan for the implementation of a strategy

👍 introduce informed deadlines for different activities

👍 allocate resources efficiently to the different activities

👍 identify float time and those activities that are critical to the success/implementation of the strategy.

The limitations of network analysis

However, network analysis has a number of limitations, including:

👎 Projects and strategies often involve multiple factors, agents and stakeholders – calculating the time taken to complete an activity can be very difficult.

👎 It does not take into account qualitative issues such as employee morale or relationships between workers.

👎 It relies on estimations. If these are correct so are the ESTs and LFTs. Strategies will not be implemented on time if this is incorrect.

👎 It does not take into account unexpected events and significant external factors beyond the business's control, such as key staff on long-term absence.

Now try this

1 What are the benefits of using network analysis when implementing a strategy?

2 What are the limitations of network analysis?

Exam skills

The following exam-style questions relate to the topics covered in Unit 3.10.3 and refer to the Cloudburst Plc–Interact Gaming Ltd merger case study on page 183.

Worked example

The information in the network analysis diagram below represents the activities involved in developing and launching Cloudburst Plc's new smartphone app to support its popular MMORPG.

Using the information in the network analysis diagram, calculate:

• the earliest start time of each activity

• the latest finish time of each activity

• the float time for each activity

• identify the critical path.

Assume that activity A can start immediately.

(1 mark)

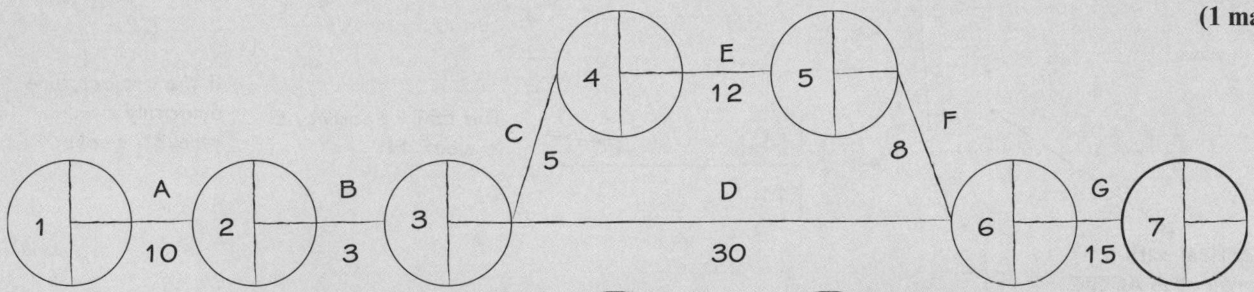

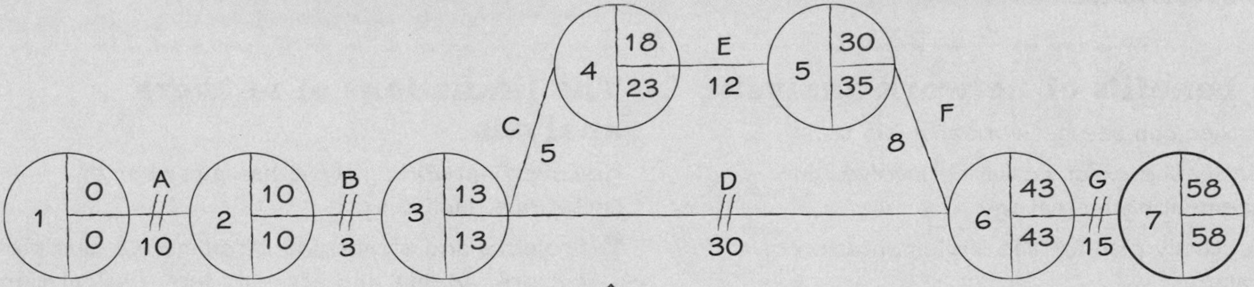

The student has completed the network diagram by identifying the earliest start times and latest finish times. They have also identified A, B, D, G as the critical path. Check the processes outlined on page 176 and see if you come up with the same calculations.

Worked example

Analyse the steps that the directors of Cloudburst Plc may take to ensure the company's strategy is implemented successfully.

(9 marks)

...A second step the directors could take is to ensure that measurable steps are identified and clear criteria and deadlines are set for the successful completion of these activities. After each activity is then complete, the employees involved should review the performance and, if necessary, be rewarded. This will help break down the implementation of the new app into clear steps so that progress can easily be monitored...

The student has identified at least one factor that should be considered when implementing business strategy. Others they could also include in their answer might be setting a clear vision for the project, ensuring key personnel have the responsibility and authority to carry out the strategy or ensuring the necessary resources are made available. It is important that the student ensures the rest of their answer is clearly linked to the Cloudburst Plc context.

Why strategies fail 1

Strategies often fail in business. Sometimes failure is beyond the control of the business, for example because of external factors like economic conditions. However, strategy can also fail because sufficient plans were not put in place, implementation failed or some other human factor was involved.

The decision-making process

All businesses will go through a decision-making process like the one below. The strategy can fail at any one of these stages.

Success may depend on a number of factors and different managers are likely to have a different perspective on what success looks like; it is very subjective.

Objectives are wrong – either not achievable or send the business down the wrong path.

Data not easily available – often business decisions are made on hunches instead of scientific data.

Poor analysis may occur when a business has little understanding or experience of the situation.

Unit 3.10.3 gives more details about the stages of strategy implementation. If a business fails to do any one of these the strategy could fail.

The wrong strategic direction could be one that is too similar to that of a competitor or one that the business does not have the resources to achieve.

Decision-making cycle: set objectives → gather data → analyse data → identify strategy → implement strategy → evaluate performance → set objectives

Planned vs emergent strategy

A planned strategy is one that is formulated and then carried out over a period of time. By contrast, an emergent strategy is one that develops as the strategic plan is implemented. Often a business will adapt the strategy because it has to respond to external forces or the managers realise that the initial plan was not appropriate.

An emergent strategy may not be what the business set out to achieve, but this does not mean that the business was not successful. A business's ability to adapt is a key factor in its long-term success.

Planned strategy

A - - - - - - - - - - - - - - - - - - - → B

- clear purpose for all employees leading to a consistent approach
- easier to measure success against
- easier to build a reputation (brand image).

Emergent strategy

A - - - - - - - - - - - - - - - - - - - → B

- allows a business to adapt to its environment
- encourages a business to learn from its mistakes.

Strategic drift

Strategic drift occurs when a business's strategy no longer matches the environment in which it operates. This can be for any of the PEST-C factors. Eventually a business will adjust its strategy or fail.

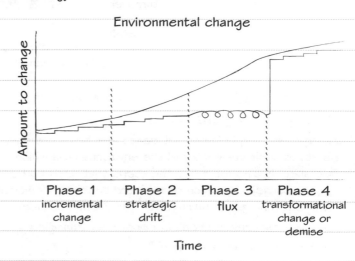

Environmental change

Amount to change / Time

Phase 1 incremental change | Phase 2 strategic drift | Phase 3 flux | Phase 4 transformational change or demise

Now try this

1 Why might business strategy fail?
2 What is an emergent strategy?
3 What might cause strategic drift?

Why strategies fail 2

The divorce between ownership and control

In large organisations the owners and managers may be different people – particularly in a Plc. Owners may not understand issues 'on the ground' and managers may make decisions based on factors that they believe are right or which might benefit themselves – perhaps short-term gains to boost profits. Where there is a divorce of ownership and control, this can create problems when implementing a strategy.

Corporate governance

Corporate governance refers to the systems and processes that are in place to monitor and control how a business is run. Corporate governance is important to ensure the interests of a particular stakeholder are not catered for over all others and to ensure the long-term success of the business.

Corporate governance might be achieved through:

👍 corporate governance policies

👍 CSR reporting

👍 non-executive directors (external).

Evaluating strategic performance

Assessing the success of a business strategy can be difficult because different stakeholders will have different perspectives. Furthermore, success of a business strategy is relative to external factors that have changed since the strategy was put in place. An emergent strategy might not be what the business originally set out to achieve, but this does not mean that it was not successful. A business can evaluate strategic performance using key performance indicators (KPIs). A business may use a number of KPIs (such as the Balanced Scorecard) and these should be:

👍 well-defined and quantifiable

👍 thoroughly communicated throughout the organisation and department

👍 crucial to achieving the business's goal (hence, they are key performance indicators)

👍 applicable to the nature of the business.

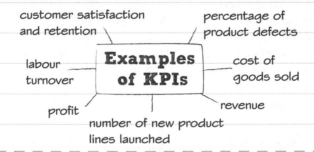

customer satisfaction and retention
percentage of product defects
labour turnover
Examples of KPIs
cost of goods sold
profit
number of new product lines launched
revenue

The value of strategic planning and contingency planning

Strategic planning is important because it helps managers understand their business and the environment in which it operates. It also identifies the steps that need to be taken and targets by which to measure success. However, strategic planning has a number of limitations because:

• the business environment is constantly changing

• strategies evolve over time

• the inaccuracy of data may limit the validity of any plan.

Contingency plans

Based on this, businesses may develop contingency plans. These are plans of action for possible but unlikely events – the 'what if' scenarios. Although contingency planning could be a waste of resources and time, it provides businesses with a fallback that they can act on should they need to. Contingency planning often considers how a business may react to the failure of a strategy.

Now try this

1 How can a divorce of ownership and control create problems for large businesses?

2 Why is contingency planning important?

Exam skills

The following exam-style question relates to the topics covered in Unit 3.10.4 and refer to the Cloudburst Plc–Interact Gaming Ltd merger case study on page 183. Context may also be drawn from the Cloudburst Plc case study from Unit 3.9 on page 167.

Worked example

To what extent could strategic drift impact the long-term success of Cloudburst Plc?   **(20 marks)**

Strategic drift occurs when the strategy of a business no longer matches the environment in which it operates. Cloudburst Plc plans to move into new markets and this is one of the reasons why it has merged with Interact Gaming Ltd. The merger has not been without complications and this could easily mean that the business's attention has been focused on making the merger a success. As a result, it could have easily lost focus on the changing business environment. Furthermore, as Cloudburst Plc will be operating in more than one market, it may have to deal with different external factors such as computer game regulations and political factors affecting international trade. This too might make it more difficult for Cloudburst Plc to maintain a strategy that is attuned to the markets it operates in.

However, business strategies do develop over time and if Cloudburst Plc is able to constantly analyse market conditions using tools such as PEST-C and SWOT analysis it may be able to develop its strategy over time. Often a business will have an emergent strategy that develops over time. This will be important for Cloudburst Plc as it works out what its strengths are following the merger and the resources it has available. For example, the success of the new app may determine the strategic direction it takes in the future.

Overall, strategic drift is a problem for all businesses. Cloudburst Plc operates in a market based around technology where new innovations are constantly being introduced. This could mean that strategic drift is more likely than if the company operated in a more stable market. The extent to which the business will experience strategic drift will depend on Cloudburst Plc's ability to stay ahead of the market and make the necessary adjustments to its strategy. In order for Cloudburst Plc to do this it is important that it continually re-evaluates the attractiveness of the markets it operates in. One way to do this would be to apply Porter's Five Forces model. It is also extremely important that Cloudburst Plc puts in place contingency plans should its strategy fail. This might include plans for retrenchment or a plan to exit the Asian markets or sell off the Interact Gaming Ltd brand.

Use the checklist below to evaluate the essay.

☐ Key terms defined and used
☐ Key issues from case study applied
☐ All points clearly explained
☐ Financial data applied and interpreted
☐ Analysis is well developed
☐ Balance shown by considering benefits and limitations
☐ Alternative perspectives and/or approaches considered
☐ Evaluation answers the question
☐ Clear justification using the key issues in the case
☐ Use of the 'depends on' rule
☐ Recommendations given where appropriate

Exam-style practice

The following exam-style questions relate to the topics covered in Unit 3.10 and refer to the Cloudburst Plc–Interact Gaming Ltd merger case study on page 183. Context may also be drawn from the Cloudburst Plc case study from Unit 3.9 on page 167. There are answers on pages 202–203.

1 Using the table below, construct a network analysis diagram for the development of a computer game

Task	Preceded by	Duration (weeks)
A – concept development	none	1
B – research	A	4
C – prototype	A	8
D – detailed artwork	B	2
E – alpha testing	B	14
F – audio production	C	8
G – first production	D, E, F	3
H – beta testing	G	1
I – debugging	H	2
J – game launch	G	6

Use the guide on page 176 to help you construct your network diagram. Draft the layout on scrap paper first before you start to add the information to the nodes and lines. You will not be required to produce a network diagram from scratch in your exam, but the process of mapping one out is good practice and will help you understand the logic behind the diagram.

2 Using your network diagram calculate the:

- earliest start times for each activity
- latest finish times for each activity
- float on each activity.

(5 marks)

Before you work this out, write down the steps required to calculate the EST, LFT and project float. Don't forget to show the critical path on your diagram using //.

3 Explain why there might be a divorce of ownership and control at Cloudburst Plc.

(5 marks)

First, define what is meant by a divorce of ownership and control. Then explain why this might be possible at a business like Cloudburst Plc. Consider its size, ownership and recent events.

4 Analyse why the directors of Cloudburst Plc might find it difficult to integrate the two companies.

(9 marks)

When answering this question think about the issues with change management and organisation culture.

5 To what extent is strategic planning essential for the long-term success of Cloudburst Plc?

(16 marks)

In your answer remember to consider the limitations of strategic planning. Are there other factors that are just as significant in the long-term success of a company like Cloudburst Plc?

6 Evaluate the approaches that the directors of Cloudburst Plc may use to overcome any resistance to change within the organisation.

(20 marks)

Before answering this question, read through Kotter and Schlesinger's theories relating to change management.

Case study

The Cloudburst Plc–Interact Gaming Ltd merger

CLOUDBURST PLC ◀ – – – ▶ **Interact**

In 2015 the board of directors agreed terms with Interact Gaming Ltd and in November a merger between the two businesses was completed, leading to a jump in Cloudburst Plc's share value by 30p per share. Cloudburst Plc became the trading name for the company, but the Interact Gaming Ltd brand was kept for existing products launched in the Asian markets.

The first step taken by the board was to move the company from a functional structure to a product structure. This was followed by the voluntary relocation of a number of former Interact Gaming Ltd game designers to Cloudburst Plc's headquarters in San Francisco.

The first new product to be launched by the company was a smartphone app to support Cloudburst Plc's popular MMORPG. The app would allow players to monitor statistics of their characters and complete transactions such as buying items for their characters to use in the game without having to log-in on a computer game console.

Initial meetings ran smoothly, but problems arose when the schedules were put in place. The former Interact Gaming Ltd game designers felt that a March 2016 launch would be feasible for the new app, but key managers at Cloudburst Plc felt that this would be too rushed and the final app might not match the quality they demanded of a Cloudburst Plc product. It also took some time for the former Interact Gaming Ltd designers to feel comfortable with the lack of autonomy they were given. Whilst working at Interact Gaming Ltd, game designers were given considerable freedom to make their own decisions. Whereas, at Cloudburst Plc project managers had to officially sign-off any big decision.

Following complications with the app, the directors of Cloudburst Plc sat down to discuss the issues. Cloudburst Plc had merged with Interact Gaming Ltd to expand into new markets, but also to benefit from the creative skills its employees possessed. It seemed that change might be needed if Cloudburst Plc was to get the most out of the company.

Answers

3.1.1

1. Why businesses exist

1 For example: Goods – car, hairdryer, pair of shoes. Services – haircut, eye test, insurance.
2 New businesses provide goods and services to satisfy the needs of consumers. New businesses also create job opportunities and lower unemployment.
3 A car manufacturer might add value by adding product features such as heated seats or a sun roof. Another way a car manufacturer might add value is by reducing the price of the car.

2. Missions and objectives

1 The purpose of a mission statement is to communicate the intentions of a business to its stakeholders.
2 Business aims are similar to a mission. They are the broad goals that a business hopes to achieve. Objectives are more specific, focused and measurable and are set by a business to help it achieve its aims.

3. Common business objectives

1 Objectives should be SMART (specific, measurable, agreed, realistic and time related) so that they are effective in helping the business achieve its aims.
2 Some objectives might be more important than others if they are linked to the survival or competitiveness of a business. The importance of an objective depends on the priorities of the business.

4. The importance of profit

1 Profit = total revenue – total costs.
2 Variable costs are linked to the product and increase with output. In the short term, fixed costs do not change with the output.
3 A business could increase its revenue by promoting its products to make them more desirable. A business could also reduce the price in order to make its products and services more competitive.

3.1.2

6. Size and form of business

1 A sole trader has complete control over their business, it is easy to set up and the owner keeps 100% of the profits.
2 Limited liability protects the owner of a business from losing their personal assets which have not been invested into the company.
3 A public limited company is allowed to raise capital by selling shares to the general public through a stock market.

7. Ownership: aims and objectives

1 Survival is an appropriate objective for a sole trader because a sole trader is normally a small business and many small businesses can fail if market conditions change.
2 When a business becomes a Plc it has external shareholders so its objectives might shift to focus on keeping these shareholders happy and improving its share price.

8. The role of shareholders

1 Shareholders are important to a company because they are the owners of the business. A shareholder has the right to be involved in decision making and is entitled to a percentage of the profits relative to their stake in the business.
2 The share price of a company may change due to its performance, the anticipated future performance of the company and the condition of the economic environment.
3 The share price of a business directly affects the value or worth of the company. The value of shares may also affect a company's ability to raise finance.

3.1.3

10. The external environment 1

1 The bargaining power of a customer will be influenced by the amount of choice they have (number of competing businesses) and how easy it is for them to switch between those competitors.
2 If a business operates in a market with a large number of competitors it may have to work hard to attract customers. To do this it may have to differentiate its products or services and provide excellent value for money.
3 Three examples of products that have seasonal demand are Christmas trees, sun cream and umbrellas.

11. The external environment 2

1 Consumers might react to an increase in interest rates by saving their money instead of spending it.
2 Three consequences of an increase in average incomes are the standard of living increasing, greater spending on luxury items and less spending on inferior goods.
3 A growing population will increase the labour market within an economy and potentially increase the tax revenue of a nation.

12. The external environment 3

1 Fairtrade produce comes from a business that does not exploit its suppliers and pays them a fair price for their goods.
2 The government imposes environmental legislation to protect the environment and limit the negative externalities caused by businesses.
3 Three external factors that may affect a business include demographic factors, legal factors and economic factors.

3.2.1

16. Management and leadership 1

1 In my opinion, the three most important roles of a manager include planning, organising and controlling the organisation.
2 One management style identified by the Blake and Mouton Grid is the 'country club' manager. This is where the manager is primarily concerned with developing good relationships with their employees. In this approach the task at hand is less important. A second management style identified by the grid is the 'authoritarian' manager. This manager is primarily concerned with achieving the task and may not be too concerned about the impact this will have on the well-being of employees.

3.2.2

19. Management decision making 1

1 Risk is the chance of a misfortune or loss occurring. It is calculated by multiplying the extent of the impact by the probability of its occurrence.
2 A business can reduce uncertainty by carrying out research and using techniques to forecast future events.
3 Intuition is important when the reliability of data is questionable or there is little evidence to base a decision on. Intuition is valuable where managers have experience in a particular aspect of business or a situation.

20. Management decision making 2

1 A manager might use a decision tree to calculate the probable outcomes of a range of decisions. Decision trees are used to calculate the financial impact of various decisions.
2 The expected value in a decision tree is the average financial result from the various outcomes anticipated by taking a course of action.

21. Management decision making 3

1 Decision trees require a probability to be attached to various outcomes. These probabilities can be inaccurate and extremely subjective. For this reason, the usefulness of a decision tree could be limited where this is the case.
2 Other decision-making tools that might be used alongside a decision tree include market maps, stakeholder maps and the product life-cycle.

3.2.3

23. The importance of stakeholders 1

1 Customers, employees, shareholders.
2 The local community will want a business to provide trade and employment opportunities, whilst at the same time reducing negative externalities such as pollution and congestion.
3 Some people may consider shareholders to be the most important stakeholder group in a business because they finance the business activities and can influence decisions within the company. Other people may consider other stakeholders, such as the government or employees, as being the most important to the long-term success of a business.

24. The importance of stakeholders 2

1 The factors that may determine the interests of a stakeholder group are the extent to which a business's activities directly impact on the lives or fortunes of that stakeholder group.
2 The power/influence of a stakeholder group may be determined by the extent to which the stakeholders can directly influence the forces on a business, such as legislation, the decisions of the business or its fortunes in terms of profitability.

3.3.1

29. Marketing objectives

1 Marketing is important to a business because it is the function that allows a business to identify and understand customer needs and is responsible for how the business communicates with its customers.
2 Three marketing objectives include increasing sales revenue, increasing brand awareness and increasing market share.
3 Marketing is linked to other business functions because it directly influences the product or services that the business will sell. For example, marketing will work closely with operations and production to ensure the product meets the needs of customers.

3.3.2

30. Market research

1 Market research allows a business to understand the needs of its potential customers, establish the level of demand in the market and assess the nature of competition from other businesses.
2 Secondary research might be an appropriate form of research for a business start-up. This is because it is relatively cheap and start-ups rarely have money to invest in market research. However, it is important for new businesses to clearly understand the market so focus groups and sampling may also be important.
3 A large supermarket chain could use market mapping to compare its position in relation to other supermarkets based on two market variables such as price and quality. This might allow it to identify its key competitor and its target market.

31. Interpreting market data

1 A correlation of 0.7 suggests that there is a visible correlation between two sets of data, but the correlation cannot be described as being strong.
2 One factor that may determine the success of sampling in market research is the extent to which the sample size is large enough and broad enough to represent the total population.
3 This is an indication of how accurate the research findings are, for example 80% = 80 per cent confidence that the results are accurate.

32. Price and income elasticity

1 A PED of 0.2 represents an inelastic product where a change in price causes a smaller change in quantity demanded.
2 Market share is the percentage of the market owned/controlled by a particular business, whereas market size represents the total sales value/volume of the entire market for all businesses.
3 Technology can aid market research by making the collection of market data simpler and faster. For example, completing a survey using smartphone technology.

3.3.3

34. Segmentation, targeting and positioning

1 A business could segment a market based on demographics, buying behaviour or income.
2 A business could use a market map and conduct market research to ensure it is positioned effectively in the market.
3 Market segmentation allows a business to identify groups of customers with similar needs. This then allows them to have a better understanding of a target market and develop products and services specific to their needs. Promotion is also more effective as the market segment can be targeted with specific forms of advertising.

35. Mass and niche markets

1 Targeting is the process of identifying a target market and using specific marketing techniques to communicate with this group of customers.
2 A niche market is a narrow/small segment of the market with specific interests and needs.

3.3.4

37. Using the marketing mix

1 The 7Ps include product, price, promotion, place, people, process and physical environment.

2 A consumer product is targeted at the general public, whereas an industrial product is targeted at other businesses. The way a consumer product is marketed may be different from an industrial product. For example, industrial products are advertised in trade magazines instead of consumer lifestyle magazines.

3 The elements of the marketing mix must complement one another in order to ensure that the whole product meets the needs of the target market. For example, a premium product may require highly skilled and knowledgeable sales staff (people) and be sold through high-end retail stores (place).

38. Product

1 Function is an important factor in product design because it ensures a product is fit for purpose. It will not matter that the product has an appealing design and is affordable if the product does not do what it is meant to do.

2 A specialty good is one that requires a high level of involvement and consideration before a consumer is willing to purchase it. For example, a car or a house.

39. Product portfolio analysis

1 When a product goes through growth it is important that the business can keep up with demand and ensure distribution channels allow the product to reach the customer.

2 The benefit of a cash cow is that it will generate regular inflow of revenue for a business. This revenue can support other projects such as new product development or promoting the 'question marks'.

3 The limitations of product-portfolio analysis are that it simplifies what can be a very complex reality. For example, it can be hard to identify the growth potential in a market or the market share of a product. Products do not always go through the same cycle and are subject to numerous external factors that can alter demand for a product.

40. Price

1 The profit margin is an important factor when setting the price of a product because it directly determines the contribution each unit will make towards paying off fixed costs and ultimately the net profit of a business.

2 A business might choose to set a premium price for a product if it believes the product is of premium quality, unique or will be highly desirable.

3 Penetration pricing is where a business offers a low price when it launches a new product in order to attract customers and break in to a market. As the product becomes more established the price will gradually rise to match that of other competitors in the market as consumers become brand loyal.

4 Price is a subjective concept because all people will place a different value on money and a different value on a product or service. Price is subjective because it depends on a number of factors including competition, incomes and necessity.

41. Promotion

1 The purpose of promotion is to create awareness, interest and the desire of customers to purchase a product.

2 Three promotion methods include advertising, public relations (PR) and sponsorship.

3 A promotion method suitable for targeting children aged 5–8 might include TV advertising early in a morning or around 4 pm when children are typically watching television. Adverts might follow children's TV programmes.

42. Distribution (place)

1 A retailer adds value to the product by providing the customer with advice, customer service and a shopping experience.

2 The role of a wholesaler is the breakdown of bulk and to help a manufacturer distribute its products to retailers.

3 A manufacturer might sell direct to its customers in order to keep its prices low and increase competitiveness. It may also allow the manufacturer to build relationships with its customers and guarantee a certain level of customer service.

3.4.1

46. Operational objectives

1 Operations can give a business a competitive advantage by finding ways to reduce costs in the production process and therefore increasing profit margins. Operations can also help a business produce and deliver a product faster than a competitor, again, providing a competitive advantage.

2 Three factors that contribute to operations objectives include cost, quality and efficiency.

3 Operations may be linked to other functional areas such as human resources. For example, a labour intensive production process will require employees to be trained and motivated in order to achieve operational targets.

3.4.2

47. Analysing operational performance

1 Productivity is the level of output relative to the input (output/input); it measures the production efficiency of a business.

2 The difference between labour productivity and unit cost is that labour productivity measures the productive efficiency of the workforce and unit cost represents the average cost to produce one unit of output.

3 Capacity utilisation is measured by dividing the current level of output by the maximum possible output for the time period.

48. Uses of operational data

1 Labour productivity data could be used to set targets for groups of workers or as a way to reward the workforce in order to motivate them to higher levels of productivity.

2 When operating at a high level of capacity utilisation unit costs are low due to economies of scale and production efficiency.

3 Variable costs are directly linked to a unit of production and will change with the level of output, whereas the unit cost takes into account the total costs of a business relative to the level of output.

3.4.3

50. Increasing efficiency and productivity

1 Efficiency is important because by improving efficiency a business can reduce the inputs required to achieve a certain level of output. This can directly impact the costs of a business and therefore its profitability.

2 A business could increase labour productivity by finding ways to motivate the workforce, redesigning jobs to make them more efficient or training employees to improve their skills.

3 The potential drawback of increasing labour productivity is that it could lead to an overworked workforce. If this happens the business could experience high rates of labour turnover and dissatisfaction amongst employees.

51. Lean production

1 In order for JIT to be successful a business will require effective systems of communication with its suppliers.
2 Three barriers to effective lean production include the responsibility and pressure it places on the workforce, the danger of devaluing the product and the potential resistance to change by the workforce.

52. Capacity and technology efficiency

1 A business might want to decrease capacity in order to increase capacity utilisation and get rid of redundant or unutilised resources.
2 Labour intensive involves production that is reliant on a workforce, whereas capital intensive production is focused on capital goods such as robots and machinery.
3 Technology can improve efficiency by removing human error and speeding up the production process.

3.4.4

54. Improving quality

1 Quality is important because it is a key way that a business can add value to its products. Quality can help build a reputation of reliability and make a business more competitive at a given price point.
2 A business could improve quality by adopting quality management techniques such as quality control and quality assurance.
3 Quality is difficult to improve because it can be expensive to implement. It is also very difficult to interpret what quality means to many customers as it is very subjective and may depend on a wide number of variables.

3.4.5

56. Inventory and supply chains 1

1 Inventory management can help a business gain a competitive advantage by allowing it to deliver its products faster than its competitors, providing a more reliable service and providing flexibility such as customisation for the customer.
2 Holding a large inventory might be a risk because it can get damaged, perish or go out of date. Holding inventory is also an opportunity cost because it ties up cash that could be spent elsewhere.
3 The target market might determine the level of customisation a business provides. For example, a specialist or niche product often offers greater customisation, whereas mass market products tend to be more standardised.

57. Inventory and supply chains 2

1 Maximum stock level, minimum stock level and re-order level are three pieces of information usually shown on an inventory control chart.
2 A business can increase flexibility when managing inventory by using computer aided manufacturing or adopting just-in-time stock control.
3 The supply chain refers to the network of providers involved in the process of getting the product to the customer.

3.5.1

61. Setting financial objectives 1

1 Operating profit is the profit left after direct costs and indirect costs have been subtracted from revenue.
2 Cash flow may be more important than profit because without managing cash flow and having sufficient working capital, a business might fail before it is able to achieve a profit at the end of the financial year.
3 A business might set itself a financial objective to reduce costs by 10% because it will help improve efficiency across the organisation and improve profitability.

62. Setting financial objectives 2

1 If a business has low gearing it means that a small proportion of the capital used to finance the business is debt.
2 Return on investment = (operating profit × 100) / capital invested.
3 The economic environment may determine the potential success of a business. For example, a business may estimate less financial success in a recession. Therefore the economic environment may influence the financial objectives set by a business.

3.5.2

64. Budgets

1 Two examples of expenditure budgets are the salaries budget and materials budget.
2 An adverse variance is one that is worse than budgeted. This would be lower on a sales budget and greater on an expenditure budget.
3 Budgets are hard to forecast because a business will often experience unforeseen costs and factors that can impact its sales revenue.

65. Cash flow forecasts

1 The opening balance is the money carried forward from the previous trading period, for example the previous day, week or month.
2 Three outflows for a business include rent, the cost of raw materials and the wages of its workforce.
3 A cash flow forecast might be used to identify any periods where a business is likely to experience a negative cash flow. If a business can identify these periods they can put in place measures to remedy the problem such as finding short-term sources of finance.
4 A cash flow forecast is calculated by (total cash inflows – total cash outflows = net cash flow + opening balance = closing balance.
5 Net cash flow is the difference between total cash inflows (receipts) minus total cash outflows (expenses).

66. Break even 1

1 Break-even = fixed cost / contribution per unit.
2 A break-even chart will include fixed costs, total revenue and total costs.
3 A business might use a break-even analysis to identify the break-even point, make decisions on price and answer 'what if' questions about different levels of production.

67. Break even 2

1 A business could lower its break-even point by reducing variable costs or increasing its price.
2 The margin of safety is the difference in units between the level of output and the break-even point. It identifies the level that output could drop before a loss is made.

3 Two limitations of break-even analysis are: it simplifies the nature of costs and revenue at different levels of output; it is also very difficult to calculate when a business produces multiple varieties of products.

68. Profitability

1 Profit for the year is the net profit generated by a business. This is the profit that can be returned to the owners or reinvested into the business.
2 Financial ratios are important because they allow managers to compare different financial variables and compare financial performance over time.
3 One limitation of financial information when making business decisions is that it does not take into account qualitative information such as brand image and motivation of the workforce.

3.5.3

72. Sources of finance 2

1 Three examples of short-term sources of finance include trade credit, an overdraft and debt factoring.
2 Retained profit is low risk because it does not have to be paid back.
3 Private limited companies (Ltd) and public limited companies (Plc) can raise finance through share capital.

3.5.4

74. Improving cash flow

1 Two ways a business could increase cash inflow would be to sell off excess stock at a discount or collect any outstanding debts from debtors.
2 A business could reduce cash outflows by agreeing trade credit with suppliers and delaying payments to creditors.
3 A business might have difficulty managing its cash flow if it fails to carry out market research into the demand for its products, has a long working capital cycle or offers trade credit terms with its customers that are too lenient.

75. Improving profitability

1 Three costs a business could reduce to improve profits are the cost of goods sold, salaries and business insurance fees.
2 Price is important to the profitability of a business because it directly affects the demand for a product and the revenue received on each item sold.
3 When trying to improve profitability a business might face problems such as a fall in quality due to cost-cutting, an inability to increase prices due to lack of value added and unforeseen costs that will directly affect forecast profits.

3.6.1

81. Human resource objectives

1 Hard HRM is the perspective that employees are a resource that need to be utilised to maximise efficiency and productivity.
2 Human resources can add value to an organisation by improving the skills and motivation of the workforce. This can improve productivity, innovation and customer service.
3 Three factors that a business may consider when setting HR objectives include the economic environment, competitive environment and the current make-up of the workforce in terms of its age, skills and growth.

3.6.2

83. Human resource performance 1

1 Labour productivity is important because by increasing labour productivity the cost per unit of output falls and this helps improve competitiveness.
2 There is an inverse relationship between labour productivity and unit labour costs because as the workforce becomes more productive a greater output is achieved from the same level of labour. For this reason, labour costs are absorbed across a greater number of units.
3 Factors that may contribute towards employee costs as a percentage of revenue include pensions, employee healthcare schemes and wage rates.

84. Human resource performance 2

1 A business could interpret a high labour turnover ratio as a result of dissatisfaction and low morale.
2 A business may want high retention rates as this will minimise the cost of recruiting new staff and maintain the skills and knowledge developed within the workforce.
3 Labour cost information might be used by a manager to set cost cutting targets, monitor the performance of the workforce and measure the impact of factors such as employee training.

3.6.3

86. Job design

1 Job design refers to the contents of a job in terms of its duties and responsibilities.
2 Two elements of the Job Characteristics Model include the core job dimensions and the critical psychological states.
3 Job enrichment involves adding more challenge and complexity to the job, whereas job enlargement involves adding variety to the job.

87. Organisation design 1

1 Delegation frees up managers and allows them to focus on strategic decision making. Delegation also benefits junior employees who benefit from the responsibility and experience of carrying out new tasks.
2 A tall organisation structure works best when the nature of the product or business requires close control and management with clearly distinguished roles and lines of authority.
3 A flat organisation structure works well with a highly skilled workforce who require little supervision and businesses where decisions need to be made quickly.

88. Organisation design 2

1 Centralisation might be appropriate for a business when the senior leaders within the organisation want to keep close control of decision making and standardise processes and products across the organisation.
2 When considering the design of the organisation a manager should consider the level of autonomy they want to give employees, how decisions will be made and the need for structure and authority.
3 Employer brand refers to a business's reputation as an employer and place of work. By having a strong employer brand the business will be able to attract the best employees.

89. Human resource flow

1 The recruitment process includes drawing up a job description and person specification, advertising the job, short-listing applicants, requesting references, inviting

candidates to interview and the necessary selection processes and identifying the best candidate and offering a contract of employment.

2 Recruitment is a key aspect of HRM because it is the process of bringing new talent and skills into the organisation. The effectiveness of the recruitment process will directly determine the quality of a company's workforce.

3 As organisations change along with the external environment, redeployment of employees is important to ensure new roles are filled and human resources are used to their full potential.

3.6.4

91. Motivational theories 1

1 Two principles of scientific management include efficiency through standardisation and the division of labour. Frederick Taylor believed that man is a rational being and is primarily motivated by financial means. Work and reward were, therefore, organised accordingly.

2 Elton Mayo's theory of motivation differs from that of Frederick Taylor in that Elton Mayo believed that human beings are primarily motivated by social interaction, whereas Taylor believed that people are rational beings and primarily motivated by financial reward.

3 Maslow's five human needs include physiological needs, security needs, love and belonging, self-esteem and self-actualisation.

92. Motivational theories 2

1 Three hygiene factors include clean working conditions, employee healthcare and a good wage.

2 Maslow believed that people are motivated to achieve a hierarchy of needs and that they aim to achieve these needs in a systematic order in all aspects of their life. Although Herzberg also identified similar motivational factors to Maslow, he believed that some factors, known as hygiene factors (similar to the lower order needs identified by Maslow), did not in fact motivate employees but prevented demotivation if they were sufficiently satisfied. Herzberg's 'motivators' correspond to the 'higher order' needs identified in Maslow's hierarchy.

3 A manager could use motivational theory to develop job design and plan remuneration so that employee needs are being met in order to maximise motivation.

93. Financial methods of motivation

1 A business might use commission as a financial motivator to reward sales staff.

2 The benefits of profit-sharing are that employees are only financially rewarded if the business performs well and generates an end of year profit. It also ensures employees are focused on the overall performance of the company and not just their own jobs.

3 The limitations of financial rewards are that they will only motivate employees to a certain extent. Financial rewards will not aid employees in achieving job satisfaction through social interactions, self-esteem and self-actualisation.

94. Non-financial methods of motivation

1 Employee training might motivate a workforce because it shows employees that the company is investing in their skills and knowledge. This helps build job security and the long-term prospects of career progression.

2 The drawbacks of teamworking are that it is difficult to identify the performance of individuals and in some circumstances social interactions at work could reduce labour productivity if they become a distraction from the task.

3 It is important to help employees achieve their 'higher order' needs as, according to Herzberg, without sufficient opportunities for career progression and personal satisfaction within a job, employees will not be motivated at work.

95. Choosing motivational methods

1 A manager might decide not to delegate decisions if the decisions are key ones or the manager does not believe their subordinates have the relevant knowledge or experience.

2 Three benefits of a highly motivated workforce are that they are more productive, will freely contribute and engage with the business and are less likely to leave the organisation.

3 The skill level of the workforce is important when considering methods of motivation because the more highly skilled the workforce, the more likely it is that employees will seek opportunities for self-actualisation. The nature of the job may also dictate the most appropriate method of payment and financial reward.

3.6.5

97. Employer–employee relations

1 A trade union is an organisation established to protect and improve the economic and working conditions of workers, such as the National Union of Teachers (NUT).

2 A works council is different from a trade union because it is not an external organisation with a specific remit and legal right to protect its members.

3 Technology such as email and internal intranet systems can improve employee communication by giving employees greater access to company information and allowing them to contribute to decisions through anonymous surveys and votes.

98. Employee disputes

1 Three benefits of effective employer–employee communication are greater involvement of employees, better understanding of the company's aims and objectives and higher levels of motivation.

2 Arbitration involves the resolution of disputes bound by a third party, whereas conciliation only involves the facilitation of negotiations by a third party.

3 Two barriers to effective communication are there being no opportunity for feedback and the misinterpretation of the message.

3.7.1

102. Mission and corporate objectives

1 Businesses use mission statements to set out and clarify the purpose of the business and communicate this purpose to all stakeholder groups.

2 Whereas a mission statement will lay down the broad purpose of a business, the corporate objectives will set out clear targets that are specific and measurable.

3 Three areas that corporate objectives may focus on include market standing, shareholder value and growth.

103. Strategy and tactics

1 Strategic decisions are broad and long term and guide the overall direction of the business, whereas tactical decisions are day-to-day decisions made by managers within the business that lead to actions which support the business strategy.

2 Examples of functional objectives include:
Marketing – to ensure 90% customer awareness of our brand.
Operations – to lower production costs by 10%.
HRM – to ensure the whole workforce are fully trained on the new IT systems by March.

104. SWOT analysis

1 SWOT stands for strengths, weaknesses, opportunities and threats.
2 A business might use SWOT analysis in order to identify its current position and form new objectives and business strategy.
3 The limitations of SWOT analysis are that often issues can be interpreted differently depending on your perspective. For example, something that is considered a strength to the business might also be a weakness.

3.7.2

106. Financial accounts 1

1 An income statement shows the revenue generated by a business, the costs it incurs and any profit generated, typically over the period of one year.
2 Gross profit is the profit that a business makes on its trading activity taking into account the direct cost of goods sold. Whereas, operating profit takes into account all other indirect costs (overheads).
3 Exceptional items are incomes and expenses that are not directly associated with the main activities of the business. These are kept separate in financial accounts in order to give a clearer indication of profit quality.

107. Financial accounts 2

1 A balance sheet is a snapshot of a business on a given day and indicates the assets and liabilities of a business. A balance sheet is an indicator of the value of a business.
2 A current asset is an item of value that the business expects to sell or use within the year.
3 Net assets are the difference between the total assets and the current liabilities.

108. Using financial ratios 1

1 The four categories of financial ratio are profitability ratios, liquidity ratios, gearing ratios and efficiency ratios.
2 Two profitability ratios include the gross profit margin ratio and the operating profit margin ratio.
3 Capital employed is the money invested into a business through share capital and long-term borrowing.

109. Using financial ratios 2

1 Liquidity refers to the ability of a business to pay its short-term liabilities.
2 A current ratio of 0.8:1 means that for every pound of liabilities the business has 80p worth of current assets.
3 A highly geared business is one that has a significant proportion of its capital employed provided through long-term borrowing. This business might face problems repaying its debts if performance falls.

110. Using financial ratios 3

1 A business might calculate its inventory turnover when it holds large inventories. The business will be interested in how quickly these inventories are turned over as this will help free up working capital.
2 Receivables are the monies owed to a business from its debtors. Payables are expenses that the business must make to its creditors.
3 The faster a business is able to retrieve debts from its debtors (receivables) the quicker cash will flow into a business, helping improve its liquidity position.

111. The value of financial accounts and financial ratios

1 One limitation of financial ratios is that they do not take into account qualitative factors such as a business's reputation, brand image or the motivation of the workforce.
2 Two stakeholder groups who might use the financial information held in financial accounts include the directors of the business to interpret the performance of the company and potential shareholders who are considering investment in the company.
3 The managers of a business might window dress their financial accounts in order to enhance the perceived performance of the company. This may boost morale within the company, attract potential shareholders and satisfy current shareholders.

3.7.3

113. Analysing the internal position

1 Two measures of marketing performance include market share and brand recognition.
2 Two measures of operational performance include quality and capacity utilisation.
3 Two measures of human resource performance include unit labour costs and labour retention.

114. Core competencies

1 A core competency is a unique ability that a business possesses that provides it with a competitive advantage.
2 A core competency can lead to a competitive advantage because it is something that a business does well. This could mean it can do this better than other businesses and if it is something that other businesses cannot copy, then it is likely to become a competitive advantage.
3 A business might assess its long-term performance by the extent it has invested in research and development or the level of employee engagement.

115. Analysing human resource performance

1 Elkington's Triple Bottom Line refers to three factors that a business should consider when evaluating its success. These include profit, people and planet. The Triple Bottom Line goes beyond simply measuring profitability and looks at how the business is succeeding with other stakeholders.
2 The value of the Balanced Scorecard and the Triple Bottom Line comes from the fact that they consider all stakeholders and not just the shareholders/owners of the business.

3.7.4

119. Political

1 The UK government encourages enterprise because new business start-ups employ people and reduce unemployment.
2 Investment in infrastructure benefits businesses because it makes it easier for businesses to operate within an economy. For example, building new roads and rail links will make it easier for a business to transport its goods and gain access to imports and exports.
3 Self-regulation involves businesses within an industry agreeing a code of conduct for trade and business practices. The purpose of self-regulation is to avoid externally imposed regulation and ensure businesses follow this code.

120. Legal

1 The drawback of legislation for a business is that new legislation may impose changes on a business such as the need to alter its products or processes. This can increase the business's costs. For example, a business may have to change labels to meet consumer protection legislation.

2 New legislation can create opportunities for businesses through creating new markets and making it easier for businesses to compete. For example, new legislation on carbon emissions could create greater demand for 'green' engines, increasing demand for cars like the BMW i3.

3 Legislation can be used to impose a tax, fines or charges on businesses that create negative externalities, such as pollution, for a third party. The money raised through such means will internalise the externality – make businesses pay the cost.

3.7.5

122. Economic change

1 Two features of an economic boom include high demand for products and services and pressure on inflation.

2 Two features of an economic slump include sustained low demand and less investment in business growth.

3 Two features of an economic recovery include businesses starting to take on new employees and increased consumer confidence.

123. Economic factors

1 When a currency is strong this benefits importers as their currency will buy more of a foreign currency. In effect, this lowers the cost of products and materials being bought from abroad. However, when the currency is weak, this has the opposite effect. A strong currency has a negative impact on exporters as this increases the price of their products in foreign markets. Unless the exporter is able to reduce their prices, demand is likely to fall. On the other hand, when the currency is weak exporters normally experience high demand due to their products being cheaper in foreign markets.

2 Businesses want a steady rate of inflation in order to manage the steady rise in costs without having to increase their prices sharply, which could have a negative impact on demand. A high rate of inflation may also mean cutbacks in households and similar falls in demand for non-essential items.

124. Fiscal and monetary policy

1 Monetary policy is a government policy concerned with the supply of money in the economy. One mechanism of monetary policy is control of interest rates.

2 Fiscal policy is concerned with government spending and taxation.

125. Trade and protectionism

1 A government might impose protectionist strategies in order to protect domestic industries and businesses from the negative impact of competition from foreign firms.

2 Three protectionist strategies a government might adopt include: favouring state procurement, imposing import quotas on certain products and imposing import tariffs on goods brought into the country.

126. Globalisation

1 Two risks of operating in international markets include the difficulties of language and cultural barriers and the danger of political insecurity – a new political regime may change policies on business activity and international trade.

2 Two potential opportunities for businesses operating in international markets is the opportunity to merge or take over international firms with experience and strong brand identities. A second opportunity may be to build a customer base and brand loyalty in small but fast growing markets as incomes grow in many developing nations.

3.7.6

128. Social change

1 Three changing demographic factors that may affect a business are the ageing population of the UK, the growth in single occupancy homes and the influx of Eastern European migrants to the UK.

2 There are many opportunities that might exist for businesses as a result of changing consumer lifestyles. For example, the prominence of smartphone technology creates new opportunities for technology companies to develop supporting software such as smartphone apps. Similarly, the growth in luxury products creates further opportunities, such as the 'glamping' trend – 'luxury' camping and people investing in their comfort when they go camping.

129. Technological change

1 The world wide web has had a significant impact on the way businesses operate over the past 20 years. Many businesses no longer require retail outlets to sell their products and instead sell directly to the customer. Businesses are also able to communicate directly with customers, targeting individuals with direct messaging and emails.

2 Two key technological advancements in recent years are: the developments in bar code scanning, such as quick response (QR) codes, which allow customers to access information quickly through a smartphone; 3D printing, with the opportunity to eventually print most products at minimal cost.

3 The risks involved with developing new technologies are that it is very expensive to invest in researching and developing new technologies, but there is no guarantee that a new technology will be accepted by an industry or the consumer. There is also the danger that a technology will become obsolete quickly and be superseded by another innovation. For example, mini discs were quickly replaced by MP3 players.

130. Corporate Social Responsibility 1

1 Two ways in which changes in technology can affect functional decisions is by changing the focus of future investments and influencing financial budgets. Technology can also affect HR decisions if employees require training when new technology is introduced.

2 Corporate Social Responsibility (CSR) is the belief that a business should act responsibly and protect the interests of its stakeholders.

3 The forces against a business investing in CSR are that it can be expensive to focus on sustainability and the interests of all stakeholders and this in turn may have an impact on short-term profitability and the interests of shareholders.

131. Corporate Social Responsibility 2

1 The shareholder concept refers to the belief that the best way for a business to be successful is to focus on the interests of its shareholders – primarily, by maximising profitability.

2 CSR is important for all businesses as it promotes long term sustainability. By focusing on the Triple Bottom Line a business will ensure that it does not have a negative impact on the environment or society and this helps ensure the conditions for businesses to operate are maintained in the long term.

3 The four responsibilities as outlined in Caroll's CSR pyramid include economic responsibility, legal responsibility, ethical responsibility and philanthropic responsibility.

3.7.7

133. The competitive environment 1

1 Porter's five competitive forces include competitive rivalry within an industry, bargaining power of suppliers, bargaining power of buyers, threat of substitutes and threat of new entrants.
2 The rivalry within a market might be determined by the number of competitors, the degree of homogeneity between brands and the extent to which businesses within the market are willing to collaborate.
3 Where suppliers have a lot of bargaining power within a market, businesses may try to establish long-term supply contracts or look for alternative sources of a substitute product or material.

134. The competitive environment 2

1 Two factors that may give buyers power in a market are the extent of their choice between rival businesses (or the availability of substitutes) and their access to information on the various competitors and their products.
2 A substitute product is one that is not the same, but could serve the same purpose or fulfil the same need for the consumer. For example, a skiing holiday might be a substitute for a cruise.
3 A business might compete with new entrants in a market by improving the quality of its products, lowering its prices to be more competitive or finding a way to differentiate themselves from rival businesses. Each of these examples are ways to add value.

3.7.8

136. Investment appraisal 1

1 Investment appraisal might be used by a business to compare alternative investments in terms of the financial and non-financial return they may bring.
2 A business might calculate payback because this will indicate how quickly a firm is able to recoup its initial investment. This is important for businesses that may have cash flow problems or need to repay a lender quickly.
3 The average rate of return is useful when making investment decisions as it allows a business to directly compare potential investments in terms of the average profit they will generate over the life of the project or asset.

137. Investment appraisal 2

1 Two non-financial factors that a business may take into consideration when comparing potential investment decisions are the level of risk associated with each investment and the impact each investment may have on the Corporate Social Responsibility of the organisation.
2 Two factors that may determine the risk associated with an investment include the length of time it takes to pay back the initial investment and the experience the business has with that particular investment. The longer the payback period, the more chance there is for conditions to change and the likelihood that the investment will lose value. The experience of managers may also be a factor in determining risk as inexperienced managers may not see potential problems or issues that could disrupt the success of any investment.
3 A business might use sensitivity analysis to identify variations in forecasts to allow for a range of outcomes. This will allow it to ask 'what if' questions and put in place contingency plans to deal with various scenarios.

3.8.1

142. Choosing strategic direction 1

1 The four strategic directions outlined by the Ansoff matrix are market penetration, market development, product development and diversification.
2 Market penetration is low risk because it involves a business dealing with customers and a market with which they are familiar without the need for expensive investment in new products that might not be successful.
3 A product development strategy is beneficial as it allows a business to develop new products that can replace others that are nearing the end of their product life-cycle. It also allows a business to spread risk and stay ahead of its competitors through innovation and adding value.

143. Choosing strategic direction 2

1 Diversification might be a suitable strategy where a business is large and has considerable economies of scale. It might also be an appropriate strategy where a business has a strong brand that may be trusted in a variety of markets or there is the opportunity to merge or take over a business in the market which the business wishes to diversify into.
2 When choosing a strategic direction a business will consider the cost of the strategy and the investment required to achieve its goal, the potential returns on the investment and how the business's core competencies may support the strategy.

3.8.2

145. Porter's strategies 1

1 A business can achieve cost leadership by being the lowest cost operator. This means that it is able to produce its products at a lower cost than any other rival. This means that it can charge a lower price than its rivals or maintain price parity and achieve higher profit margins.
2 A business could differentiate its product in a number of ways. These might include its design, features, brand image, quality or the services that come with the product, such as after sales service.

146. Porter's strategies 2

1 Customer loyalty is important with a segmentation strategy because the business is operating in a niche (focused) market. As this means there are fewer potential customers, the business must retain as many as possible if it is going to maintain sales.
2 A niche market is a market with a relatively small number of potential customers with specific needs which separate them from the mass market.

147. Bowman's strategic clock

1 Bowman's strategic clock is a business tool that outlines a number of strategic positions that a business may take in the market based on the value of a product compared to its price.
2 Bowman's strategic clock differs from Porter's strategies as it offers a far wider range of potential positions and represents these strategies based on a price point and not the cost to the business. Furthermore, Bowman believed that businesses can compete where value does not justify the price.
3 Some of the strategies identified by Bowman's strategic clock are risky as they represent a low value product being sold at a high price. In effect, these strategies, such as monopoly pricing or risky high margins, do not offer customers value for money and in some circumstances may take advantage of customers. These strategies are risky because reputation and loyalty can easily be damaged if customers do not believe they are being treated fairly.

149. The value of strategic positioning

1 Two factors that might influence the strategic position that a business takes include the relative strategic positions adopted by its competitors and the business's strengths in the form of its core competencies. For example, having a highly skilled workforce may lead to the business choosing to differentiate on customer service.

2 The strategic position of a business may change over time as the market it operates in will also change. For example, social and legal factors will change, leading to different customer needs and new regulations. These factors might erode the value or feasibility of the current strategy and mean a new position has to be taken in order to remain competitive.

3 A business can achieve a sustainable competitive advantage through innovation, architecture or reputation. Innovation refers to a business's ability to create new ideas, products and processes that are better than those of competitors. Architecture refers to the internal relationships between stakeholders that build synergy, understanding, trust and effective working relationships; reputation refers to the brand image that the business builds over time.

3.9.1

152. Assessing a change in scale 1

1 Organic growth is steady and gradual. Whereas, external growth is very sudden and can bring about significant change in an organisation.

2 Economies of scope refers to the benefits a business experiences by operating with a wide variety of products in a number of markets. These benefits include reduced costs shared across the different product lines and spreading the risk of any one product failing.

3 Financial economies of scale are experienced when a large business has more collateral and can therefore raise more capital through loans than a smaller business can.

153. Assessing a change in scale 2

1 Two diseconomies of scale a business might experience include communication problems and flexibility. Large businesses might find it more difficult to communicate with all stakeholders and guarantee the right message is received across the organisation. Large organisations also take longer to make decisions and implement them and this can reduce their ability to change quickly.

2 Overtrading refers to a business that grows too fast and overstretches its financial resources such as cash. Overtrading can lead to operational inefficiencies, such as lost orders, and cash flow problems.

154. Managing growth

1 Greiner's model of growth identifies the likely phases a business may go through as it grows in scale. If a manger understands these phases, then they can take steps to address some of the problems associated with each stage. For example, at the 'leadership crisis' phase the manager may choose to employ supervisors or put in place clear policies to govern how tasks should be done.

2 As a business grows, the operations function may be affected in a number of ways. First, operations must be able to increase capacity whilst maintaining efficiency and quality. Operations may also have to consider different methods of production. For example, a batch production approach may no longer be feasible and the business may have to adopt flow production as demand increases.

155. Types and methods of growth

1 A business may choose to seek a joint venture instead of an acquisition because this model of growth will not require the capital investment required to buy the other company. Acquisitions can also result in resistance from internal stakeholders; this is less likely in a joint venture as growth involves partnership and not takeover.

2 Franchising is a popular method of expansion as the risks associated with growth, such as the business failing in new markets, are passed on to the franchisee. The capital required to start the new business or branch is provided by someone else who wishes to gain the benefits of a reputable brand.

3 A business might choose to take over a supplier so that it can guarantee and control the supply of materials or products. The cost of these resources is also reduced as there is no longer a mark-up added by the supplier.

3.9.2

157. Assessing innovation 1

1 There is pressure on businesses to keep innovating because the competitive environment around them does not stop changing. For example, competitors release new and improved products, customer needs change and technology advances. If any business is to remain competitive, it must find ways to better what it does – improving productivity and efficiency, lowering costs and adding value in new ways.

2 The factors that might contribute to an innovative business culture include rewarding innovation, an acceptance of failure (low fear of innovative ideas not working), and a willingness to listen to new ideas amongst the organisation's leaders.

158. Assessing innovation 2

1 Disruptive innovation refers to innovation that considerably alters a market. Any disruptive innovation might concern the managers of a business because there is potential for this innovation to make their current products and processes obsolete. Furthermore, if the business is unable to keep up with the innovation in an industry, it is likely to fall behind and lose competitiveness.

2 A business should innovate because it is one way to improve competitiveness through better quality, faster delivery, lower costs or improved service. Innovation can directly influence each of these. Furthermore, without innovation a business will lose ground on its competitors, leading to a loss of market share and possibly failure.

3 A business can protect the design of a new product through design rights – these do not need to be registered and are similar to copyright.

3.9.3

160. Assessing internationalisation 1

1 Some firms choose to operate in international markets because they offer significant growth opportunities through market development. Some businesses may also benefit from lower costs of production due to lower costs of resources and labour costs.

2 Internationalisation is closely linked to the Ansoff matrix because it may be a key component of the market development and diversification strategies.

3 There are a number of options for a business looking to expand abroad. Two options include choosing to export its products into foreign markets or via direct investment, which involves setting up production facilities and retail outlets in a foreign country.

161. Assessing internationalisation 2

1 Three factors that a business might consider when choosing which international markets to operate in include the competitive rivalry of businesses within the market, the political stability of the country and the relative similarities to its home market, which it has experience of.

2 A business might choose to re-shore production if there is pressure for the business to support employment in its home nation. It may also choose to re-shore if it has experienced diseconomies of scale from operating abroad.

3 The difference between a global strategy and a multi-domestic strategy is that a global strategy involves creating a standardised product for all international markets, whereas a multi-domestic strategy involves products being specifically tailored for the local conditions of each international market.

162. Assessing internationalisation 3

1 The benefit of running a transnational business is that it is completely responsive to local trends and needs within the market, whilst maintaining the benefits of size and economies of scale.

2 The risks associated with running an international business are that slight modifications for each market can be very costly and erode any advantages the business might have received through economies of scale.

3.9.4

164. Assessing the use of digital technology 1

1 Data mining is a process of analysing business data to identify patterns and relationships between a number of variables, for example demographics and buying behaviour in supermarkets.

2 E-commerce is not suitable for all forms of business because some products are not suitable for shipping because they are very delicate. Furthermore, a customer may prefer to try out a product before they purchase it, for example to see if it fits or see how it works.

3 Enterprise resource planning (ERP) might be useful to link functional aspects of a business such as the ordering of stock and details of customer accounts. For example, this might be appropriate when customers are buying a new car.

165. Assessing the use of digital technology 2

1 Digital technology can benefit a business by making important information available to employees wherever they are in order to make important decisions. This could include access to other employees with knowledge and experience or information on projects, products and customer information.

2 Some of the risks in investing in digital technologies are that technology is constantly changing and technology can very quickly become obsolete or lose its value when replaced with more effective and efficient technologies. This is risky as a business can easily invest energy and time into systems that need replacing, lowering the return on investment.

3.10.1

168. Managing change 1

1 External forces could include technological change or political change. Both of these forces may require a business to adapt its products in order to remain competitive. For example, changing a product to meet new regulations or investing in new technology to innovate its product range.

2 Lewin's force field analysis model is a tool used to identify the various forces driving change and opposing change. A manager may use this model to identify any resistance to a new business strategy and develop and put in place measures to remove these barriers. A manager may also use the model to evaluate whether any form of change is worthwhile.

169. Managing change 2

1 One factor that may change within a business is its workforce. Over time, employees will leave and retire. A business must plan for the future needs of its workforce and put in place measures to ensure employees are replaced and trained. Furthermore, when managing workforce change a business must also plan for growth or the downsizing of the organisation. This could involve creating new jobs, or in the latter example, redundancies.

2 Two reasons why employees might resist change include a focus on their own self-interests, which might be affected by the change, or a lack of understanding of the change, the need for it and how it might affect them.

3 Two ways that a manager might ensure the process of change runs smoothly is to ensure the change is thoroughly communicated to the workforce and they understand why it is necessary for the long-term success of the business. A manager should also ensure their workforce is involved in the decision-making process and that key issues are negotiated.

3.10.2

171. Managing organisational culture 1

1 Business cultures differ across nations in a number of ways. For example, some nations demonstrate a big power distance between managers and employees. This involves the relationships that might exist between these two groups. Where power distance is big, employees may not form friendships with their managers outside of work and may maintain very formal relationships in work. Whereas in businesses in countries which have a small power distance, employees may speak frankly with their bosses and have an informal relationship.

2 Organisation culture can be classified in a number of ways. For example, Charles Handy identified four cultural types based on the relationships between employees and managers. These include power culture, role culture, task culture and person culture. Geert Hofstede also identified that nations have different cultural traits. These vary from country to country and involve factors such as power distance, individualism, masculinity and uncertainty avoidance.

172. Managing organisational culture 2

1 Factors that may influence organisational culture include the leaders within the organisation, the values and beliefs, the structure of the business and the norms and traditions.

2 A business might choose to change its culture if the managers believe that it is not effective and could lead to failure. For example, if the organisation has a culture of making key decisions slowly, the managers may try to change this if they believe it will help make the business more responsive to customer needs, and therefore, more competitive.

3 Changing organisational culture is very difficult because many factors that contribute to an organisation's culture, such as the values and beliefs of employees, are not always obvious or 'visible'. People are also often resistant to any form of change because it brings with it uncertainty and many people will see this as risk.

3.10.3

174. Managing strategic implementation

1 Strategic implementation involves the stages a business will go through to plan, implement and evaluate its strategy.

2 There are a number of steps a business can take to ensure its strategy is implemented successfully. These steps might include communicating the strategy effectively to all employees, ensuring resources are made available to implement the strategy and identifying the key performance indicators (KPIs) that will be used to measure the success of the strategy.

3 Communication is vital if business strategy is to be implemented successfully. Effective communication will ensure that all employees understand what they should be doing and why they are doing it.

175. The role of organisational structure in strategic implementation

1 Two structures that a business might adopt in order to implement its strategy include a product structure or a regional structure. A product structure might be adopted if customer needs centre on the specific products a business offers or a regional structure might be adopted if the business is a multinational and has operations across different countries.

2 A business might choose to decentralise decision making in order to give regional managers more autonomy to make their own decisions. This might be important where the regional businesses are required to adapt what they do to meet the needs of local customers.

176. Network analysis 1

1 On a network diagram the EST refers to the earliest start time of a task or stage of a project. The LFT refers to the latest finish time of a particular task or project so that it does not delay other stages of the project.

2 The 'float' on an activity refers to the amount of additional time (hours, days or weeks) that a task can take without having an impact on the preceding task. The float is useful to know as it helps managers identify those tasks which are flexible versus those that are critical to meeting the project deadline.

3 The 'critical path' refers to those activities or tasks within a project where there is no flexibility in terms of float time, and therefore, are critical to the projected finish time of the whole project.

177. Network analysis 2

1 The benefits of using network analysis when implementing a strategy are that it helps managers to meet a deadline, identify critical tasks in the implementation of a strategy and effectively manage all resources involved in implementing the strategy.

2 The limitations of network analysis are that often the duration of a task within a project is difficult to predict and durations are often estimates. Furthermore, network analysis does not guarantee the project will be a success; all tasks still have to be managed effectively.

3.10.4

179. Why strategies fail 1

1 A business strategy might fail for a number of reasons. However, one of the most frequent reasons is that the external environment, including the political, legal and competitive landscape, is constantly changing. As a result, the original strategy may no longer be suitable as time goes by. If a business is unable to adapt its strategy then it is likely to fail.

2 An emergent strategy is one that develops as the strategic plan is implemented. Often a business will adapt the strategy because it has to respond to external forces or the managers realise that the initial plan was not appropriate.

3 Strategic drift occurs when a business's strategy no longer matches the environment in which it operates. This may occur when a business is not flexible and does not adapt its approach to meet the ever changing environment in which it operates.

180. Why strategies fail 2

1 A divorce of ownership and control exists in businesses where the pressure from shareholders forces the managers of the business to focus on short-term incentives such as shareholder value. This can cause problems for a business because it can discourage managers from making decisions that may be in the long-term interest of the business and its stakeholders. For example, failing to invest in employees' training in order to boost profits.

2 Contingency planning is important because it provides businesses with a fallback that they can act on should they need to. Contingency planning often considers how a business may react to the failure of a strategy.

Exam-style practice answers

Unit 3.1

1 C

2 A

3 C (£10 000 − 10% = a reduction in costs of £1000. Therefore profits will rise by £1000.)

4 Total revenue − total contribution = total variable costs
£25 000 − £17 700 = £7300
Total costs − total variable costs = fixed costs
£21 000 − £7300 = £13 700

5 If an electrician sets up their business as a private limited company (Ltd) they will be protected with limited liability. This means that their liability is limited to the capital invested in the business. As it is a competitive local market there is the possibility that the business could fail. If the business does fail the owner will not lose their personal assets such as their house or car.

6 A fall in GDP means that fewer goods and services are being bought in the UK. As a national delivery business relies on other businesses and individuals to ship goods this will directly affect the demand for their service. As a result, the business might experience a fall in revenue and may have to make cuts in order to maintain profits and reduce excess capacity in their warehouses and fleets of delivery vans.

7 Dividend pay-outs are important to the success of a business because dividend payments is one way that shareholders earn a return on their investment. If shareholders receive a high dividend yield then this will keep them satisfied with the performance of the company. As a result, the shareholders are more likely to let the managers of the company make decisions without interference; for example, signing off an agreement for bonus payments to the managers or the investment in new products if they believe these initiatives will continue to grow

the business and guarantee future dividends. This will mean that the managers of the company can make decisions to encourage long-term growth without shareholder input. On the other hand, some shareholders may be happy not to receive a significant pay-out. For example, Standard Chartered's shareholders may be satisfied with the 14.4p pay-out if they appreciate that the company is operating in a difficult economic climate. There are also other ways for shareholders to make money on their investment, such as rising share prices.

Overall, the long-term success of a Plc will be determined by many other factors than the dividends they return to shareholders. This may include the competitive advantage the company holds over its rivals and the extent that the business invests for the future. Nevertheless, there is considerable pressure on Plcs to satisfy their shareholders but there are many ways that they can do this without having to pay high dividends. If a business is able to reassure its shareholders that long-term sustainable growth is likely most shareholders will accept this and support the managers of the business.

Unit 3.2

1 C
2 A
3 Increasing advertising of current products: $(0.8 \times 25\,000 = £20\,000) + (0.2 \times 2\,000 = £400) = £20\,400 - £3\,000 = £17\,400$

Launch new product range: $(0.7 \times 50\,000 = £35\,000) + (0.3 \times 0 = 0) = £35\,000 - £5\,000 = £30\,000$

Launching a new product range is the best option.
4 Dave Nutton currently has an autocratic leadership style. This is where the manager takes control of decision making and gives instruction to their employees. This is demonstrated by Dave's insistence that he sees every design before it is approved for print. As the business grows Dave will have a larger team to manage and this might mean that he has to delegate more decisions as he will not be able to do everything. A democratic or laissez-faire leadership style might be more appropriate as his company grows.
5 Risk is the chance of incurring misfortune or loss. The decision to invest in a new garment printing machine is a relatively high risk strategy as the capital required to purchase the machinery is £50 000. It is unclear how Dave will finance the expansion and it is also likely that he will have to finance this growth with borrowing. This too will increase the level of risk as the business will have to make loan repayments as it grows.

Another factor that suggests this is a high risk venture is the lack of research or data that Dave has based the decision on. Dave has almost 10 years' experience in the industry, but the closure of a major competitor is only a rumour. Without a clear understanding of the UK printing market it is unclear whether there is sufficient demand for the expansion. Nevertheless, Print Eastwood is a successful business and along with Dave's experience could reduce the risk associated with his expansion plans.
6 From the stakeholder map we can see that Dave's suppliers have a high level of interest in his business. This might be because he is a successful business that continues to grow. For this reason a considerable amount of the suppliers' trade may come from Print Eastwood – they are a significant customer. As the printing materials supplied to Print Eastwood are fairly generic, Dave might be able to find a cheaper supplier elsewhere and this might suggest that working with his supplier is less important than with some other stakeholders, especially as they have limited power over his business. Nevertheless, by working closely with his suppliers Dave may be able to negotiate favourable conditions of supply at a discounted rate. In the long term this will help lower his business costs and the overall profitability through economies of scale.

7 The stakeholder map suggests that Print Eastwood's local community has significant power, but relatively little interest in the business. The high power may come from the fact that most of Print Eastwood's customers come from the local area, and any negative publicity could significantly affect sales. The lower level of interest may be because Print Eastwood is only a small business and not a significant employer in the local area. Neither is it likely that the business poses any negative externalities. Dave has ensured that his business works closely with the local community and as much of his trade comes from Eastwood then the local community is a significant factor in the long-term success of the company.

However, Print Eastwood is a growing business and if Dave's expansion plans pay off it is likely that his customer base will extend beyond the local area into other areas around Nottingham or the UK. As a result, keeping the local community happy may be less important than developing close links with a major supplier or building a cohesive workforce as the company grows.

Overall, the power and influence of the local community will become less important for the long-term success of Print Eastwood. However, the interest of the local community may grow if Print Eastwood becomes a significant employer or the local community is affected by negative externalities as a result of Print Eastwood's expansion. Ultimately, the extent to which the local community will influence the long-term success of Print Eastwood may be determined by the objectives Dave sets for his company and the value he places on supporting the local area of Eastwood.

Unit 3.3

1 B
2 C
3 $1\,288\,00 \times 0.03 = 38\,640$ vinyl records
4 Market segmentation will allow Rick White to understand the needs of his customers. This is because segmentation allows a business to group its customers into homogenous groups with similar needs. Rick has identified males aged 35 plus and university students. Therefore, it might be appropriate for Rick to segment his market based on income. This would allow him to target customers with different prices. Another benefit of segmentation is that it helps a business target customers with different promotion methods. Rick might therefore be able to use suitable channels to target local students, such as a university newspaper or flyers at a students' union.
5 If Round Round Records decided to distribute its products solely through e-commerce, this would allow Rick White to close down his record store. The benefits of not using a retail outlet is that it could save him the fixed costs of renting the property. However, he may still require storage facilities to keep his stock of records. Through e-commerce he may also be able to make it easier for his customers to search for products and reach a wider geographical market beyond the local areas.

However, Rick has realised that many of his customers visit his store for the 'shopping experience' and to meet other music enthusiasts. If Rick only sold through e-commerce he may lose this aspect, which could be a USP for his business. Furthermore, much of his trade may come through passing trade and without a retail store this may limit potential trade. At the moment 60% of Rick's trade comes through e-commerce; therefore it is a very important distribution channel for his business. Nevertheless, he should not close his retail store because this allows him to add value to his business and considering vinyl records are a traditional product many customers will probably want to buy them through a traditional channel. In the long term the channels of distribution that Rick uses may depend on what proportion of his sales are generated through e-commerce and the cost of running his shop.

6 'People' refers to how employees are used to add value to the marketing of a product. As Rick's business sells records 'people' is an important aspect of the marketing mix. People visit Rick's shop for the shopping experience and part of this will be how they interact with sales staff in the store. People enjoy buying music and the expertise of Rick and his staff will add value to the shopping experience.

On the other hand, there are aspects of the marketing mix that are just as important as 'people'. For example, 'Physical environment' will represent the décor and atmosphere within the store. Making records easy to browse and in an environment where people will want to shop will go hand in hand with 'people' and if done right will help Rick add value. Overall, 'People' is an important aspect of the marketing mix because it is key to offering customer service. However, without appropriately addressing other aspects of the marketing mix, such as price and promotion, Round Round Records would not be a successful business.

7 A premium price is one that is high in comparison to other competitors due to the value or prestige of the product. Pricing decisions are very important in order to maximise profit. If Rick is able to understand the demand and rarity of different records then he may be able to set a price that is appropriate and will maximise the profit margin on each record sold. This will help Round Round Records maximise sales revenue and the overall profits of the business.

Other factors that are important in maximising profits are Rick's ability to manage his overheads and the cost he pays to acquire his records. Running his retail store and paying wages for additional staff will be expensive and if he is not able to control these costs it will eat into his profits. Furthermore, charging a premium price will not help Rick maximise profits if the cost of purchasing his stock is high.

Overall, the price of a vinyl record will be determined by market forces. There is little that Rick can do to add value to his products apart from the service he gives and the shopping experience in his shop. Therefore, the most important factor that will influence profitability is Rick's ability to lower his operating costs. The ability for Rick to charge a premium price may also depend on the extent to which the vinyl market continues to grow in the future.

Unit 3.4

1 B

2 £12 000 + £7000 + £5750 = £24 750 ÷ 1300 = £19.04

3 The introduction of new ovens will increase the efficiency of the business by reducing the cooking times and increasing the quantity of food that can be cooked in a given time period. At the moment the capacity of the Cleethorpes restaurant is 65 tables per evening. With the new ovens this could increase the capacity of each restaurant and allow the waiters to serve a greater number of tables. As the hours worked will not increase, labour productivity will rise.

4 Capacity utilisation is the percentage of the total capacity that a business is operating at. If Tasty Tapas is able to maximise capacity utilisation it will reduce the average cost of each meal. This is because waiters will be paid the same for working a shift but will have turned over more tables, generating higher revenues for the business.

5 Operations management involves inventory management. One way that effective inventory management could increase Tasty Tapas's competitive advantage is by making sure the restaurant has all of the ingredients it needs to cook all of the meals on its menu. Occasionally it may not be able to serve every meal and this could put some customers off. By having systems in place for speedy delivery of all its ingredients this will help ensure this never happens. Furthermore, effective inventory management will help the business meet demand as the company grows and the

restaurants reach full capacity as was seen through June. Another way that operations management could help Tasty Tapas achieve a competitive advantage is through introducing elements of lean production. Lean production includes techniques such as Kaizen and JIT. Lean production helps a business improve efficiency by cutting out unnecessary processes and waste that do not add value to the business. This could help Tasty Tapas speed up its processes and serve meals quicker. This is particularly important considering that the business has received a number of complaints recently referring to the slow service in the restaurants.

6 Outsourcing involves contracting out certain tasks or processes to another business. If Tasty Tapas outsources aspects of food preparation it may allow it to speed up the production of meals and serve more tables if the food is prepared quicker. Not only will this help combat the problem of complaints about slow service, it will also serve more tables. This will increase capacity and the potential to generate higher revenue from serving more customers. Indeed, the maximum capacity of the restaurant may rise from 65 tables per evening.

On the other hand, outsourcing production to another business could reduce the authenticity of the Spanish cuisine. There is also no guarantee that outsourcing food preparation will make the process faster and it could lower the overall quality of food. As a result, the reputation of Tasty Tapas could be damaged.

Overall, the pressure on capacity seems to be an issue with the waiters and not the preparation of food and the new ovens may also alleviate some of the pressure in the kitchens. I do not feel that outsourcing food preparation will 'ease pressure on the kitchens' because it will no longer be in the control of the chefs; therefore more mistakes or faults could be incurred. Nevertheless, outsourcing can help improve efficiency by allowing workers to specialise and outsourcing basic food preparation could reduce costs.

7 Operating with a good supplier is important for a business like Tasty Tapas because it is a restaurant and will be receiving deliveries every day. Most restaurants deal with a variety of suppliers, therefore managing the supply chain is extremely important. Tasty Tapas also operates in a very competitive market so the cost of its ingredients will be important so that it can maximise profitability. For this reason, finding a cheap yet reliable supplier is very important. Furthermore, a good supplier will also be flexible and be able to offer trade credit to Tasty Tapas. Flexibility is important as Katie may want to vary the menu depending on the season or have different meal options on the 'specials board'. Trade credit is also very important as it can help Tasty Tapas manage its cash flow and ensure revenue is received before inventory has been paid.

However, other operational factors may be just as important as finding a good supplier. For example, ensuring the workforce is highly productive is also very important. If the workforce is not productive, for example being slow to serve meals, then this could reduce the competitiveness of Tasty Tapas in terms of developing a reputation for slow service and serving fewer meals in a day. For productivity to be high it is important that the workforce is highly motivated and uses processes that are effective and efficient. For example, making sure the hand held ordering devices are being used properly to streamline the ordering process.

Overall, a good supplier is very important for a restaurant like Tasty Tapas, but the most important operational issue at the moment is capacity utilisation. A good supplier cannot help increase capacity utilisation; therefore it is not the most important operational factor. The introduction of new ovens might help Tasty Tapas increase capacity utilisation in the future if it helps it cook more food in a shorter time period. The success of the new ovens may depend on whether or not they ease pressure in the kitchens and for this to happen staff may need training. It is also important for Katie to resolve the 'teething problems' with the touch screen devices if the benefits of new ovens are to translate into more meals being served.

Unit 3.5

1. Break-even = fixed costs ÷ contribution per unit
   £900 ÷ (£45 − 16) = **31.03 cakes**
2. 75 − 45 = 30 cakes (growth between Qr1 and Qtr 4)
   30 ÷ 45 − 100 = 66% **growth in forecasted sales**
3.

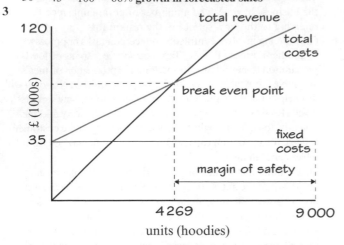

4. Revenue is the income generated through sales of Jaume's hoodies. In order to increase revenue one option is for Jaume to lower the price of his hoodies. If the product is relatively elastic then reducing price could help increase the volume of sales even though the contribution per hoodie would have fallen. This would be an effective strategy in a competitive market such as personalised hoodies.

5. Cash flow forecasting involves forecasting future cash inflows and outflows from a business. Cash flow forecasting is a valuable management tool for all businesses, but especially start-up businesses who may have more cash flow problems as they establish a customer base. Jaume will be able to use cash flow forecasting to identify periods within his first year when he may need extra capital or have a dip in sales. If he can identify any potential periods of negative cash flow, such as during the autumn when schools are not looking to purchase hoodies, then he can make arrangements to access extra cash, such as taking out a bank overdraft. However, cash flow can be very difficult to predict and without experience his forecasts are likely to be inaccurate.

   Other factors that may be important for Jaume include the budgets he sets. Jaume must have a clear understanding of his revenue and expenditure budgets as without these he will not be able to construct an accurate cash flow forecast. His budgets will also act as financial targets that he can set his objectives against.

   Overall, cash flow forecasting is very important to Jaume as many small businesses fail because they are unable to effectively manage this area of the business. However, Jaume must also put in place realistic budgets if he is going to manage his cash flow effectively. The accuracy of his cash flow forecasts may also depend on the accuracy and extent of his market research.

6. Issuing capital through the sale of new shares is an appropriate form of financing the business considering it is looking to expand. Issuing new shares through a stock market might attract lots of interest, especially as the company is already floated on the stock market and is profitable. As the business has plans for expansion, potential shareholders will see this as an opportunity to invest in a growing company and demand for the shares could be high. The benefit of raising finance through issuing new shares is that Hands On Plc will not be subject to high interest loan repayments.

   On the other hand, issuing new shares could dilute the directors' control of the company further. In the long-

term this could hinder business decision making, make the company vulnerable to takeover and limit the extent to which profits can be reinvested back into the business because shareholders will expect dividends from the annual profits. Raising finance through issuing new shares is a relatively safe option for Hands On Plc, considering they are a profitable and growing business. However, gearing has fallen over recent years and this suggests that a lower percentage of the capital in the business has come from borrowing. In order to balance the capital structure of the business, Hands On Plc could choose to borrow the money for the new product line from a bank. However, this may depend on the economic context and how willing the banks are to lend.

7. A financial objective is one that sets out the financial performance of the company and may flow from the corporate objectives. One objective that the owners of Hands on Plc might set is to balance the capital structure of the company so that it is evenly proportioned between share capital and long-term borrowing. At the moment the gearing ratio has fallen over recent years from 60% to 30%. This suggests that the business has paid off long-term debt. As the business is looking to expand further with a new line of products, one option may be to finance the expansion through a long-term loan instead of issuing new shares.

   Another objective for Hands On Plc might be to improve profitability. The data suggests that the company is effective at generating gross profit through its direct trading activity, but since 2013 operating profit has fallen slightly. Although this may not be a worry for the company it could suggest it is struggling to manage operating costs. As a result, operating profit and profit for the year might be a suitable area to focus on in order to stop the declining trend. However, there may be a good reason for the overall fall in operating profit, such as the investment in new machinery or growth in the workforce.

   As Hands On Plc is also looking to launch a new product line a suitable financial objective could be to set targets for the return on investment. The directors might set this target based on the return on investment of previous toy lines. However, the return on investment may be a long-term objective if they expect the payback to be over a number of years.

   Overall, the key issue is that Hands On Plc is a growing business that exports to the USA and Western Europe. Therefore, appropriate financial objectives might be based around growth. For this reason, the most appropriate financial objectives might be based around sales revenue growth and gross profit and in the long term operating profit and net profit once expansion has taken place. In order to hit these targets Hands On Plc should invest in marketing to promote its products to a wider customer base and establish export links with new agents. If it is able to do this it is likely that sales will grow and directly impact the overall profitability of the company.

Unit 3.6

1. C
2. A suitable human resource objective that Louise could set would be to reduce labour turnover and retain the best employees. This would seem to be an appropriate objective considering the labour turnover for the first 18 months. Setting this objective will help boost morale within the tea room as the team become settled and established. As a result, the settled employees will start to work as a team and productivity will rise.
3. QTR 1: £12 000 ÷ £20 000 × 100 = 60%
   QTR 4: £35 000 ÷ £72 000 × 100 = 49%
   Change in labour costs as a percentage of revenue fell by 11% between QTR 1 and QTR 4.
4. Job design refers to the contents of a job in terms of its duties and responsibilities. One way that Paul could improve job design would be to introduce job rotation across the workforce. For example, this might involve factory workers joining the delivery team for a day or carpenters working with

the upholsterers. This would add more variety to the work of Paul's employees and help them to appreciate how other areas of the business function. As a result, employee motivation may rise as they appreciate that they are part of a bigger team. Another aspect of job design is the extent to which decisions and tasks are delegated to Paul's subordinates. Paul could delegate some of his tasks to the factory managers in order to develop their skills and give them more autonomy over their jobs. This is a form of job enrichment and could help the managers achieve their self-esteem needs along with the opportunity for career progression.

5 Paul has introduced two new fringe benefits for employees that are types of financial rewards in the form of a staff discount and 2 more days' holiday which is part of the employees' contract and working conditions. This will help motivate employees because it shows that Paul cares for his staff. It may also help retain employees because they have an extra incentive to work for Retro Homes. In terms of motivation these additions may help employees achieve some of their basic needs as outlined by Maslow, in particular, their physiological needs.

On the other hand, Herzberg would consider holiday entitlement and staff discounts as 'hygiene factors' that will only prevent demotivation and not motivation of the workforce. Furthermore, neither of these initiatives will help employees achieve the 'higher order needs' or support the social aspects of work life. In order for Paul to truly motivate his workforce, he must think beyond simply financial methods of motivation and consider non-financial methods linked to job design.

Overall, these initiatives will help motivate staff as they improve the overall working conditions at Retro Home and reward staff with a discount on furniture. Nevertheless, if Paul wants a highly motivated workforce he must consider other factors such as the critical psychological states as outlined Hackman and Oldman's Job Characteristics Model. For example, ensuring work is meaningful, that employees have responsibility for their work and that they see the results of their work. The extent to which Paul develops a highly motivated workforce may depend on how he designs the job of his employees to maximise these factors.

6 The key change to Retro Homes' organisational structure is that Paul has brought in an extra level of management. This includes a production manager, a tea room manager and a showroom manager. The impact of this change is that Retro Homes now has a tall organisation structure. The benefit of this is that it will allow greater supervision and management of each team within the business. This could help improve productivity as each manager will be able to focus on their own area of the business and ensure their team is performing to the best of their ability. The new managers will also increase specialisation within the company and will reduce the span of control beneath Paul. Consequently, Paul and Louise can focus on strategic decisions and growing the company. However, employing three new managers will not be cheap and it will add considerably to the wage bill of the company. Recently labour costs as a percentage of revenue has fallen but it is likely that this will rise again in the near future. Paul will have to be careful that some employees do not become demotivated by these changes. For example, both factory managers may lose some of the authority and autonomy to make their own decisions if the production manager is autocratic and wants to influence most of the decisions made in either factory. Nevertheless, with a longer chain of command come opportunities for promotion and this could motivate employees in the long-run.

Overall, the key to success at Retro Homes may be how well the various areas of the business work together. As Paul and Louise have more time to focus on strategic decisions and not the day to day management of the business, this might be easier to achieve in the new organisation structure. Nevertheless, performance in terms of unit costs and labour productivity may fall in the short term, but if the new managers are effective each area of the business should improve over time through greater efficiencies and productivity. In order to encourage a high performing workforce, Paul and Louise must agree the job design in terms of enrichment, enlargement and delegation so that all employees are motivated to work hard under the new organisation structure.

Unit 3.7 (sub-topics 3.7.1–3.7.3)

1 The lead time of a suit refers to the time it takes for it to be delivered from the time it was ordered. If Sartorial Ltd can reduce its lead time, perhaps by moving production to the UK, it will mean that customers can receive their suits quicker. Although many people may expect it to take time to make a bespoke suit, shortening this process will certainly add value and some customers may be willing to pay an additional premium for a service that is quicker. Indeed, some customers may want a suit quickly, therefore, a shorter lead time will help meet their needs.

Another factor that may help Sartorial Ltd meet customer needs by reducing the lead time, is that the suits may be produced in the UK, and not the Czech Republic, in order for this to happen. Some customers may see a British made suit as being more prestigious, and again, this may add value to the product. As many customers looking for a bespoke suit are also looking for premium quality the 'made in Britain' may be desirable.

2 Quality refers to how well a product is 'fit for purpose' and meets the specification. Quality is also very subjective and can mean different things to different people. This makes it difficult to measure. However, Sartorial Ltd has set a target of 'zero defects or complaints' and this might be one way to measure quality of their suits. If no one complains then this would suggest that they are happy with their purchase and this might mean that Sartorial Ltd is achieving its mission of giving customers a 'suit they are proud to wear'.

On the other hand, quality can be difficult to measure. This is because it is subjective and can mean different things to different people. It is also very difficult to determine when providing customers with a service, as is the case when making bespoke suits. Furthermore, as the suits are bespoke it could be very difficult to standardise the product and set a benchmark for the desired quality. As a result, the quality of each suit and customer experience might be difficult to measure.

3 Financial performance can be measured by revenue or profitability. It can also be measured in terms of return on investment and liquidity. The gross profit margin is important for Sartorial Ltd because it gives an indication of the profitability of its main trading activity – selling suits. As the gross profit margin has fallen by 6 percentage points between 2014 and 2015, this could indicate that Sartorial Ltd's direct costs have increased, or that it is not generating as much revenue per sale. Although other profitability measures need to be considered, such as the operating profit and profit for the year, the gross profit margin gives a good indication of the performance before indirect costs have been deducted.

However, financial performance indicators need to be viewed alongside other indicators of long-term success. For example, the Triple Bottom Line or the Balanced Scorecard. These concepts take into account other factors such as the planet, learning and growth and the impact on stakeholders, to name but a few. Without considering these factors when analysing performance, it is unlikely that a business will have sustainable success if it is only focusing on the bottom line. For example, without considering the engagement and motivation of the workforce Sartorial Ltd could lose a key asset in its highly trained tailors, which will have a knock-on effect on profitability.

Overall, Sartorial Ltd must measure profitability because without it the business will struggle to grow and become the UK market leader for bespoke suits. Nevertheless, measuring profitability alone is likely to result in a detrimental effect on long-term performance. The importance of profitability may also depend on the current situation, both internally and externally. For example, a business looking to expand may sacrifice profitability as it reinvests profit into expansion. Profits may also be less important in a recession, where many businesses will be focusing on survival.

4   Functional targets are those set out by managers at a functional level and are set in order to help the business achieve its corporate objectives, and ultimately, its mission statement. Sartorial Ltd has set operational objectives to achieve 100% satisfaction of good or better and this is one way that it will be able to achieve its mission of 'a special experience for every customer'. However, although this is the objective, it is not clear how the business will ensure that all customers feel this way. Avoiding defects and complaints will similarly help Sartorial Ltd to achieve its mission, but again, it is not clear how this will be achieved. One way to do this might be to adopt quality assurance techniques or provide customer service training for all of its tailors.

Although operational targets are very important in achieving Sartorial Ltd's mission statement, it must also understand its customers in order to provide them with a 'special experience'. For this to happen the business must carry out market research through questionnaires and focus groups. Sartorial Ltd must also be able to manage its costs in order to provide suits that are affordable for a mass market. If its suits are too expensive customers may be proud to wear them, but it will narrow down the potential number of new customers and possibly prevent Sartorial Ltd from becoming the market leader.

Overall, operational targets are very important and achieving them will certainly contribute towards its mission statement. Nevertheless, Sartorial Ltd must have a clear strategy and know how it is going to achieve these targets over the next few years. In order to achieve its operational targets the company must first manage moving its production facilities to the UK. It is likely that there will be some teething problems with this, which could have an impact on the logistics of the business. Although it is likely that lead times may fall, costs may rise and efficiency could fall as the production facilities get set up.

Unit 3.7 (Sub-topics 3.7.4–3.7.8)

1   The data indicates that some public transport costs, such as rail fares, have trebled in the period between 1987 and 2013, with a sharp rise between 2009 and 2013. This increase may make it less accessible for some parts of the population to access public transport, lowering their mobility and access to jobs. As a result the standard of living in the UK will also fall. As motoring costs have not risen as sharply, this may mean more people opt to use cars instead of public transport. As a result, this will contribute to congestion and pollution, particularly in large cities.

2   The data suggests that government public sector spending increased considerably between 2006 and 2010. However, cutbacks were made between 2010 and 2013. The growth in spending may have included spending on infrastructure and subsidising public transport. This may have removed barriers to entry and made it easier for new public transport companies to enter the market. This may have increased consumer choice and improved the standard of public transport in the UK.

If the government were investing in infrastructure, this would create a number of opportunities for contract firms to build and improve roads and rail networks. This would create more demand in the market and opportunities for growth in heavy construction and road maintenance. The competitive rivalry within the industry will be very high as these companies bid to win the government contracts to build new roads and rail links.

3   The extract suggests that there are a number of technological advancements that will improve the standard of car safety and the opportunities for associated businesses. One way that these changes may lead to growth in the automobile industry is through creating cars that are more desirable to consumers. As new technologies are introduced there will always be a group of consumers known as the 'first movers' who will desire this new technology and be willing to purchase new cars that feature this technology. Furthermore, 'comprehensive vehicle tracking' may reduce insurance costs and this could lower the costs of running a car, particularly for younger drivers, consequently, increasing demand.

On the other hand, it is unlikely that this new technology will actually make cars cheaper or influence the number of cars on UK roads. For this reason, it is unlikely that we will see a significant increase in the demand for cars, but instead, increased demand for car manufacturers that are able to innovate and adopt this technology within their new models. Overall, demand may increase for some businesses that lead in developing these technologies, but long-term growth will mainly be determined by other factors such as population growth and fluctuations in the business cycle. Technology will increase demand where it makes products cheaper or more accessible to customers.

4   Uber's partnership with Facebook may help it increase its competitiveness because it creates a barrier for other companies who want to enter the market. Should other companies wish to start up a taxi hailing app the link with Facebook, a leading social media platform, limits the routes other firms can take to reach customers online. This move also gives Uber greater bargaining power. The partnership makes it even easier to use Uber's service, and therefore, reduces the bargaining power of customers because Uber is the easiest and most accessible option.

Nevertheless, the partnership with Facebook would mean sharing some revenue and Uber must compare this option to other investments. The ARR of 4% may be attractive, but this should be compared to other investments. A drawback of the partnership is the negative publicity the business has received. Uber will have to consider the impact the partnership may have on CSR and how this could affect the long-term success of the company. For example, Uber should consider Carroll's CSR pyramid and its 'legal' and 'philanthropic responsibilities'. It is possible that Uber may have to pay legal costs due to the pending lawsuits. For this reason, Uber may consider the payback of this investment and whether it may need these funds within the next 5 years in order to pay legal fees.

Overall, Uber is a private limited company driven by profit. The partnership with Facebook helps it protect its market share and improves competitiveness and is therefore the right choice. However, in the long term this may depend on the popularity of Facebook as a social media site and how the partnership is perceived and valued by Uber's customers. If few customers access Uber's services through Facebook the partnership may have little value.

5   Sustained growth of 2% GDP between 2017 and 2020 will be good for UK businesses. A steady rate of growth means that the economy will steadily grow throughout this period. This will mean more products and services are being bought. As a result, this will encourage start-ups and employment will rise. Therefore, the overall standard of living will increase in the UK. Furthermore, as growth is fairly gradual at a rate of 2%, this will make it easier for the government to control inflation. Businesses and consumers can manage steady increase in RPI, leading to a stable economy.

Nevertheless, the economic forecast for other countries is not as hopeful. In particular, there is an expected slowdown in large economies such as China and India, which have been growing fast over the past 10 years. A slowdown in these countries could have a negative impact on the UK as many of our industries are linked, such as financial services and tourism.

Overall, forecast growth of 2% is good for the UK. However, forecasts change and can be inaccurate. During this period there could be any number of internal or external shocks that affect the UK economy and this means it is very hard to guarantee sustainable growth. Furthermore, growth may depend on other countries that the UK trades with and not all businesses may experience growth. For example, UK exporters may find it difficult if demand from China slows. In order to maintain growth of 2% the government will have to use a range of policies to help correct any fluctuations in the business cycle. This may include fiscal or monetary policy. International trade policy will also be very important if the UK is to maintain good trading relationships with other large economies.

Unit 3.8

1 One factor that may influence the strategy adopted by Right Plumbing Ltd is the political factors around renewable energy. Political factors refer to government policy and how this can affect markets and business activity. For example, it is possible that the government will want to encourage households to adopt renewable energy in the future and may therefore subsidise this technology. This could make the market more attractive for businesses like Right Plumbing Ltd by lowering the cost of the technology and boosting demand.

2 Strategic positioning involves a business taking up a strategic position that is unique from other competitors in its market. These strategic positions might be based on business models such as Porter's Generic Strategies or Bowman's strategic clock.
Strategic positioning will allow Right Plumbing Ltd to compete in its market by offering its customers something unique that they cannot get from other plumbing businesses. For example, this may be the excellent customer service that differentiates Right Plumbing Ltd from other businesses. By focusing on this core competency, Right Plumbing Ltd will build a reputation for delivering excellent customer service and this will add value for its customers.
On the other hand, strategic positioning on this level may not provide a sustainable competitive advantage as other businesses could also focus on customer service as a differentiating feature. Although Right Plumbing Ltd has received lots of positive publicity about its customer service, this does not mean other businesses could not build a similar reputation and position.

3 Diversification involves a business moving into a new customer market with a new product. As a result, diversification can be a high risk strategy.
Right Plumbing Ltd could diversify by moving its operation into Lancashire and supplying renewable energy. This may be an appropriate strategy as Right Plumbing Ltd is a successful business that is looking to expand. Diversification will allow the business to seek out new opportunities and spread the risk should demand in its current market fall. It also seems that Right Plumbing Ltd has a core competency to deliver excellent customer service. This is surely valued in all markets and this therefore gives it a chance to succeed in a completely new area.
Nevertheless, Jeremy will have to employ new plumbers if he expands into Lancashire and it will take time for him to train them in the procedures and policies used by Right Plumbing Ltd. Furthermore, as Jeremy has little experience with renewable energy, such as solar panels, it is possible that there may be more problems when it comes to installing the technology and this could damage the reputation and customer service that his business has become associated with.

Overall, diversification is a realistic strategy for Right Plumbing Ltd, but at the moment this might be too risky. The success of diversification may depend on the quality of the new contractors and how quickly Jeremy's company is able to learn about and adopt the new technology.

4 A sustainable competitive advantage is one that is unique, not easily copied and may take a long time to achieve. One way that Right Plumbing Ltd could develop a sustainable competitive advantage is through innovation. Jeremy is looking to provide customers with renewable energy such as solar panels and wind turbines. Although his business has not developed this technology he may be able to find a unique way to bring this technology to households in an affordable way. Although his business may be one of the first companies to do this effectively, it will be difficult to protect unless he can develop a process that he is able to patent.
Another factor that may lead to competitive advantage is the reputation his business has for delivering excellent customer service. This reputation becomes the brand image associated with his business and a good reputation can take a long time for a business to develop. It can also be damaged very quickly. This may also lead to a sustainable competitive advantage if customers associate his business with excellent service, but it does not mean that other companies cannot imitate this in the long term.
Overall, the reputation of Right Plumbing Ltd for excellent customer service is, perhaps, the most likely source of competitive advantage. However, it is very difficult for the business to protect this position as service is something that all businesses can develop. It does not depend on unique knowledge or skills. The sustainability of this competitive advantage may depend on Jeremy's ability to protect this position. One way to do this might be to achieve a quality mark for customer service. This may involve the business being assessed by an external body. This, along with the positive publicity, will reinforce its reputation and strengthen its strategic position.

Unit 3.9

1 Cloudburst Plc could use data mining to improve efficiency. Data mining involves analysing data to find patterns and relationships across large quantities of data. This may help Cloudburst Plc improve efficiency as it will be able to find trends in what its game players are looking for, such as the content they enjoy or how they play the game, which would allow it to create more content and games like this. This would improve efficiency because it would stop designers creating content and features that are not wanted by customers.

2 A diseconomy of scale is a negative impact on a business that it might experience as it grows in scale, often leading to costs rising and inefficiencies. One diseconomy that Cloudburst Plc might experience is poor communication. As the company merges with Interact Gaming Ltd there will be far more employees to communicate with and this will make effective communication more difficult, leading to slower communication and miscommunication. This problem might be amplified due to the fact that Interact Gaming Ltd is a Chinese firm with a different language and culture.

3 Innovation involves developing commercially viable products and processes. For example, new computer games or technology that powers computer games. One factor that could contribute to Cloudburst Plc's ability to innovate is the skills of its workforce. If Cloudburst Plc merges with Interact it will be acquiring a creative team of designers. These designers are likely to help Cloudburst Plc develop new games. In turn, this can help it enter new segments of the market and replace outdated titles.
Another factor that may contribute to Cloudburst Plc's ability to innovate will be the amount of capital the directors are

willing to invest in research and development. Although this might not help it design creative new games it could help the company improve the technology it uses, such as better game graphics and fewer bugs. However, investment in research and development does not guarantee that Cloudburst Plc will develop new and effective technologies to enhance its games.

4   The Bartlett and Ghoshal matrix considers the different approaches a business might take towards internationalisation. The matrix considers two variables – the level of responsiveness to local markets and the drive for a standardised global product. Cloudburst Plc could use this model to identify the strategy it wishes to use. As Cloudburst Plc sells its games in international markets it will use the model to decide which aspects of the games might need changing to meet the various needs. For example, if Cloudburst Plc adopted an 'international strategy' it would make slight amendments to its game for different markets. For example, it could change the language and a few features to make the game culturally acceptable in different countries. On the other hand, Cloudburst Plc might adopt a global strategy and keep all aspects of its game consistent, no matter what market it operates in. The benefit of this strategy is that Cloudburst Plc will benefit from economies of scale through standardisation and reduce costs by not having to create multiple versions of the game. Nevertheless, this may then mean the game is not as desirable or suitable in certain countries.

5   A disruptive innovation is one that replaces an accepted and established technology. Disruptive innovation can cause significant problems for businesses as they have to make the choice between adopting new technology, processes and products, or sticking with what they know.
Disruptive innovation is likely to affect Cloudburst Plc because new games and new games consoles are released on a regular basis. As new consoles are released, new games are required and this is an opportunity for other companies to capture Cloudburst Plc's market share. This also leads to older games becoming obsolete. As a result, Cloudburst Plc must decide how quickly it will develop new games with the risk that a new game could quickly become superseded without generating the maximum return on its initial investment.
On the other hand, Cloudburst Plc have a very successful brand and established titles. This means that console manufacturers are more likely to involve Cloudburst Plc in the development of new technology and this will be even more likely should the partnership with the console manufacturer go ahead. Furthermore, Cloudburst Plc's leading game is the market leader and this means that customers are likely to be loyal to the brand, limiting any impact of disruptive innovation introduced by other firms.
Overall, Cloudburst Plc operates in a high-tech industry that is used to innovation and ethnological advancement, and for this reason, it will anticipate and expect disruptive innovation and should be able to deal with this. The extent to which any disruptive innovation may impact Cloudburst Plc may depend on its ability to remain creative and continue to introduce new games.

6   The first option that Cloudburst Plc has considered is the merger with Interact Gaming Ltd. As Interact Gaming Ltd is a Chinese business, this will help Cloudburst Plc break into the Chinese market, and other Eastern markets, where there is a high rate of economic growth and demand for leisure products such as computer games. By merging with Interact, Cloudburst Plc will own the brand and this will make it easier for them to launch new products that are immediately accepted by Chinese consumers. Furthermore, Cloudburst Plc will have the intellectual capital of the company and the creative design skills of Interact's employees. However, both companies currently operate in very different markets and have significant differences in approach and culture. If the

merger is to result in long-term success for Cloudburst Plc, the two businesses will have to be integrated effectively.
The second option of a partnership with a leading console manufacturer is very attractive as it will give Cloudburst Plc a USP and competitive advantage over its rivals. This is because its games will be promoted alongside the games console. As a result, Cloudburst Plc's reputation will be enhanced and potentially help it break into new markets where the console is sold. As games designers supply the games for console manufacturers, a close partnership is likely to benefit Cloudburst Plc and help it gain an advantage over other game designers. This is the 'architecture' that leads to a sustainable competitive advantage and refers to the relationships a business has with its stakeholders that are difficult to develop and copy.
Overall, the strategy that is most likely to lead to long-term success is the merger with Interact Gaming Ltd. This is because the move will not only help Cloudburst Plc adopt a market development strategy, but it will also improve innovation across the company, which is of key importance to a business in an industry that is driven by creativity and technological advancement. The success of the merger will, however, depend on how well these two businesses can integrate – for example, how well the Chinese designers settle into the Cloudburst Plc way of doing things. In order for the long-term success to be guaranteed, it is important for the directors of Cloudburst Plc to have a clear vision and ensure this is understood and accepted by all areas of the company.

Unit 3.10

1   A network diagram should be constructed from the table and look similar to the one below.

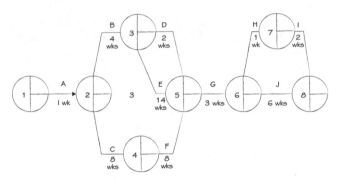

2   Network diagram showing earliest start time, latest finish time and float on each activity.

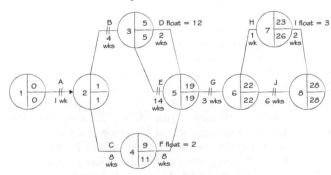

3   A divorce of ownership refers to the different interests that might exist between the managers and owners (shareholders) of a business. In a large organisation the owners and managers may be different people, particularly in a Plc such as Cloudburst Plc. Owners may not understand issues 'on the ground' and managers may make decisions based on factors which they believe are right or which might benefit themselves – perhaps short-term gains to boost profits. As Cloudburst Plc has taken on a new Chinese company, the shareholders may not appreciate the needs of the organisation or what is required for the company to be successful in the long term.

This could result in short-term decisions being made to boost profits at the expense of integrating the two companies effectively.

4   One reason why the directors at Cloudburst Plc may find it difficult to integrate the two companies is that they are likely to have very different cultures. For example, at Cloudburst Plc big decisions are kept with project managers and this might represent a power. Whereas, at Interact Gaming Ltd game designers have much more freedom, perhaps representative of a role culture. Culture can be very difficult to change as it is embedded in people's values and beliefs.

Another factor that might make integration difficult is the fact that the employees of Interact Gaming Ltd are used to a different organisational structure. As Interact Gaming Ltd previously adopted a functional structure it may not be used to working in a product structure. This may cause problems because the employees may not know how their roles relate to those of other employees and the different ways of working required from a product orientated approach instead of a functional approach, such as a dedicated marketing team supporting all areas of the business.

5   Strategic planning involves analysis of a business's context, the setting of appropriate objectives and then choosing a strategy that utilises the business's strengths. To do this a business might use a number of theoretical models including the Ansoff matrix or Five Forces analysis.

Strategic planning is important because it helps a business understand its current position in terms of internal and external factors. For example, Cloudburst Plc may identify that its brand and most successful game are its key strengths and that the Asian markets might be a significant opportunity for it to exploit. Without appropriate analysis of the business context and clear objectives the business strategy may not be appropriate and is likely to fail.

Nevertheless, the external business environment is constantly changing and no matter how much planning goes into strategic implementation there will inevitably be strategic drift. Indeed, for many businesses an emergent strategy is more likely to occur, which involves the strategy being developed over time with changes being made based on external factors that are often unforeseen. For this reason, strategic planning has limited significance on the long-term success of a business.

Overall, strategic planning is very important for the long-term success of Cloudburst Plc. This is because it will be entering new markets and new product areas, such as smartphone apps, over the coming years. As there is much uncertainty in diversification, strategic planning will be very important in order to identify the opportunities and threats.

6   One approach that the directors of Cloudburst Plc may take in order to overcome any resistance to change might be to educate and communicate with the workforce. This will involve ensuring all employees fully understand the rationale behind the change and why it is necessary for the long-term success of the company. For example, this might involve holding a seminar with all employees so that they all have the correct information and explanation. It will also be important to allow all employees the opportunity to ask questions. As Cloudburst Plc is merging with Interact Gaming Ltd, it will be important that both sets of employees are spoken to together so that they feel part of the same team.

Another approach that the directors might take to overcome resistance to change might be to bring on board key leaders within the organisation to help them implement the change. This might involve the promotion of some Interact Gaming Ltd employees in order to help them manipulate the Chinese game designers and bring them on board. By doing this they will be using key leaders within the workforce to help them embed any new strategy.

Overall, the methods the directors use to counteract any resistance to change will depend on the needs of the individual employee group. For example, some employees may simply need support and training, such as training on how to develop apps or the characteristics of the Asian market for computer games, whilst others may need to be negotiated with. The latter approach is likely to be very important with managers of Interact Gaming Ltd. As they are the leaders of the company that has effectively been taken over, it is important that they have a say in how the company moves forward so that they see that they are part of the same team and the merger is not something simply happening to them without any control of strategic direction. Indeed, it is very important that the managers of Interact are involved in any strategy formation, considering that they have all the expertise in the markets Cloudburst Plc hopes to break into.

Notes